# AMERICA IN THE COLD WAR

*Twenty Years of Revolutions and Response, 1947-1967*

HOSSAIN S. FAROQUI
1979

# PROBLEMS IN AMERICAN HISTORY

Series Editor:
**LOREN BARITZ**
University of Rochester

# AMERICA IN THE
# COLD WAR

*Twenty Years of Revolutions
and Response, 1947-1967*

EDITED BY

*Walter LaFeber*

Cornell University

*John Wiley & Sons, Inc.*
New York  London  Sydney  Toronto

Library of Congress Catalog Card Number: 70-78475
Cloth: SBN 471 51132 3   Paper: SBN 471 51133 1
Printed in the United States of America

# PART ONE

## Four Alternative Views

# SERIES PREFACE

This series is an introduction to the most important problems in the writing and study of American history. Some of these problems have been the subject of debate and argument for a long time, although others only recently have been recognized as controversial. However, in every case, the student will find a vital topic, an understanding of which will deepen his knowledge of social change in America.

The scholars who introduce and edit the books in this series are teaching historians who have written history in the same general area as their individual books. Many of them are leading scholars in their fields, and all have done important work in the collective search for better historical understanding.

Because of the talent and the specialized knowledge of the individual editors, a rigid editorial format has not been imposed on them. For example, some of the editors believe that primary source material is necessary to their subjects. Some believe that their material should be arranged to show conflicting interpretations. Others have decided to use the selected materials as evidence for their own interpretations. The individual editors have been given the freedom to handle their books in the way that their own experience and knowledge indicate is best. The overall result is a series built up from the individual decisions of working scholars in the various fields, rather than one that conforms to a uniform editorial decision.

A common goal (rather than a shared technique) is the bridge of this series. There is always the desire to bring the reader as close to these problems as possible. One result of this objective is an emphasis of the nature and consequences of problems and events, with a de-emphasis of the more purely historiographical issues. The goal is to involve the student in the reality of crisis, the inevitability of ambiguity, and the excitement of finding a way through the historical maze.

v

Above all, this series is designed to show students how experienced historians read and reason. Although health is not contagious, intellectual engagement may be. If we show students something significant in a phrase or a passage that they otherwise may have missed, we will have accomplished part of our objective. When students see something that passed us by, then the process will have been made whole. This active and mutual involvement of editor and reader with a significant human problem will rescue the study of history from the smell and feel of dust.

*Loren Baritz*

# CONTENTS

# AMERICA IN THE COLD WAR

*Twenty Years of Revolutions and Response, 1947-1967*

# 1 Lyndon B. Johnson: Our Foreign Policy Must Always Be An Extension of This Nation's Domestic Policy (August 26, 1966)

*By the middle of his presidential term (1963–1969), Lyndon Johnson (1908– ) confronted a crisis in American urban areas and an increasingly costly and unproductive war in Vietnam. In the following speech, the President related the two tragedies, suggesting that the tactics used to solve the domestic problem could also ameliorate foreign policy dilemmas. The assumptions underlying his belief in such a relationship merit close examination. For example, the President's belief that "social justice" is the same to all Americans and to Vietnamese alike is a questionable proposition in view of the different traditions and political institutions of each of these peoples. Does the attempted extension of "a great, liberal, and progressive democracy" beyond American borders into foreign lands help or injure American foreign policy?*

---

. . . Today, I am not going to speak of particular countries or particular policies or of the particular problems of conflict and negotiation which now engage our attention. Instead, I am going to suggest some of the rules or principles which, as President, I believe should control our conduct of the foreign policy of this country. This will help us to understand better how we react and how we should react to the endless succession of problems which daily pour in upon Washington from all of the six continents and across all the many seas.

The overriding rule which I want to affirm today is this: that our foreign policy must always be an extension of this nation's domestic policy. Our safest guide to what we do abroad is always to take a good look at what we are doing at home.

The great creative periods of American foreign policy have

SOURCE. *Department of State Bulletin*, Vol. LV, September 19 1966, pp. 406–409.

been the great periods of our domestic achievement. Abraham Lincoln, Woodrow Wilson, and Franklin D. Roosevelt, to mention but three, projected their image of concern and accomplishment to the entire world. I would mistrust any expert on foreign affairs, however deeply he might be informed, if he confessed ignorance of the politics of the United States of America.

The reason for this is quite simple. Politics are the means by which men give their collective voice to their hopes and aspirations. Can we suppose that these are so very different for Americans than for the people of the other lands from which our parents came? Certainly not. Nor will we long have the confidence and respect of other people if we hold what is necessary for Americans is too good for other people. . . . Let me offer you some concrete examples.

I think first of the problems of these last years in our large cities. We do not condone violence; we do not hold innocent those people who incite it. We know that there are men who feed on the misery of others, and we know there are men who seek to turn disorder and protest to their own gain. They have neither the interests of the poor nor the interests of our country at heart, for their intent is usually to tear down and not to build.

But when violence breaks out, our instinct is to ask: "Why? What is the cause? And what can we do about it?" We look for the deeper causes on which anger and tension grow and feed. We look for privation and indignity and evidence of past oppression or neglect.

And so it is abroad. We do not, if we are wise, see the hand of a villain in every outbreak against authority. There, as at home, it is the sound American instinct always to ask if oppression, privation, and neglect are not the root cause.

It has often seemed to me that a visitor from Mars—brought back, perhaps as an exchange fellow from one of the more memorable space probes of Jim Webb [James E. Webb, Administrator, National Aeronautics and Space Administration] and the Johnson administration—will not be greatly impressed by the fact that the people on this planet speak different languages, are of a different color, or even, at first glance, that they live under different political systems.

He will notice, rather, that there is an area of comparative economic well-being that is spreading over the northern part of this hemisphere and all of Europe. It extends deeply into the Soviet Union. Here, most of the people have, at a minimum, enough to eat. Most have enough to wear. They have schools to attend. . . .

And our visitor will observe that, in general and except perhaps in election years in the United States, this is a zone of political tranquillity. Governments are stable. Revolutions are rare. Even as between nations, he will notice that, while there is not complete peace, the wars for the last 20 years have at least been conducted largely in words. Words wound. But as a veteran of more than 12 years in the United States Senate, I happily attest that words do not kill.

But our tourist from Mars will soon notice that there is another part of the world where governments are insecure; where people take readily to the streets; where guerrillas lurk in the jungles; where armies eye each other across unstable frontiers and all too frequently they exchange shots; and where, on frequent occasions, landless peasants or unemployed workers rise up in strong protest.

And this world, our traveler, I think, by then will have noticed, is a very poor one. He will form his own conclusions as to what makes for tranquillity within a country and as between countries. And he will not be wrong. I may ask this gentleman to stay on in a high position in my administration.

Let me give you a second application of this rule.

Here in the United States we do not like violence. We know that otherwise peaceful men can sometimes be driven to its use. We regard it as a manifestation of failure. When it occurs, whether it occurs in an urban slum during a demonstration or whether it occurs on a picket line, we count it a manifestation of failure. We seek to reestablish the rule of law. We try to get negotiations going again. To negotiate is never to admit failure. To negotiate is to show good sense. . . .

And so also is it in foreign policy. There, too, violence is one face of failure. There, too, the rule of law and the resort to the bargaining table are the hallmarks of success. The man who deals in principles is sometimes accused of dealing in generalities. . . .

Let me say accordingly, as I have said often before, this rule applies without qualification to Vietnam. We shall count it a mark of success when all the parties to that dispute come to the conference table. We Americans are experienced in bargaining; we have nothing to fear from negotiation. And we Americans know the nature of a fair bargain. No people ever need fear negotiating with Americans.

Let me give you a third application of the rule.

Here in the United States we do not like being told what to do. We like even less being told what to think. Not every action that my administration has taken since I became President has been universally popular. I doubt that everything we do in the future will be acclaimed by all people.

But we defend, and I intend to defend, the right of everyone to disagree, if he wants to, with everything that we urge or do. We ask only in return that when we dissent from their dissent that it be recognized as an exercise of the very right that we defend, the right of free speech. . . .

And again, we find that American policy provides the guide to foreign policy. All people want the dignity that goes with constitutional and civil liberty. All people wish the right to speak their minds. And all men are diminished by dictatorship and by thought control.

Here again, let me be not content with just enunciating a rule. Let me apply it. The United States has no mandate to interfere wherever government falls short of our specifications. But we shall have—and deserve—the respect of the people of other countries only as they know what side America is on.

In the Communist countries we are on the side of those who, year by year, seek to enlarge the spectrum of discussion. As long as these men and women persist, communism will be in a state of change, and the change will be good.

In the Latin American countries we are on the side of those who want constitutional governments. We are not on the side of those who say that dictatorships are necessary for efficient economic development or as a bulwark against communism. We have already made it amply clear that where personal freedom is threatened we are not on the side of unbridled authority.

In Africa we are on the side of those who are working toward full equality between the races. . . .

In Vietnam we are on the side of fair and orderly elections

that give, in the troubled land, the widest possible expression to the will of the people who live there. We have already made it amply clear, I think, that what is freely and fairly expressed by that will, the United States of America will accept.

You will notice, I think, that there is no application of these rules which, were it the United States, we would not accept and very nearly accept it as a matter of course. You will see, I think, why I think that domestic policy is a good guide to our foreign policy and what we should do abroad.

Let me give you a fourth and final application of the rule. . . .

The United States is, by the standards that the world community applies, a very successful society. We have here at home much to do. But in our brief span of 200 years—a lesser period than encompassed by the military campaigns known to history as the Crusades—we have accomplished quite a lot. Nor have we been backward in reflecting on the reasons.

We know that we are an energetic people. We think we are intelligent. We early appreciated the importance of public education. We had a continent that was rich in resources. We had a sound idea for our economic system. And, without doubt, we were truly smiled upon by our Creator.

But I wonder if this explains our relative good fortune. . . .

Our advantage, I think, then, is that we early discovered that social justice is very efficient. We discovered that by assuring to everyone the fruits of his own labor—and that is what social justice really means—we made him a productive force of untold power. He became subject to the most exacting of all employers, namely himself. Deny a man this sense of fair reward and his effort and his productivity are cut to a fraction. . . .

And here also is a rule that applies to our shores. It is the theory which underlies our efforts in Latin America and in South Asia and wherever applicable in other parts of the world. . . .

We are a great and liberal and progressive democracy up to our frontiers. And we are the same beyond. Let us never imagine for a moment that Americans can wear one face in Denver and Des Moines and Seattle and Brooklyn and another in Paris and Mexico City and Karachi and Saigon. Nor, may I say, do we have a different face for Moscow or for Peking or for Hanoi. . . .

## 2   Barry Goldwater: Why We Must Be Stronger Militarily (September 23, 1964)

*When Barry Goldwater (1909–    ), a Senator from Arizona, ran against Lyndon Johnson in the 1964 presidential election, the challenger personified the hope of many Americans who, in their frustrations over the nearly two-decade-old Cold War, wanted to cut through the complexities of international affairs with military force. However, to justify the threat or the use of such power, Senator Goldwater had to define the opponent carefully but in bold terms. Is he correct in stating in his key assumption that "Communism is the only major threat to the peace of the world anywhere in this world today. . . ."? After President Johnson defeated Senator Goldwater in the 1964 election, the Johnson Administration accelerated the American military commitment to Vietnam. Do you see the seeds of this commitment when you compare President Johnson's speech (Reading 1) with Senator Goldwater's statement?*

---

. . . I want to talk today about peace. No man anywhere wants peace more than I do, and no man anywhere wants to avoid war more than I do. I know war, and I have sons and daughters and grandchildren who I do not want touched by war. I think one war in a man's life is par for the course. . . .

I believe that in the first place, we must recognize that it's not possible or at least not honest, to talk about peace without talking about and understanding Communism.

Now, the great, harsh fact of today's troubled world is that Communism is at war, and it's at war against us, at war against all non-Communist nations.

The great, harsh fact is that Communism is the only major

SOURCE. Barry Goldwater, Speech of September 23, 1964, in *Vital Speeches of the Day*, Vol. XXXI, October 15, 1964, pp. 5–7. Reprinted by permission of the City News Publishing Company and Barry Goldwater.

threat to the peace of the world anywhere in this world today, and the sooner we realize this the better.

The great, harsh fact is that Communism wants the whole world. In Cuba, in the Congo, at the Berlin wall, in Indonesia, in Vietnam—wherever the flames of conflict are being fanned, Communism is the cause.

Now, the methods it uses in its unrelenting drive to conquer the world are based solely upon expediency. What Communism will do, how far it will go, at any given moment, depends upon their hardheaded, cold-blooded assessment of the risks that they must face.

If they can bury us, as they've promised to do—if they can win the world, as they've said they will—if they can do this without nuclear war, then they will try to avoid nuclear war.

But remember this: it is not compassion or decency which prevents their attacking us. It's not concern for our children. It's just plain fear. They respect our power and they fear provoking its use against them.

Now, this is the reason that we must maintain peace, through preparedness. . . .

I needn't remind you of this, but sometimes it's necessary to remind the American people that whenever free world leaders have shrunk from responsible use of power at critical moments in history, they have permitted little problems to grow into gigantic and infinitely more dangerous problems. This, let me remind you, has always been true—from Munich to the Bay of Pigs—and it's high time that our leaders faced the fact.

If we follow in this country the notion that a "let's be friends" approach, coupled with a defense establishment we are reluctant to use, can save us from Communism, we will run a very, very grave risk of war.

Now, the balance of power can't remain static forever. The threat of a technological breakthrough by the Soviets must be considered. And if the Communists believe the odds favor them, they will not hesitate to hit us with their most fearsome weapons.

Therefore, the first and central duty of the Federal Government is to provide for the common defense, and in the present state of the world, military spending is and must be high. But it alone amounts to less than one-half of the total Federal expenditures. In the 12 months ending June 30, 1964, the Federal Government spent the astounding total of $120 billion, or nearly $650 for every man, woman and child in the United States. Of this amount, $55 billion was spent on our military forces. Nondefense expenses, however, amounted to $65 billion.

And more importantly, the sharp rise in Federal spending in the present Administration has been mainly for purposes other than our common defense. In 1960, the final full year of the Eisenhower Administration, the Federal Government spent $94 billion, of which $46 billion was for defense.

And in the four years since, total expenditures have risen by nearly $30 billion, or by about one-third, and this is what this Administration calls economy. Federal expenses, for example, on our military forces have risen by $10 billion, so two-thirds of the rise in expenditures was for other purposes. Nondefense expenditures alone rose by 40 per cent in the last four years.

Currently, the Administration proposes actually to cut our military spending in order to provide funds for sticking the Government's fingers in still a larger mess of pies—for handouts here, subsidies there, and all, no doubt, said to be for the good purposes but, like past efforts in these directions, likely to end up having effects quite the opposite of those intended, yet draining the public purse.

That way lies national suicide. There is no surer way to condemn this nation to the status of a second-rate power, incapable of exerting influence in the world at large, than to fritter away taxable capacity in do-gooder schemes that waste our substance. Let me remind you that the experience of Britain is a striking example of how this can happen. We must not let it happen here.


3    *J. William Fulbright: The Great Society Is a Sick Society (August 8, 1967)*


J. William Fulbright (1905–    ), Democratic Senator from Arkansas, since the early 1940's has been one of the leading internationalists in

*Congress. Until 1965, he fully supported the American commitment in Vietnam and, as Chairman of the powerful Senate Foreign Relations Committee, helped President Johnson wage that conflict. However, in 1965, Fulbright began to withdraw his support from the Johnson foreign policies. The next selection, from a widely read speech made in the Senate in August 1967, indicates why the Arkansas legislator changed his mind. What examples does Senator Fulbright offer as he attacks President Johnson's assumption that social justice at home can be expanded into social justice abroad, and how does he turn the argument against the President? Besides the obvious dissimilarities between Senators Fulbright and Goldwater (Reading 2) on the matter of how much military power should be emphasized, in what other ways do their statements differ?*

---

Standing in the smoke and rubble of Detroit, a Negro veteran said: "I just got back from Vietnam a few months ago, but you know, I think the war is here."

There are in fact two wars going on. One is the war of power politics which our soldiers are fighting in the jungles of southeast Asia. The other is a war for America's soul which is being fought in the streets of Newark and Detroit and in the halls of Congress, in churches and protest meetings and on college campuses, and in the hearts and minds of silent Americans from Maine to Hawaii. I believe that the two wars have something to do with each other, not in the direct, tangibly causal way that bureaucrats require as proof of a connection between two things, but in a subtler, moral and qualitative way that is no less real for being intangible. Each of these wars might well be going on in the absence of the other, but neither, I suspect, standing alone, would seem so hopeless and demoralizing.

The connection between Vietnam and Detroit is in their conflicting and incompatible demands upon traditional American values. The one demands that they be set aside, the other that they be fulfilled. The one demands the acceptance by America

SOURCE. *Congressional Record*, 90th Congress, 1st Session, August 9, 1967, pp. 22126–22129.

of an imperial role in the world, or of what our policy makers like to call the "responsibilities of power," or of what I have called the "arrogance of power." The other demands freedom and social justice at home, an end to poverty, the fulfillment of our flawed democracy, and an effort to create a role for ourselves in the world which is compatible with our traditional values. The question, it should be emphasized, is not whether it is *possible* to engage in traditional power politics abroad and at the same time the perfect democracy at home, but whether it is possible for *us Americans*, with our particular history and national character, to combine morally incompatible roles.

Administration officials tell us that we can indeed afford both Vietnam and the Great Society, and they produce impressive statistics of the gross national product to prove it. The statistics show financial capacity but they do not show moral and psychological capacity. They do not show how a President preoccupied with bombing missions over North and South Vietnam can provide strong and consistent leadership for the renewal of our cities. They do not show how a Congress burdened with war costs and war measures, with emergency briefings and an endless series of dramatic appeals, with anxious constituents and a mounting anxiety of their own, can tend to the workaday business of studying social problems and legislating programs to meet them. Nor do the statistics tell how an anxious and puzzled people, bombarded by press and television with the bad news of American deaths in Vietnam, the "good news" of enemy deaths—and with vividly horrifying pictures to illustrate them—can be expected to support neighborhood anti-poverty projects and national programs for urban renewal, employment and education. . . .

At present much of the world is repelled by America and what America seems to stand for in the world. Both in our foreign affairs and in our domestic life we convey an image of violence; I do not care very much about images as distinguished from the things they reflect, but this image is rooted in reality. Abroad we are engaged in a savage and unsuccessful war against poor people in a small and backward nation. At home—largely because of the neglect from twenty-five years of preoccupation with foreign involvements—our cities are exploding in violent protest against generations of social injustice. America, which only a few years ago seemed to the world to be a model of democracy and social justice, has become a symbol of violence and undisciplined power. . . . By our undisciplined use of physical power we have divested ourselves of a greater power: the power of example. How, for example, can we commend peaceful compromise to the Arabs and the Israelis when we are unwilling to suspend our relentless bombing of North Vietnam? How can we commend democratic social reform to Latin America when Newark, Detroit, and Milwaukee are providing explosive evidence of our own inadequate efforts at democratic social reform? How can we commend the free enterprise system to Asians and Africans when in our own country it has produced vast, chaotic, noisy, dangerous and dirty urban complexes while poisoning the very air and land and water? . . .

While the death toll mounts in Vietnam, it is mounting too in the war at home. During a single week of July 1967, 164 Americans were killed and 1,442 wounded in Vietnam, while 65 Americans were killed and 2,100 were wounded in city riots in the United States. We are truly fighting a two-front war and doing badly in both. Each war feeds on the other and, although the President assures us that we have the resources to win both wars, in fact we are not winning either.

Together the two wars have set in motion a process of deterioration in American society and there is no question that each of the two crises is heightened by the impact of the other. Not only does the Vietnam war divert human and material resources from our festering cities; not only does it foster the conviction on the part of slum Negroes that their country is indifferent to their plight. In addition the war feeds the idea of violence as a way of solving problems. If, as Mr. Rusk tells us, only the rain of bombs can bring Ho Chi Minh to reason, why should not the same principle apply at home? Why should not riots and snipers' bullets bring the white man to an awareness of the Negro's plight when peaceful programs for housing and jobs and training have been more rhetoric than reality? Ugly and shocking thoughts are in the American air and they were forged in the Vietnam crucible. Black power extremists talk of "wars of liberation" in the urban ghettoes of America. . . .

Priorities are reflected in the things we spend money on. Far from being a dry accounting of bookkeepers, a nation's budget is full of moral implications; it tells what a society cares about and what it does not care about; it tells what its values are.

Here are a few statistics on America's values: Since 1946 we have spent over $1,578 billion through our regular national budget. Of this amount over $904 billion, or 57.29 percent of the total, have gone for military power. By contrast, less than $96 billion, or 6.08 percent, were spent on "social functions" including education, health, labor and welfare programs, housing and community development. The Administration's budget for fiscal year 1968 calls for almost $76 billion to be spent on the military and only $15 billion for "social functions."

I would not say that we have shown ourselves to value weapons five or ten times as much as we value domestic social needs, as the figures suggest; certainly much of our military spending has been necessitated by genuine requirements of national security. I think, however, that we have embraced the necessity with excessive enthusiasm, that the Congress has been too willing to provide unlimited sums for the military and not really very reluctant at all to offset these costs to a very small degree by cutting away funds for the poverty program and urban renewal, for rent supplements for the poor and even for a program to help protect slum children from being bitten by rats. . . .

While the country sickens for lack of moral leadership, a most remarkable younger generation has taken up the standard of American idealism. Unlike so many of their elders, they have perceived the fraud and sham in American life and are unequivocally rejecting it. Some, the hippies, have simply withdrawn, and while we may regret the loss of their energies and their sense of decency, we can hardly gainsay their evaluation of the state of society. Others of our youth are sardonic and skeptical, not, I think, because they do not want ideals but because they want the genuine article and will not tolerate fraud. Others—students who wrestle with their consciences about the draft, soldiers who wrestle with their consciences about the war, Peace Corps volunteers who strive to light the spark of human dignity among the poor of India or Brazil, and VISTA volunteers who try to do the same for our own poor in Harlem or Appalachia—are striving to keep alive the traditional values of American democracy.

They are not really radical, these young idealists, no more radical, that is, than Jefferson's idea of freedom, Lincoln's idea of equality, or Wilson's idea of a peaceful community of nations. Some of them, it is true, are taking what many regard as radical action, but they are doing it in defense of traditional values and in protest against the radical departure from those values embodied in the idea of an imperial destiny for America.

The focus of their protest is the war in Vietnam and the measure of their integrity is the fortitude with which they refused to be deceived about it. By striking contrast with the young Germans who accepted the Nazi evil because the values of their society had disintegrated and they had no normal frame of reference, these young Americans are demonstrating the vitality of American values. . . .

It may be that the challenge will succeed, that America will succumb to becoming a traditional empire and will reign for a time over what must surely be a moral if not a physical wasteland, and then, like the great empires of the past, will decline or fall. Or it may be that the effort to create so grotesque an anachronism will go up in flames of nuclear holocaust. But if I had to bet my money on what is going to happen, I would bet on this younger generation—this generation who reject the inhumanity of war in a poor and distant land, who reject the poverty and sham in their own country, this generation who are telling their elders what their elders ought to have known, that the price of empire is America's soul and that price is too high.

4    *Carl Oglesby: "How Can We Continue to Sack the Ports of Asia and Still Dream of Jesus?"* (*November 27, 1965*)

*Carl Oglesby, President of the Students for a Democratic Society, gave the following speech at the mammoth march on Washington in the late autumn of 1965. The march was organized to demonstrate the massive dissent, particularly among younger Americans, from Presi-*

*dent Johnson's policies in Vietnam and from his foreign and domestic
policies in general. Oglesby spoke during a time when the "New Left"
protest movement was redirecting its primary attention from the civil
rights issue at home to the Vietnam conflict abroad. In what way does
Oglesby tie these two problems (civil rights and Vietnam) together?
Why does he single out the "liberals" for attack? Most important, in
what particulars does he read the historical record differently than
President Johnson, Senator Goldwater, or even Senator Fulbright?*

---

Seven months ago at the April March on Washington, Paul
Potter, then President of Students for a Democratic Society,
stood in approximately this spot and said that we must name the
system that creates and sustains the war in Vietnam—name it,
describe it, analyze it, understand it, and change it.

Today I will try to name it—to suggest an analysis which, to
be quite frank, may disturb some of you—and to suggest what
changing it may require of us.

We are here again to protest against a growing war. Since it
is a very bad war, we acquire the habit of thinking that it must
be caused by very bad men. But we only conceal reality, I think,
to denounce on such grounds the menacing coalition of industrial
and military power, or the brutality of the blitzkrieg we are waging against Vietnam, or the ominous signs around us that heresy
may soon no longer be permitted. We must simply observe, and
quite plainly say, that this coalition, this blitzkrieg, and this demand for acquiescence are creatures, all of them, of a government
that since 1932 has considered itself to be fundamentally *liberal*.

The original commitment in Vietnam was made by President
Truman, a mainstream liberal. It was seconded by President Eisenhower, a moderate liberal. It was intensified by the late President
Kennedy, a flaming liberal. Think of the men who now engineer
that war—those who study the maps, give the commands, push the

SOURCE. Speech by Carl Oglesby on November 27, 1965 printed in Jacob
and Saul Landau, *The New Radicals*, (1966). Copyright 1966 by Students for
a Democratic Society (international). Reprinted by permission of Students
for a Democratic Society.

buttons, and tally the dead: Bundy, McNamara, Rusk, Lodge, Goldberg, the President himself.

They are not moral monsters.

They are all honorable men.

They are all liberals.

But so, I'm sure, are many of us who are here today in protest. To understand the war, then, it seems necessary to take a closer look at this American liberalism. Maybe we are in for some surprises. Maybe we have here two quite different liberalisms: one authentically humanist, the other not so human at all.

Not long ago, I considered myself a liberal. And if someone had asked me what I meant by that, I'd perhaps have quoted Thomas Jefferson or Thomas Paine, who first made plain our nation's unprovisional commitment to human rights. But what do you think would happen if these two heroes could sit down now for a chat with President Johnson and McGeorge Bundy?

They would surely talk of the Vietnam war. Our dead revolutionaries would soon wonder why their country was fighting against what appeared to be a revolution. The living liberals would hotly deny that it is one: there are troops coming in from outside, the rebels get arms from other countries, most of the people are not on their side, and they practice terror against their own. Therefore, *not* a revolution.

What would our dead revolutionaries answer? They might say: "What fools and bandits, sirs, you make then of us. Outside help? Do you remember Lafayette? Or the three thousand British freighters the French navy sank for our side? Or the arms and men we got from France and Spain? And what's this about terror? Did you never hear what we did to our own loyalists? Or about the thousands of rich American Tories who fled for their lives to Canada? And as for popular support, do you not know that we had less than one third of our people with us? That, in fact, the colony of New York recruited more troops for the British than for the revolution? Should we give it all back?"

Revolutions do not take place in velvet boxes. They never have. It is only the poets who make them lovely. What the National Liberation Front is fighting in Vietnam is a complex and vicious war. This war is also a revolution, as honest a revolution as you can find anywhere in history. And this is a fact which all our intricate official denials will never change.

But it doesn't make any difference to our leaders anyway. Their aim in Vietnam is really much simpler than this implies. It is to safeguard what they take to be American interests around the world against revolution or revolutionary change, which they always call Communism—as if that were that. In the case of Vietnam, this interest is, first, the principle that revolution shall not be tolerated anywhere, and second, that South Vietnam shall never sell its rice to China—or even to North Vietnam.

There is simply no such thing now, for us, as a just revolution—never mind that for two thirds of the world's people the twentieth century might as well be the Stone Age; never mind the terrible poverty and hopelessness that are the basic facts of life for most modern men; and never mind that for these millions there is now an increasingly perceptible relationship between their sorrow and our contentment.

Can we understand why the Negroes of Watts rebelled? Then why do we need a devil theory to explain the rebellion of the South Vietnamese? Can we understand the oppression in Mississippi, or the anguish that our Northern ghettos make epidemic? Then why can't we see that our proper human struggle is not with Communism or revolutionaries, but with the social desperation that drives good men to violence, both here and abroad?

To be sure, we have been most generous with our aid, and in Western Europe, a mature industrial society, that aid worked. But there are always political and financial strings. And we have never shown ourselves capable of allowing others to make those traumatic institutional changes that are often the prerequisites of progress in colonial societies. For all our official feeling for the millions who are enslaved to what we so self-righteously call the yoke of Communist tyranny, we make no real effort at all to crack through the much more vicious right-wing tyrannies that our businessmen traffic with and our nation profits from every day. And for all our cries about the international red conspiracy to take over the world, we take only pride in our six thousand military bases on foreign soil.

We gave Rhodesia a grave look just now—but we keep on

buying her chromium, which is cheap because black slave labor mines it.

We deplore the racism of Verwoerd's fascist South Africa— but our banks make big loans to that country and our private technology makes it a nuclear power.

We are saddened and puzzled by random back-page stories of revolt in this or that Latin American state—but are convinced by a few pretty photos in the Sunday supplement that things are getting better, that the world is coming our way, that change from disorder can be orderly, that our benevolence will pacify the distressed, that our might will intimidate the angry.

Optimists, may I suggest that these are quite unlikely fantasies? They are fantasies because we have lost that mysterious social desire for human equity that from time to time has given us genuine moral drive. We have become a nation of young, bright-eyed, hard-hearted, slim-waisted, bullet-headed make-out artists. A nation—may I say it?—of beardless liberals.

You say I am being hard? Only think.

This country, with its thirty-some years of liberalism, can send two hundred thousand young men to Vietnam to kill and die in the most dubious of wars, but it cannot get a hundred voter registrars to go into Mississippi.

What do you make of it?

The financial burden of the war obliges us to cut millions from an already pathetic War on Poverty budget. But in almost the same breath, Congress appropriates $140 million for the Lockheed and Boeing companies to compete with each other on the super-sonic transport project—that Disneyland creation that will cost us all about $2 billion before it's done.

What do you make of it?

Many of us have been earnestly resisting for some years now the idea of putting atomic weapons into West German hands, an action that would perpetuate the division of Europe and thus the Cold War. Now just this week we find out that, with the meager-est of security systems, West Germany has had nuclear weapons in her hands for the past six years.

What do you make of it?

Some will make of it that I overdraw the matter. Many will ask: What about the other side? To be sure, there is the bitter ugliness of Czechoslovakia, Poland, those infamous Russian tanks in the streets of Budapest. But my anger only rises to hear some say that sorrow cancels sorrow, or that *this* one's shame deposits in *that* one's account the right to shamefulness.

And others will make of it that I sound mighty anti-American. To these, I say: Don't blame *me* for *that*! Blame those who mouthed my liberal values and broke my American heart.

Just who might they be, by the way? Let's take a brief factual inventory of the latter-day Cold War.

In 1953 our Central Intelligence Agency managed to overthrow Mossadegh in Iran, the complaint being his neutralism in the Cold War and his plans to nationalize the country's oil resources to improve his people's lives. Most evil aims, most evil man. In his place we put in General Zahedi, a World War II Nazi collaborator. New arrangements on Iran's oil gave twenty-five-year leases on 40 percent of it to three United States firms, one of which was Gulf Oil. The CIA's leader for this coup was Kermit Roosevelt. In 1960 Kermit Roosevelt became a vice-president of Gulf Oil.

In 1954 the democratically elected Arbenz of Guatamala wanted to nationalize a portion of United Fruit Company's plantations in his country, land he needed badly for a modest program of agrarian reform. His government was overthrown in a CIA-supported right-wing coup. The following year, General Walter Bedell Smith, director of the CIA when the Guatemala venture was being planned, joined the board of directors of the United Fruit Company.

Comes 1960 and Castro cries we are about to invade Cuba. The Administration sneers "poppycock," and we Americans believe it. Comes 1961 and the invasion. Comes with it the awful realization that the United States government had lied.

Comes 1962 and the missile crisis, and our Administration stands prepared to fight global atomic war on the curious principle that another state does not have the right to its own foreign policy.

Comes 1963 and British Guiana, where Cheddi Jagan wants independence from England and a labor law modeled on the Wagner Act. And Jay Lovestone, the AFL-CIO foreign policy chief, acting, as always, quite independently of labor's rank and file, arranges with our government to finance an eleven-week dock strike that brings Jagan down, ensuring that the state will remain *British* Guiana, and that any workingman who wants a wage better than fifty cents a day is a dupe of Communism.

Comes 1964. Two weeks after Undersecretary Thomas Mann announces that we have abandoned the *Alianza's* principle of no aid to tyrants, Brazil's Goulart is overthrown by the vicious right-winger Ademar Barros, supported by a show of American gun-boats at Rio de Janeiro. Within twenty-four hours the new head of state, Mazzilli, receives a congratulatory wire from our President.

Comes 1965. The Dominican Republic. Rebellion in the streets. We scurry to the spot with twenty thousand neutral Marines and our neutral peacemakers—like Ellsworth Bunker, Jr., Ambassador to the Organization of American States. Most of us know that our neutral Marines fought openly on the side of the junta, a fact that the Administration still denies. But how many also know that what was at stake was our new Caribbean sugar bowl? That this same neutral peace-making Bunker is a board member and stock owner of the National Sugar Refining Company, a firm his father founded in the good old days, and one which has a major interest in maintaining the status quo in the Dominican Republic? Or that the President's close personal friend and ad-visor, our new Supreme Court Justice Abe Fortas, has sat for the past nineteen years on the board of the Sucrest Company, which imports black-strap molasses from the Dominican Republic? Or that the rhetorician of corporate liberalism and the late President Kennedy's close friend, Adolf Berle, was chairman of that same board? Or that our roving ambassador Averell Harriman's brother Roland is on the board of National Sugar? Or that our former Ambassador to the Dominican Republic, Joseph Farland, is a board member of the South Peurto Rico Sugar Co., which owns 275,000 acres of rich land in the Dominican Republic and is the largest employer on the island—at about one dollar a day?

Neutralists! God save the hungry people of the world from such neutralists!

We do not say these men are evil. We say, rather, that good men can be divided from their compassion by the institutional system that inherits us all. Generation in and out, we are put to use. People become instruments. Generals do not hear the screams of the bombed; sugar executives do not see the misery of the cane cutters: for to do so is to be that much *less* the general, that much *less* the executive.

The foregoing facts of recent history describe one main aspect of the estate of Western liberalism. Where is our American humanism here? What went wrong?

Let's stare our situation coldly in the face. All of us are born to the colossus of history, our American corporate system—in many ways an awesome organism. There is one fact that describes it: with about 5 percent of the world's people, we consume about half the world's goods. We take a richness that is in good part not our own, and we put it in our pockets, our garages, our split-levels, our bellies, and our futures.

On the *face* of it, it is a crime that so few should have so much at the expense of so many. Where is the moral imagination so abused as to call this just? Perhaps many of us feel a bit uneasy in our sleep. We are not, after all, a cruel people. And perhaps we don't really need this super-dominance that deforms others. But what can we do? The investments are made. The financial ties are established. The plants abroad are built. Our system *exists*. One is swept up into it. How intolerable—to be born moral, but addicted to a stolen and maybe surplus luxury. Our goodness threatens to become counterfeit before our eyes—unless we change. But change threatens us with uncertainty—at least.

Our problem, then, is to justify this system and give its theft another name—to make kind and moral what is neither, to perform some alchemy with language that will make this injustice seem to be a most magnanimous gift.

A hard problem. But the Western democracies, in the heyday of their colonial expansionism, produced a hero worthy of the task.

Its name was free enterprise, and its partner was an *illiberal liberalism* that said to the poor and the dispossessed: What we acquire of your resources we repay in civilization. The white man's burden. But this was too poetic. So a much more hard-headed theory was produced. This theory said that colonial status is in fact a *boon* to the colonized. We give them technology and bring them into modern times.

But this deceived no one but ourselves. We were delighted with this new theory. The poor saw in it merely an admission that their claims were irrefutable. They stood up to us, without gratitude. We were shocked—but also confused, for the poor seemed again to be right. How long is it going to be the case, we wondered, that the poor will be right and the rich will be wrong?

Liberalism faced a crisis. In the face of the collapse of the European empires, how could it continue to hold together our twin need for richness and righteousness? How can we continue to sack the ports of Asia and still dream of Jesus?

The challenge was met with a most ingenious solution: the ideology of anti-Communism. This was the bind: we cannot call revolution bad, because we started that way ourselves, and because it is all too easy to see why the dispossessed should rebel. So we will call revolution *Communism*. And we will reserve for ourselves the right to say what Communism means. We take note of revolution's enormities, wrenching them where necessary from their historical context and often exaggerating them, and say: Behold, Communism is a bloodbath. We take note of those reactionaries who stole the revolution, and say: Behold, Communism is a betrayal of the people. We take note of the revolution's need to consolidate itself, and say: Behold, Communism is a tyranny.

It has been all these things, and it will be these things again, and we will never be at a loss for those tales of atrocity that comfort us so in our self-righteousness. Nuns will be raped and bureaucrats will be disemboweled. Indeed, revolution is a *fury*. For it is a letting loose of outrages pent up sometimes over centuries. But the more brutal and longer-lasting the suppression of this energy, all the more ferocious will be its explosive release.

Far from helping Americans deal with this truth, the anti-Communist ideology merely tries to disguise it so that things may stay the way they are. Thus, it depicts our presence in other lands not as a coercion, but a protection. It allows us even to say that the napalm in Vietnam is only another aspect of our humanitarian love—like those exorcisms in the Middle Ages that so often killed the patient. So we say to the Vietnamese peasant, the Cuban intellectual, the Peruvian worker: "You are better dead than red. If it hurts or if you don't understand why—sorry about that."

This is the action of *corporate liberalism*. It performs for the corporate state a function quite like what the Church once performed for the feudal state. It seeks to justify its burdens and protect it from change. As the Church exaggerated this office in the Inquisition, so with liberalism in the McCarthy time—which, if it was a reactionary phenomenon, was still made possible by our anti-Communist corporate liberalism.

Let me then speak directly to humanist liberals. If my facts are wrong, I will soon be corrected. But if they are right, then you may face a crisis of conscience. Corporatism or humanism; which? For it has come to that. Will you let your dreams be used? Will you be grudging apologists for the corporate state? Or will you help try to change it—not in the name of this or that blueprint or ism, but in the name of simple human decency and democracy and the vision that wise and brave men saw in the time of our own Revolution?

And if your commitment to human value is unconditional, then disabuse yourselves of the notion that statements will bring change, if only the right statements can be written, or that interviews with the mighty will bring change if only the mighty can be reached, or that marches will bring change if only we can make them massive enough, or that policy proposals will bring change if only we can make them responsible enough.

We are dealing now with a colossus that does not want to be changed. It will not change itself. It will not cooperate with those who want to change it. Those allies of ours in the government— are they really our allies? If they *are*, then they don't need advice, they need *constituencies*; they don't need study groups, they need a *movement*. And if they are *not*, then all the more reason for building that movement with a most relentless conviction.

There are people in this country today who are trying to build that movement, who aim at nothing less than a humanist reformation. And the humanist liberals must understand that it is this movement with which their own best hopes are most in tune. We radicals know the same history that you liberals know, and we can understand your occasional cynicism, exasperation, and even distrust. But we ask you to put these aside and help us risk a leap. Help us find enough time for the enormous work that needs doing here. Help us build. Help us shake the future in the name of plain human hope.

# PART TWO

## The Historical Context

# 5  Alexis de Tocqueville: Americans Love Change, But They Dread Revolutions (1840)

*Alexis Charles Henri Clerel de Tocqueville (1805–59) arrived in the United States from France for a visit in May 1831. From his observations of Jacksonian America, Tocqueville wrote* Democracy in America, *the most famous analysis of American society ever written by a foreign visitor. Both awed and amused by the traditions (or lack thereof), economic enterprise, and political interests that he discovered in the United States, Tocqueville's greatness as a social observer lay in his ability to reach general conclusions from his specific observations. An example of this genius is his analysis of why Americans would be antirevolutionary (unless, as he carefully added, these revolutions would "be brought about by the presence of the black race on the soil of the United States."). Can you discover evidences of Tocqueville's theme in the Johnson, Goldwater, and Fulbright readings? Are there characteristics of these readings, and of Oglesby's in particular, that Tocqueville failed to perceive when he concluded that Americans would be antirevolutionary?*

---

A people who have existed for centuries under a system of castes and classes, can only arrive at a democratic state of society by passing through a long series of more or less critical transformations, accomplished by violent efforts, and after numerous vicissitudes; in the course of which, property, opinions, and power are rapidly transferred from one to another. Even after this great revolution is consummated, the revolutionary habits produced by it may long be traced, and it will be followed by deep commotion. As all this takes place at the very time when social conditions are becoming more equal, it is inferred that some concealed relation and secret tie exists between the principle of equality

SOURCE. Alexis de Tocqueville, *Democracy in America*, Henry Reeve, tr., edited with notes by Henry Bowen, Cambridge: Sever and Francis, 1862, II, pp. 308–323.

itself and revolution insomuch that the one cannot exist without giving rise to the other. . . .

But is this really the case? Does the equality of social conditions habitually and permanently lead men to revolution. . . . ? I do not believe it; and as the subject is important, I beg for the reader's close attention.

Almost all the revolutions which have changed the aspect of nations have been made to consolidate or to destroy social inequality. Remove the secondary causes which have produced the great convulsions of the world, and you will almost always find the principle of inequality at the bottom. Either the poor have attempted to plunder the rich, or the rich to enslave the poor. If, then, a state of society can ever be founded in which every man shall have something to keep, and little to take from others, much will have been done for the peace of the world. . . .

Not only are the men of democracies not naturally desirous of revolutions, but they are afraid of them. All revolutions more or less threaten the tenure of property: but most of those who live in democratic countries are possessed of property; not only are they possessed of property, but they live in the condition where men set the greatest store upon their property. . . .

I have shown, in another part of this work, that the equality of conditions naturally urges men to embark in commercial and industrial pursuits, and that it tends to increase and to distribute real property: I have also pointed out the means by which it inspires every man with an eager and constant desire to increase his welfare. Nothing is more opposed to revolutionary passions than these things. It may happen that the final result of a revolution is favorable to commerce and manufactures; but its first consequence will almost always be the ruin of manufacturers and mercantile men, because it must always change at once the general principles of consumption, and temporarily upset the existing proportion between supply and demand.

I know of nothing more opposite to revolutionary manners than commercial manners. Commerce is naturally adverse to all the violent passions; it loves to temporize, takes delight in compromise, and studiously avoids irritation. It is patient, insinuating, flexible, and never has recourse to extreme measures until obliged by the most absolute necessity. Commerce renders men independent of each other, gives them a lofty notion of their personal importance, leads them to seek to conduct their own affairs, and teaches how to conduct them well; it therefore prepares men for freedom, but preserves them from revolutions. . . .

Moreover, whatever profession men may embrace, and whatever species of property they may possess, one characteristic is common to them all. No one is fully contented with his present fortune; all are perpetually striving, in a thousand ways, to improve it. Consider any one of them at any period of his life, and he will be found engaged with some new project for the purpose of increasing what he has; talk not to him of the interests and the rights of mankind, this small domestic concern absorbs for the time all his thoughts, and inclines him to defer political agitations to some other season. This not only prevents men from making revolutions, but deters men from desiring them. Violent political passions have but little hold on those who have devoted all their faculties to the pursuit of their well-being. The ardor which they display in small matters calms their zeal for momentous undertakings. . . .

I do not assert that men living in democratic communities are naturally stationary; I think, on the contrary, that a perpetual stir prevails in the bosom of those societies, and that rest is unknown there; but I think that men bestir themselves within certain limits, beyond which they hardly ever go. They are forever varying, altering, and restoring secondary matters; but they carefully abstain from touching what is fundamental. They love change, but they dread revolutions.

Although the Americans are constantly modifying or abrogating some of their laws, they by no means display revolutionary passions. . . . In no country in the world is the love of property more active and more anxious than in the United States; nowhere does the majority display less inclination for those principles which threaten to alter, in whatever manner, the laws of property.

I have often remarked, that theories which are of a revolutionary nature, since they cannot be put in practice without a complete and sometimes a sudden change in the state of property and persons, are much less favorably viewed in the United States than in the great monarchical countries of Europe: if some men profess them, the bulk of the people reject them with instinctive abhorrence. I do not hesitate to say, that most of the maxims commonly called democratic in France would be proscribed by the democracy of the United States. This may easily be understood; in America, men have the opinions and passions of democracy; in Europe, we have still the passions and opinions of revolution.

If ever America undergoes great revolutions, they will be brought about by the presence of the black race on the soil of the United States; that is to say, they will owe their origin, not to the equality, but to the inequality of condition. . . .

The observations I have here made on events may also be applied in part to opinions. Two things are surprising in the United States,—the mutability of the greater part of human actions, and the singular stability of certain principles. Men are in constant motion; the mind of man appears almost unmoved. When once an opinion has spread over the country and struck root there, it would seem that no power on earth is strong enough to eradicate it. In the United States, general principles in religion, philosophy, morality, and even politics, do not vary, or at least are only modified by a hidden and often an imperceptible process; even the grossest prejudices are obliterated within incredible slowness, amidst the continual friction of men and things.

I hear it said that it is in the nature and the habits of democracies to be constantly changing their opinions and feelings. This may be true of small democratic nations, like those of the ancient world, in which the whole community could be assembled in a public place, and then excited at will by an orator. But I saw nothing of the kind amongst the great democratic people which dwells upon the opposite shores of the Atlantic Ocean. What struck me in the United States was, the difficulty of shaking the majority in an opinion once conceived, or of drawing it off from a leader once adopted. Neither speaking nor writing can accomplish it; nothing but experience will avail, and even experience must be repeated. . . .

Amidst the ruins which surround me, shall I dare to say that revolutions are not what I most fear for coming generations? If men continue to shut themselves more closely within the narrow circle of domestic interests, and to live upon that kind of excitement, it is to be apprehended that they may ultimately become inaccessible to those great and powerful public emotions which perturb nations, but which develop them and recruit them. When property becomes so fluctuating, and the love of property so restless and so ardent, I cannot but fear that men may arrive at such a state as to regard every new theory as a peril, every innovation as an irksome toil, every social improvement as a stepping-stone to revolution, and so refuse to move altogether for fear of being moved too far. I dread, and I confess it, lest they should at last so entirely give way to a cowardly love of present enjoyment, as to lose sight of the interests of their future selves and those of their descendants; and prefer to glide along the easy current of life, rather than to make, when it is necessary, a strong and sudden effort to a higher purpose.

# PART THREE

*Documents (1947-1967)*

# CHAPTER I
## "MR. X" (1947-1950)

It was twenty years ago today,
Sgt. Pepper taught the band to play
They've been going in and out of style
But they're guaranteed to raise a smile.
So may I introduce to you
The act you've known for all these years,
Sgt. Pepper's Lonely Hearts Club Band.

The Beatles, *Sgt. Pepper's Lonely Hearts Club Band*, 1967.
Copyright 1967 by Northern Songs Ltd. (Used by permission;
all rights reserved.)

## 6  George F. Kennan ("Mr. X"): The Sources of Soviet Conduct (July 1947)

George Kennan (1904–    ) began his career as a Foreign Service
Officer in the Department of State in 1927. In 1933 he was a member
of the American mission to Moscow that helped to establish the first
formal diplomatic ties between the United States and the Soviet
Union. During the next 13 years he served in Vienna, Prague, Berlin,
Lisbon, London, and in 1945 returned to the American Embassy in
Moscow. While in Russia during 1945 and part of 1946, he sent the
State Department long telegrams analyzing Soviet foreign policy.
Kennan warned that, because of Marxist ideology and Stalinist politi-
cal strategies, the Russians could not be the trusted allies of the United

*States in the postwar world. His messages came to the attention of high Washington officials, including Secretary of the Navy (and later Secretary of Defense) James Forrestal, who were arguing for a tougher policy against the Soviets. Kennan returned to Washington in 1946, soon became the most influential member of the State Department's Policy Planning Staff, was instrumental in shaping the Truman Doctrine and the Marshall Plan and, in the Mr. "X" article which follows, made public the assumptions that guided the Truman Administration's foreign policies in the early years of the Cold War. Notice very carefully the history on which Kennan bases his suggestions for future policy. Is this historical record sufficiently accurate and complete to justify his policy of "containment?" What meaning does this article have for American attitudes toward revolutions? Does Kennan indicate an awareness of the American attitudes described in the Tocqueville selection (Reading 5)?*

---

The political personality of Soviet power as we know it today is the product of ideology and circumstances: ideology inherited by the present Soviet leaders from the movement in which they had their political origin, and circumstances of the power which they now have exercised for nearly three decades in Russia. There can be few tasks of psychological analysis more difficult than to try to trace the interaction of these two forces and the relative role of each in the determination of official Soviet conduct. Yet the attempt must be made if that conduct is to be understood and effectively countered.

It is difficult to summarize the set of ideological concepts with which the Soviet leaders came into power. Marxian ideology, in its Russian-Communist projection, has always been in process of subtle evolution. The materials on which it bases itself are extensive and complex. But the outstanding features of Communist thought as it existed in 1916 may perhaps be summarized as fol-

SOURCE. "X," "The Sources of Soviet Conduct," in *Foreign Affairs*, Vol. XXV, July 1947, pp. 566–582. Copyright by the Council on Foreign Relations, Inc., New York. Reprinted by special permission from *Foreign Affairs*, July 1947 issue.

lows: (a) that the central factor in the life of man, the fact which determines the character of public life and the "physiognomy of society," is the system by which material goods are produced and exchanged; (b) that the capitalist system of production is a nefarious one which inevitably leads to the exploitation of the working class by the capital-owning class and is incapable of developing adequately the economic resources of society or of distributing fairly the material goods produced by human labor; (c) that capitalism contains the seeds of its own destruction and must, in view of the inability of the capital-owning class to adjust itself to economic change, result eventually and inescapably in a revolutionary transfer of power to the working class; and (d) that imperialism, the final phase of capitalism, leads directly to war and revolution.

The rest may be outlined in Lenin's own words: "Unevenness of economic and political development is the inflexible law of capitalism. It follows from this that the victory of Socialism may come originally in a few capitalist countries or even in a single capitalist country. The victorious proletariat of that country, having expropriated the capitalists and having organized Socialist production at home, would rise against the remaining capitalist world, drawing to itself in the process the oppressed classes of other countries." It must be noted that there was no assumption that capitalism would perish without proletarian revolution. A final push was needed from a revolutionary proletariat movement in order to tip over the tottering structure. But it was regarded as inevitable that sooner or later that push be given. . . .

The circumstances of the immediate post-Revolution period—the existence in Russia of civil war and foreign intervention, together with the obvious fact that the Communists represented only a tiny minority of the Russian people—made the establishment of dictatorial power a necessity. The experiment with "war Communism" and the abrupt attempt to eliminate private production and trade had unfortunate economic consequences and caused further bitterness against the new revolutionary regime. While the temporary relaxation of the effort to communize Russia, represented by the New Economic Policy, alleviated some of this economic distress and thereby served its purpose, it also made it evident that the "capitalistic sector of society" was still prepared to profit at once from any relaxation of governmental pressure, and would, if permitted to continue to exist, always constitute a powerful opposing element to the Soviet regime and a serious rival for influence in the country. Somewhat the same situation prevailed with respect to the individual peasant who, in his own small way, was also a private producer.

Lenin, had he lived, might have proved a great enough man to reconcile these conflicting forces to the ultimate benefit of Russian society, though this is questionable. But be that as it may, Stalin, and those whom he led in the struggle for succession to Lenin's position of leadership, were not the men to tolerate rival political forces in the sphere of power which they coveted. Their sense of insecurity was too great. Their particular brand of fanaticism, unmodified by any of the Anglo-Saxon traditions of compromise, was too fierce and too jealous to envisage any permanent sharing of power. From the Russian-Asiatic world out of which they had emerged they carried with them a skepticism as to the possibilities of permanent and peaceful coexistence of rival forces. Easily persuaded of their own doctrinaire "rightness," they insisted on the submission or destruction of all competing power. Outside of the Communist Party, Russian society was to have no rigidity. There were to be no forms of collective human activity or association which would not be dominated by the Party. No other force in Russian society was to be permitted to achieve vitality or integrity. Only the Party was to have structure. All else was to be an amorphous mass.

And within the Party the same principle was to apply. The mass of Party members might go through the motions of election, deliberation, decision and action; but in these motions they were to be animated not by their own individual wills but by the awesome breath of the Party leadership and the overbrooding presence of "the world". . . .

Now the outstanding circumstance concerning the Soviet regime is that down to the present day this process of political consolidation has never been completed and the men in the Kremlin have continued to be predominantly absorbed with the struggle to secure and make absolute the power which they seized in November 1917. They have endeavored to secure it primarily against forces at home, within Soviet society itself. But they have also endeavored to secure it against the outside world. For ideology, as we have seen, taught them that the outside world was hostile and that it was their duty eventually to overthrow the political forces beyond their borders. The powerful hands of Russian history and tradition reached up to sustain them in this feeling. Finally, their own aggressive intransigence with respect to the outside world began to find its own reaction; and they were soon forced, to use another Gibbonesque phrase, "to chastise the contumacy" which they themselves had provoked. It is an undeniable privilege of every man to prove himself right in the thesis that the world is his enemy; for if he reiterates it frequently enough and makes it the background of his conduct he is bound eventually to be right.

Now it lies in the nature of the mental world of the Soviet leaders, as well as in the character of their ideology, that no opposition to them can be officially recognized as having any merit or justification whatsoever. Such opposition can flow, in theory, only from the hostile and incorrigible forces of dying capitalism. As long as remnants of capitalism were officially recognized as existing in Russia, it was possible to place on them, as an internal element, part of the blame for the maintenance of a dictatorial form of society. But as these remnants were liquidated, little by little, this justification fell away; and when it was indicated officially that they had been finally destroyed, it disappeared altogether. And this fact created one of the most basic of the compulsions which came to act upon the Soviet regime: since capitalism no longer existed in Russia and since it could not be admitted that there could be serious or widespread opposition to the Kremlin springing spontaneously from the liberated masses under its authority, it became necessary to justify the retention of the dictatorship by stressing the menace of capitalism abroad.

This began at an early date. In 1924, Stalin specifically defended the retention of the "organs of suppression," meaning, among others, the army and the secret police, on the ground that "as long as there is a capitalist encirclement there will be danger of intervention with all the consequences that flow from that danger." In accordance with that theory, and from that time on, all internal opposition forces in Russia have consistently been portrayed as the agents of foreign forces of reaction antagonistic to Soviet power.

By the same token, tremendous emphasis has been placed on the original Communist thesis of a basic antagonism between the capitalist and Socialist worlds. It is clear, from many indications, that this emphasis is not founded in reality. The real facts concerning it have been confused by the existence abroad of genuine resentment provoked by Soviet philosophy and tactics and occasionally by the existence of great centers of military power, notably the Nazi regime in Germany and the Japanese government of the late 1930's, which did indeed have aggressive designs against the Soviet Union. But there is ample evidence that the stress laid in Moscow on the menace confronting Soviet society from the world outside its borders is founded not in the realities of foreign antagonism but in the necessity of explaining away the maintenance of dictatorial authority at home. . . .

## II

So much for the historical background. What does it spell in terms of the political personality of Soviet power as we know it today?

Of the original ideology, nothing has been officially junked. Belief is maintained in the basic badness of capitalism, in the inevitability of its destruction, in the obligation of the proletariat to assist in that destruction and to take power into its own hands. But stress has come to be laid primarily on those concepts which relate most specifically to the Soviet regime itself: to its position as the sole truly Socialist regime in a dark and misguided world, and to the relationships of power within it.

The first of these concepts is that of the innate antagonism between capitalism and Socialism. We have seen how deeply that concept has become imbedded in foundations of Soviet power. It has profound implications for Russia's conduct as a member of international society. It means that there can never be on Moscow's side any sincere assumption of a community of aims between the Soviet Union and powers which are regarded as capitalism. It must invariably be assumed in Moscow that the aims of the capitalist world are antagonistic to the Soviet regime and, therefore, to the interests of the peoples it controls. If the Soviet government occasionally sets its signature to documents which would indicate the contrary, this is to be regarded as a tactical maneuver permissible in dealing with the enemy (who is without honor) and should be taken in the spirit of *caveat emptor*. Basically, the antagonism remains. It is postulated. And from it flow many of the phenomena which we find disturbing in the Kremlin's conduct of foreign policy: the secretiveness, the lack of frankness, the duplicity, the war suspiciousness, and the basic unfriendliness of purpose. These phenomena are there to stay, for the foreseeable future. There can be variations of degree and of emphasis. When there is something the Russians want from us, one or the other of these features of their policy may be thrust temporarily into the background; and when that happens there will always be Americans who will leap forward with gleeful announcements that "the Russians have changed," and some who will even try to take credit for having brought about such "changes." But we should not be misled by tactical maneuvers. These characteristics of Soviet policy, like the postulate from which they flow, are basic to the internal nature of Soviet power, and will be with us, whether in the foreground or the background, until the internal nature of Soviet power is changed.

This means that we are going to continue for a long time to find the Russians difficult to deal with. It does not mean that they should be considered as embarked upon a do-or-die program to overthrow our society by a given date. The theory of the inevitability of the eventual fall of capitalism has the fortunate connotation that there is no hurry about it. The forces of progress can take their time in preparing the final *coup de grace*. Meanwhile, what is vital is that the "Socialist fatherland"—that oasis of power which has been already won for Socialism in the person of the Soviet Union—should be cherished and defended by all good Communists at home and abroad, its fortunes promoted, its enemies badgered and confronted. The promotion of premature, "adventuristic" revolutionary projects abroad which might embarrass Soviet power in any way would be an inexcusable, even a counter-revolutionary act. The cause of Socialism is the support and promotion of Soviet power, as defined in Moscow.

This brings us to the second of the concepts important to contemporary Soviet outlook. That is the infallibility of the Kremlin. The Soviet concept of power, which permits no focal points of organization outside the Party itself, requires that the Party leadership remain in theory the sole repository of truth. For if truth were to be found elsewhere, there would be justification for its expression in organized activity. But it is precisely that which the Kremlin cannot and will not permit.

The leadership of the Communist Party is therefore always right and has been always right ever since in 1929 Stalin formalized his personal power by announcing that decisions of the Politburo were being taken unanimously.

On the principle of infallibility there rests the iron discipline of the Communist Party. In fact, the two concepts are mutually self-supporting. Perfect discipline requires recognition of infallibility. Infallibility requires the observance of discipline. And the two together go far to determine the behaviorism of the entire Soviet apparatus of power. But their effect cannot be understood unless a third factor be taken into account: namely, the fact that the leadership is at liberty to put forward for tactical purposes any particular thesis which it finds useful to the cause at any particular moment and to require the faithful and unquestioning acceptance of that thesis by the members of the movement as a whole. This means that truth is not a constant but is actually created, for all intents and purposes, by the Soviet leaders themselves. It may vary from week to week, from month to month. It is nothing absolute and immutable—nothing which flows from objective reality. It is only the most recent manifestation of the wisdom of those in whom the ultimate wisdom is supposed to reside, because they represent the logic of history. The accumulative effect of these factors is to give to the whole subordinate apparatus of Soviet power an unshakeable stubborness and steadfastness in its orientation. This orientation can be changed at will by the Kremlin but by no other power. Once a given party line has been laid down on a given issue of current policy, the whole Soviet governmental machine, including the mechanism of diplomacy, moves inexorably along the prescribed path, like a persistent toy automobile wound up and headed in a given direction, stopping only when it meets with some unanswerable force. The individuals who are the components of this machine are unamenable to argument or reason which comes to them from outside sources. Their whole training has taught them to mistrust and discount the glib persuasiveness of the outside world. Like the white dog before the phonograph, they hear only the "master's voice." And if they are to be called off from the purposes last dictated to them, it is the master who must call them off. . . .

But we have seen that the Kremlin is under no ideological compulsion to accomplish its purposes in a hurry. Like the Church, it is dealing in ideological concepts which are of long-term validity, and it can afford to be patient. It has no right to risk the existing achievements of the revolution for the sake of vain baubles of the future. The very teachings of Lenin himself require great caution and flexibility in the pursuit of Communist purposes. Again, these precepts are fortified by the lessons of Russian history: of centuries of obscure battles between nomadic forces over the stretches of a vast unfortified plain. Here caution, circumspection, flexibility and deception are the valuable qualities; and their value finds natural appreciation in the Russian or the oriental mind. Thus the Kremlin has no compunction about retreating in the face of superior force. And being under the compulsion of no timetable, it does not get panicky under the necessity for such retreat. Its political action is a fluid stream which moves constantly, wherever it is permitted to move, toward a given goal. Its main concern is to make sure that it has filled every nook and cranny available to it in the basin of world power. But if it finds unassailable barriers in its path, it accepts these philosophically and accommodates itself to them. The main thing is that there should always be pressure, increasing constant pressure, toward the desired goal. There is no trace of any feeling in Soviet psychology that that goal must be reached at any given time.

These considerations make Soviet diplomacy at once easier and more difficult to deal with than the diplomacy of individual aggressive leaders like Napoleon and Hitler. On the one hand it is more sensitive to contrary force, more ready to yield on individual sectors of the diplomatic front when that force is felt to be too strong, and thus more rational in the logic and rhetoric of power. On the other hand it cannot be easily defeated or discouraged by a single victory on the part of its opponents. And the patient persistence by which it is animated means that it can be effectively countered not by sporadic acts which represent the momentary whims of democratic opinion but only by intelligent long-range policies on the part of Russia's adversaries—policies no less steady in their purpose, and no less variegated and resourceful in their application, than those of the Soviet Union itself.

In these circumstances it is clear that the main element of any United States policy toward the Soviet Union must be that of a long-term, patient but firm and vigilant containment of Russian expansive tendencies. It is important to note, however, that such a policy has nothing to do with outward histrionics: with threats or blustering or superfluous gestures of outward "toughness." While the Kremlin is basically flexible in its reaction to political realities, it is by no means unamenable to considerations of prestige. Like almost any other government, it can be placed by tactless and threatening gestures in a position where it cannot afford to yield even though this might be dictated by its sense of realism. The Russian leaders are keen judges of human psychology, and as such they are highly conscious that loss of temper and of self-control is never a source of strength in political affairs. They are quick to exploit such evidences of weakness. For these reasons, it is a *sine qua non* of successful dealing with Russia that the foreign government in question should remain at all times cool and collected and that its demands on Russian policy should be put forward in such a manner as to leave the way open for a compliance not too detrimental to Russian prestige.

### III

In the light of the above, it will be clearly seen that the Soviet pressure against the free institutions of the Western world is something that can be contained by the adroit and vigilant application of counter-force at a series of constantly shifting geographical and political points, corresponding to the shifts and maneuvers of Soviet policy, but which cannot be charmed or talked out of existence. The Russians look forward to a duel of infinite duration, and they see that already they have scored great successes. It must be borne in mind that there was a time when the Communist Party represented far more of a minority in the sphere of Russian national life than Soviet power today represents in the world community.

But if ideology convinces the rulers of Russia that truth is on their side and that they can therefore afford to wait, those of us on whom that ideology has no claim are free to examine objectively the validity of that premise. The Soviet thesis not only implies complete lack of control by the West over its own economic destiny, it likewise assumes Russian unity, discipline and patience over an infinite period. Let us bring this apocalyptic vision down to earth, and suppose that the Western world finds the strength and resourcefulness to contain Soviet power over a period of ten to fifteen years. What does that spell for Russia itself?

The Soviet leaders, taking advantage of the contributions of modern technique to the arts of despotism, have solved the question of obedience within the confines of their power. Few challenge their authority; and even those who do are unable to make that challenge valid as against the organs of suppression of the state.

The Kremlin has also proved able to accomplish its purpose of building up in Russia, regardless of the interests of the inhabitants, an industrial foundation of heavy metallurgy, which is, to be sure, not yet complete but which is nevertheless continuing to grow and is approaching those of the other major industrial countries. All of this, however, both the maintenance of internal political security and the building of heavy industry, has been carried out at a terrible cost in human life and in human hopes and energies. It has necessitated the use of forced labor on a scale unprecedented in modern times under conditions of peace. It has involved the neglect or abuse of other phases of Soviet economic life, particularly agriculture, consumers' goods production, housing and transportation.

To all that, the war has added its tremendous toll of destruction, death and human exhaustion. In consequence of this, we have in Russia today a population which is physically and spiritually tired. The mass of the people are disillusioned, skeptical and no longer as accessible as they once were to the magical attraction which Soviet power still radiates to its followers abroad. The avidity with which people seized upon the slightest respite accorded to the Church for tactical reasons during the war was eloquent testimony to the fact that their capacity for faith and devotion found little expression in the purposes of the regime.

In these circumstances, there are limits to the physical and nervous strength of people themselves. These limits are absolute ones, and are binding even for the cruelest dictatorship, because beyond them people cannot be driven. . . .

In addition to this, we have the fact that Soviet economic development, while it can list certain formidable achievements, has been precariously spotty and uneven. Russian Communists who speak of the "uneven development of capitalism" should blush at the contemplation of their own national economy. Here certain branches of economic life, such as the metallurgical and machine industries, have been pushed out of all proportion to other sectors of economy. Here is a nation striving to become in a short period one of the great industrial nations of the world while it still has no highway network worthy of the name and only a relatively primitive network of railways. . . .

It is difficult to see how these deficiencies can be corrected at an early date by a tired and dispirited population working largely under the shadow of fear and compulsion. And as long as they are not overcome, Russia will remain economically a vulnerable, and in a certain sense an impotent, nation, capable of exporting its enthusiasms and of radiating the strange charm of its primitive political vitality but unable to back up those articles of export by the real evidences of material power and prosperity.

Meanwhile, a great uncertainty hangs over the political life of the Soviet Union. That is the uncertainty involved in the transfer of power from one individual or group of individuals to others.

This is, of course, outstandingly the problem of the personal position of Stalin. We must remember that his succession to Lenin's pinnacle of pre-eminence in the Communist movement was the only such transfer of individual authority which the Soviet Union has experienced. That transfer took twelve years to consolidate. It cost the lives of millions of people and shook the state to its foundations. The attendant tremors were felt all through the international revolutionary movement, to the disadvantage of the Kremlin itself.

It is always possible that another transfer of preeminent power may take place quietly and inconspicuously, with no repercus-

sions anywhere. But again, it is possible that the questions involved may unleash, to use some of Lenin's words, one of those
"incredibly swift transitions" from "delicate deceit" to "wild
violence" which characterize Russian history, and may shake
Soviet power to its foundations. . . .

Thus the future of Soviet power may not be by any means as
secure as Russian capacity for self-delusion would make it appear
to the men in the Kremlin. That they can keep power themselves, they have demonstrated. That they can quietly and easily
turn it over to others remains to be proved. Meanwhile, the
hardships of their rule and the vicissitudes of international life
have taken a heavy toll of the strength and hopes of the great
people on whom their power rests. It is curious to note that the
ideological power of Soviet authority is strongest today in areas
beyond the frontiers of Russia, beyond the reach of its police
power. This phenomenon brings to mind a comparison used by
Thomas Mann in his great novel *Buddenbrooks*. Observing that
human institutions often show the greatest outward brilliance at
a moment when inner decay is in reality farthest advanced, he
compared the Buddenbrook family, in the days of its greatest
glamour to one of those stars whose light shines most brightly on
this world when in reality it has long ceased to exist. And who
can say with assurance that the strong light still cast by the
Kremlin on the dissatisfied peoples of the Western world is not
the powerful afterglow of a constellation which is in actuality
on the wane? This cannot be proved. And it cannot be disproved.
But the possibility remains (and in the opinion of this writer it is
a strong one) that Soviet power, like the capitalist world of its
conception, bears within it the seeds of its own decay, and that
the sprouting of these seeds is well advanced.

## IV

It is clear that the United States cannot expect in the foreseeable
future to enjoy political intimacy with the Soviet regime. It must
continue to regard the Soviet Union as a rival, not a partner, in
the political arena. It must continue to expect that Soviet policies
will reflect no abstract love of peace and stability, no real faith
in the possibility of a permanent happy coexistence of the Socialist and capitalist worlds, but rather a cautious, persistent

pressure toward the disruption and weakening of all rival influence and rival power.

Balanced against this are the facts that Russia, as opposed to the Western world in general, is still by far the weaker party, that Soviet policy is highly flexible, and that Soviet society may well contain deficiencies which will eventually weaken its own total potential. This would of itself warrant the United States entering with reasonable confidence upon a policy of firm containment, designed to confront the Russians with unalterable counter-force at every point where they show signs of encroaching upon the interests of a peaceful and stable world. . . .

It would be an exaggeration to say that American behavior unassisted and alone could exercise a power of life and death over the Communist movement and bring about the early fall of Soviet power in Russia. But the United States has it in its power to increase enormously the strains under which Soviet policy must operate, to force upon the Kremlin a far greater degree of moderation and circumspection than it has had to observe in recent years, and in this way to promote tendencies which must eventually find their outlet in either the breakup or the gradual mellowing of Soviet power. For no mystical, Messianic movement—and particularly not that of the Kremlin—can face frustration indefinitely without eventually adjusting itself in one way or another to the logic of that state of affairs.

Thus the decision will really fall in large measure in this country itself. The issue of Soviet-American relations is in essence a test of the over-all worth of the United States as a nation among nations. To avoid destruction the United States need only measure up to its own best traditions and prove itself worthy of preservation as a great nation.

Surely, there was never a fairer test of national quality than this. In the light of these circumstances, the thoughtful observer of Russian-American relations will find no cause for complaint in the Kremlin's challenge to American society. He will rather experience a certain gratitude to a Providence which, by providing the American people with this implacable challenge, has made their entire security as a nation dependent on their pulling themselves together and accepting the responsibilities of moral and political leadership that history plainly intended them to bear.

## 7   Harry S. Truman: The Truman Doctrine (March 12, 1947)

*Harry S. Truman ( 1884–       ) served as President of the United States during the critical years of 1945 to 1953 when American tactics in the Cold War were formed and hardened. In perspective, none of them surpassed the Truman Doctrine in shaping the framework within which American foreign policy was to be carried out. In this Doctrine, delivered to Congress in March 1947, the President defined the nature of the Soviet challenge and the requirements for an American response. He so sharply drew the picture of "aggressive movements that seek to impose . . . totalitarian regimes" that Congress quickly reacted by sending the requested aid to Greece and Turkey and (along with the American people as a whole) dedicated itself to "containing" the "aggressive movements" as Mr. "X" and President Truman asked. The tone of the message, the President's definition of the threats that "aggressive movements" posed, and the labeling of the speech as a "doctrine" are particularly significant. What are the implications of calling a foreign policy message of this kind a "doctrine?" Does it imply an ideological commitment not usually associated with what we like to think is a "pragmatic" American foreign policy? Why does the President draw distinctions between Greece and Turkey? Do his conclusions at the end of the message culminate naturally from his remarks concerning Greece and Turkey and his general reading of American-Russian relations historically? What are the implications of this doctrine for American responses to revolutionary outbreaks?*

---

Mr. President, Mr. Speaker, Members of the Congress of the United States:

The gravity of the situation which confronts the world today necessitates my appearance before a joint session of the Congress.

SOURCE. *Public Papers of the Presidents . . . Harry S. Truman . . . 1947,* Washington, D. C.: Government Printing Office, 1963, pp. 176–180.

The foreign policy and the national security of this country are involved.

One aspect of the present situation, which I wish to present to you at this time for your consideration and decision, concerns Greece and Turkey.

The United States has received from the Greek Government an urgent appeal for financial and economic assistance. Preliminary reports from the American Economic Mission now in Greece and reports from the American Ambassador in Greece corroborate the statement of the Greek Government that assistance is imperative if Greece is to survive as a free nation.

I do not believe that the American people and the Congress wish to turn a deaf ear to the appeal of the Greek Government.

Greece is not a rich country. Lack of sufficient natural resources has always forced the Greek people to work hard to make both ends meet. Since 1940 this industrious and peace-loving country has suffered invasion, four years of cruel enemy occupation, and bitter internal strife. . . .

The very eixstence of the Greek state is today threatened by the terrorist activities of several thousand armed men, led by Communists, who defy the Government's authority at a number of points, particularly along the northern boundaries. A commission appointed by the United Nations Security Council is at present investigating disturbed conditions in northern Greece and alleged border violations along the frontier between Greece on the one hand and Albania, Bulgaria, and Yugoslavia on the other.

Meanwhile, the Greek Government is unable to cope with the situation. The Greek Army is small and poorly equipped. It needs supplies and equipment if it is to restore authority to the Government throughout Greek territory.

Greece must have assistance if it is to become a self-supporting and self-respecting democracy.

The United States must supply that assistance. We have already extended to Greece certain types of relief and economic aid, but these are inadequate.

There is no other country to which democratic Greece can turn.

No other nation is willing and able to provide the necessary support for a democratic Greek Government.

The British Government, which has been helping Greece, can give no further financial or economic aid after March 31. Great Britain finds itself under the necessity of reducing or liquidating its commitments in several parts of the world, including Greece.

We have considered how the United Nations might assist in this crisis. But the situation is an urgent one requiring immediate action, and the United Nations and its related organizations are not in a position to extend help of the kind that is required.

It is important to note that the Greek Government has asked for our aid in utilizing effectively the financial and other assistance we may give to Greece, and in improving its public administration. It is of the utmost importance that we supervise the use of any funds made available to Greece, in such a manner that each dollar spent will count toward making Greece self-supporting, and will help to build an economy in which a healthy democracy can flourish.

No government is perfect. One of the chief virtues of a democracy, however, is that its defects are always visible and under democratic processes can be pointed out and corrected. The Government of Greece is not perfect. Nevertheless it represents 85 percent of the members of the Greek Parliament who were chosen in an election last year. Foreign observers, including 692 Americans, considered this election to be a fair expression of the views of the Greek people.

The Greek Government has been operating in an atmosphere of chaos and extremism. It has made mistakes. The extension of aid by this country does not mean that the United States condones everything that the Greek Government has done or will do. We have condemned in the past, and we condemn now, extremist measures of the right or the left. We have in the past advised tolerance, and we advise tolerance now.

Greece's neighbor, Turkey, also deserves our attention.

The future of Turkey as an independent and economically sound state is clearly no less important to the freedom-loving peoples of the world than the future of Greece. The circumstances in which Turkey finds itself today are considerably different from those of Greece. Turkey has been spared the disasters that have beset Greece. And during the war the United States and Great Britain furnished Turkey with material aid.

Nevertheless, Turkey now needs our support.

Since the war Turkey has sought additional financial assistance from Great Britain and the United States for the purpose of effecting that modernization necessary for the maintenance of its national integrity.

That integrity is essential to the preservation of order in the Middle East.

The British Government has informed us that, owing to its own difficulties, it can no longer extend financial or economic aid to Turkey.

As in the case of Greece, if Turkey is to have the assistance it needs, the United States must supply it. We are the only country able to provide that help.

I am fully aware of the broad implications involved if the United States is the creation of conditions in which we and other nations will be able to work out a way of life free from coercion. This was a fundamental issue in the war with Germany and Japan. Our victory was won over countries which sought to impose their will, and their way of life upon other nations.

To insure the peaceful development of nations, free from coercion, the United States has taken a leading part in establishing the United Nations. The United Nations is designed to make possible lasting freedom and independence for all its members. We shall not realize our objectives, however, unless we are willing to help free peoples to maintain their free institutions and their national integrity against aggressive movements that seek to impose upon them totalitarian regimes. This is no more than a frank recognition that totalitarian regimes imposed upon free peoples, by direct or indirect aggression, undermine the foundations of international peace and hence the security of the United States.

The peoples of a number of countries of the world have recently had totalitarian regimes forced upon them against their will. The Government of the United States has made frequent protests against coercion and intimidation, in violation of the Yalta agreement, in Poland, Rumania, and Bulgaria. I must also state that in a number of other countries there have been similar developments.

At the present moment in world history nearly every nation

must choose between alternative ways of life. The choice is too often not a free one.

One way of life is based upon the will of the majority, and is distinguished by free institutions, representative government, free elections, guaranties of individual liberty, freedom of speech and religion, and freedom from political oppression.

The second way of life is based upon the will of a minority forcibly imposed upon the majority. It relies upon terror and oppression, a controlled press and radio, fixed elections, and the suppression of personal freedoms.

I believe that it must be the policy of the United States to support free peoples who are resisting attempted subjugation by armed minorities or by outside pressures.

I believe that we must assist free peoples to work out their own destinies in their own way.

I believe that our help should be primarily through economic and financial aid which is essential to economic stability and orderly political processes.

The world is not static, and the *status quo* is not sacred. But we cannot allow changes in the *status quo* in violation of the Charter of the United Nations by such methods as coercion, or by such subterfuges as political infiltration. In helping free and independent nations to maintain their freedom, the United States will be giving effect to the principles of the Charter of the United Nations.

It is necessary only to glance at a map to realize that the survival and integrity of the Greek nation are of grave importance in a much wider situation. If Greece should fall under the control of an armed minority, the effect upon its neighbor, Turkey, would be immediate and serious. Confusion and disorder might well spread throughout the entire Middle East.

Moreover, the disappearance of Greece as an independent state would have a profound effect upon those countries in Europe whose peoples are struggling against great difficulties to maintain their freedoms and their independence while they repair the damages of war.

It would be an unspeakable tragedy if these countries, which have struggled so long against overwhelming odds, should lose that victory for which they sacrificed so much. Collapse of free institutions and loss of independence would be disastrous not only for them but for the world. Discouragement and possibly failure would quickly be the lot of neighboring peoples striving to maintain their freedom and independence.

Should we fail to aid Greece and Turkey in this fateful hour, the effect will be far-reaching to the West as well as to the East.

We must take immediate and resolute action.

I therefore ask the Congress to provide authority for assistance to Greece and Turkey in the amount of $400,000,000 for the period ending June 30, 1948. In requesting these funds, I have taken into consideration the maximum amount of relief assistance which would be furnished to Greece out of the $350,000,000 which I recently requested that the Congress authorize for the prevention of starvation and suffering in countries devastated by the war.

In addition to funds, I ask the Congress to authorize the detail of American civilian and military personnel to Greece and Turkey, at the request of those countries, to assist in the tasks of reconstruction, and for the purpose of supervising the use of such financial and material assistance as may be furnished. I recommend that authority also be provided for the instruction and training of selected Greek and Turkish personnel.

Finally, I ask that the Congress provide authority which will permit the speediest and most effective use, in terms of needed commodities, supplies, and equipment, of such funds as may be authorized.

If further funds, or further authority, should be needed for purposes indicated in this message, I shall not hesitate to bring the situation before the Congress. On this subject the Executive and Legislative branches of the Government must work together.

This is a serious course upon which we embark.

I would not recommend it except that the alternative is much more serious.

The United States contributed $341,000,000,000 toward winning World War II. This is an investment in world freedom and world peace.

The assistance that I am recommending for Greece and Turkey amounts to little more than one-tenth of one percent of this investment. It is only common sense that we should safeguard this investment and make sure that it was not in vain.

The seeds of totalitarian regimes are nurtured by misery and want. They spread and grow in the evil soil of poverty and strife. They reach their full growth when the hope of a people for a better life has died.

We must keep that hope alive.

The free peoples of the world look to us for support in maintaining their freedoms.

If we falter in our leadership, we may endanger the peace of the world—and we shall surely endanger the welfare of our own Nation.

Great responsibilities have been placed upon us by the swift movement of events.

I am confident that the Congress will face these responsibilities squarely.

8   *Undersecretary of State Dean Acheson: The Marshall Plan; Relief and Reconstruction Are Chiefly Matters of American Self-Interest (May 8, 1947)*

*Dean Gooderham Acheson (1893–    ) had served as Undersecretary of the Treasury in 1933 but then resigned because of his dislike of New Deal financial policies. With the outbreak of war in Europe, he left a highly lucrative Washington law practice to reenter government—first as Assistant Secretary of State and then, between 1945 and 1947, as Undersecretary of State. He returned as Secretary of State from 1949 to 1953. As Undersecretary, Acheson played a pivotal role in shaping the Marshall Plan, that massive effort of relief and rehabilitation which by 1951 had done much to restore war-shattered Western Europe. In these selections from a speech made at Cleveland, Mississippi, in May 1947, Acheson describes why such aid would not be merely an altruistic act. What is Acheson's main argument for an aid program? If his assessment of the American economy is correct, what does this*

*mean for any so-called "isolationist" foreign policy? Does he suggest
or imply any alternative programs for the American economy if that
economy cannot find sufficient export markets in a reconstructed
world economy? What is the meaning of this speech for American
policies toward revolutionary disturbances?*

---

. . . Here are some of the basic facts of life with which we are
primarily concerned today in the conduct of foreign relations:

The first is that most of the countries of Europe and Asia are
today in a state of physical destruction or economic dislocation,
or both. Planned, scientific destruction of the enemy's resources
carried out by both sides during the war has left factories destroyed, fields impoverished and without fertilizer or machinery
to get them back in shape, transportation systems wrecked, populations scattered and on the borderline of starvation, and long-
established business and trading connections disrupted.

Another grim fact of international life is that two of the greatest workshops of Europe and Asia—Germany and Japan—upon
whose production Europe and Asia were to an important degree
dependent before the war, have hardly been able even to begin
the process of reconstruction because of the lack of a peace
settlement. . . .

A third factor is that unforeseen disasters—what the lawyers
call "acts of God"—have occurred to the crops of Europe. For
two successive years unusually severe droughts have cut down
food production. And during the past winter storms and floods
and excessive cold unprecedented in recent years have swept
northern Europe and England with enormous damage to agricultural and fuel production. . . .

The accumulation of these grim developments has produced a
disparity between production in the United States and production
in the rest of the world that is staggering in its proportions. The
United States has been spared physical destruction during the
war. Moreover, we have been favored with unusually bountiful

SOURCE. *Department of State Bulletin*, Vol. XVI, May 18, 1947, pp.
991–994.

agricultural crops in recent years. Production in this country is today running at the annual rate of 210 billion dollars.

Responding to this highly abnormal relationship between production in the United States and production in the rest of the world, the United States Government has already authorized and is carrying out an extensive program of relief and reconstruction. We have contributed nearly 3 billion dollars to foreign relief. . . .

These measures of relief and reconstruction have been only in part suggested by humanitarianism. Your Congress has authorized and your Government is carrying out a policy of relief and reconstruction today chiefly as a matter of national self-interest. For it is generally agreed that until the various countries of the world get on their feet and become self-supporting there can be no political or economic stability in the world and no lasting peace or prosperity for any of us. Without outside aid, the process of recovery in many countries would take so long as to give rise to hopelessness and despair. In these conditions freedom and democracy and the independence of nations could not long survive, for hopeless and hungry people often resort of desperate measures. The war will not be over until the people of the world can again feed and clothe themselves and face the future with some degree of confidence.

The contribution of the United States towards world livelihood and reconstruction is best measured today not in terms of money but in terms of the commodities which we ship abroad. It is commodities—food, clothing, coal, steel, machinery—that the world needs. . . .

Our exports of goods and services to the rest of the world during the current year, 1947, are estimated to total 16 billion dollars, an all-time peacetime high. Before the war our exports of goods and services fluctuated around 4 billion dollars annually.

It is difficult to imagine 16 billion dollars' worth of commodities. This represents one month's work for each man and woman in the United States, one month's output from every farm, factory, and mine.

Let me give you another indication of the extent of our exports. The volume of commodities now moving out of east coast and Gulf ports of the United States is twice as great as the peak volume which moved out of those ports during the war when we were transporting and supplying not only our own huge armies abroad but a tremendous volume of lend-lease supplies. . . .

It is extremely difficult under present circumstances to increase the volume of our exports further. For in this country, too, there is a great demand for commodities, and foreign customers must compete with American customers. The character and composition of our exports will probably change. . . . But the total volume of exports is not likely to increase substantially until the world gets soundly on its feet and a genuine world prosperity may carry a healthy multilateral trade to higher levels.

In return for the commodities and services which we expect to furnish the world this year, we estimate that we will receive commodities and services from abroad to the value of about 8 billion dollars. This is just about half as much as we are exporting. This volume of imports is equal to about two weeks' work of all the factories, farms, mines, and laborers of the United States, and consists largely of things which are not produced in this country in sufficient quantity. We wish that the imports were larger, but the war-devastated world is just not able to supply more.

The difference between the value of the goods and services which foreign countries must buy from the United States this year and the value of the goods and services they are able to supply to us this year will therefore amount to the huge sum of about 8 billion dollars.

How are foreigners going to get the U.S. dollars necessary to cover this huge difference? And how are they going to get the U.S. dollars to cover a likely difference of nearly the same amount next year? These are some of the most important questions in international relations today.

Of this year's difference between imports and exports, more than 5 billion dollars is being financed by loans and grants-in-aid from the United States Government, through such instruments as direct relief, the Export-Import Bank, the International Bank, the International Fund, and the loan to Great Britain. . . . The remainder of this year's deficit will be covered by private investments, remittances of American citizens abroad, and by drawing down the extremely limited foreign reserves of gold and foreign exchange.

But what of next year, and the year after that? . . .

What do these facts of international life mean for the United States and for United States foreign policy?

They mean first that we in the United States must take as large a volume of imports as possible from abroad in order that the financial gap between what the world needs and what it can pay for can be narrowed. There is no charity involved in this. It is simply common sense and good business. We are today obliged from considerations of self-interest and humanitarianism to finance a huge deficit in the world's budget. The only sound way to end this deficit financing is by accepting increased quantities of goods from abroad. There can never be any stability or security in the world for any of us until foreign countries are able to pay in commodities and services for what they need to import and to finance their equipment needs from more normal sources of investment. . . .

The Geneva conference [of 17 nations to negotiate mutual reduction of world-wide trade barriers and to encourage international trade] must succeed not only because of the emergency supply and financial situation that exists today, but also because our position as the world's greatest producer and creditor nation demands that for a long period to come we accept an even larger volume of imports. When the process of reconversion at home is completed, we are going to find ourselves far more dependent upon exports than before the war to maintain levels of business activity to which our economy has become accustomed.

The facts of international life also mean that the United States is going to have to undertake further emergency financing of foreign purchases if foreign countries are to continue to buy in 1948 and 1949 the commodities which they need. . . .

This leads directly to a third imperative for our foreign policy. Since world demand exceeds our ability to supply, we are going to have to concentrate our emergency assistance in areas where it will be most effective in building world political and economic stability, in promoting human freedom and democratic institutions, in fostering liberal trading policies, and in strengthening the authority of the United Nations.

This is merely common sense and sound practice. It is in keeping with the policy announced by President Truman in his special message to Congress on March 12 on aid to Greece and

Turkey. Free peoples who are seeking to preserve their independence and democratic institutions and human freedoms against
totalitarian pressures, either internal or external, will receive top
priority for American reconstruction aid. . . .

The fourth thing we must do in the present situation is to push
ahead with the reconstruction of those two great workshops of
Europe and Asia—Germany and Japan—upon which the ultimate
recovery of the two continents so largely depends. . . . European
recovery cannot be complete until the various parts of Europe's
economy are working together in a harmonious whole. And the
achievement of a coordinated European economy remains a
fundamental objective of our foreign policy. . . .

## 9   Walter Lippman: Mr. "X" Policy Is Misconceived and Must Result in a Misuse of American Power (1947)

*For a half century, Walter Lippmann (1889–    ) has been one of the
most widely-read and influential of American authors and journalists.
His ideas and observations made an important contribution to the
shaping of the Marshall Plan in 1947. Lippmann, however, sharply
differentiated between the Marshall Plan, on the one hand, and the
Mr. "X" article and the Truman Doctrine, on the other. In a series of
newspaper columns, later collected in a book, Lippmann vigorously
attacked the Mr. "X" essay. In the selection that follows, he countered
nearly the entire range of assumptions and policy suggestions of Mr.
"X." Perhaps the most fundamental difference between Kennan and
Lippmann is their view of Soviet motivation. How does Lippmann's
reading of history differ from Kennan's, and how does each man's
analysis of the historical record lead to different assessments of Soviet
foreign policy objectives? Does Lippmann's expressed fear that "containment" will weaken the United States Constitution have any coun-
terpart in the Kennan or Truman selections (Readings 6 and 7)? How*

*does Lippmann's definition of the "decisive problem" in international affairs differ from Kennan's view? As implied by Lippman, how should the United States view revolutions?*

---

. . . I agree entirely with Mr. X that the Soviet pressure cannot "be charmed or talked out of existence." I agree entirely that the Soviet power will expand unless it is prevented from expanding because it is confronted with power, primarily American power, that it must respect. But I believe, and shall argue, that the strategical conception and plan which Mr. X recommends is fundamentally unsound, and that it cannot be made to work, and that the attempt to make it work will cause us to squander our substance and our prestige.

We must begin with the disturbing fact . . . that Mr. X's conclusions depend upon the optimistic prediction that the "Soviet power . . . bears within itself the seeds of its own decay, and that the sprouting of these seeds is well advanced". . . .

Of this optimistic prediction Mr. X himself says that it "cannot be proved. And it cannot be disproved." Nevertheless, he concludes that the United States should construct its policy on the assumption that the Soviet power is inherently weak and impermanent, and that this unproved assumption warrants our entering "with reasonable confidence upon a policy of firm containment. . . ."

I do not find much ground for reasonable confidence in a policy which can be successful only if the most optimistic prediction should prove to be true. Surely a sound policy must be addressed to the worst and hardest that may be judged to be probable, and not to the best and easiest that may be possible. . . .

Surely it is by no means proved that the way to lead mankind is to spend the next ten or fifteen years, as Mr. X proposes we

SOURCE. Walter Lippmann, *The Cold War: A Study in U.S. Foreign Policy*, New York: Harper & Row, 1947, pp.10–17, 21–24, 30–31, 33–35, 40, 46–47, 50, 51, 58–59, and 60–61. Copyright 1947 by Walter Lippmann. Reprinted by permission of Harper & Row, Publishers.

should, in reacting at "a series of constantly shifting geographical and political points, corresponding to the shifts and maneuvers of Soviet policy." For if history has indeed intended us to bear the responsibility of leadership, then it is not leadership to adapt ourselves to the shifts and maneuvers of Soviet policy at a series of constantly shifting geographical and political points. For that would mean for ten or fifteen years Moscow, not Washington, would define the issues, would make the challenges, would select the ground where the conflict was to be waged, and would choose the weapons. And the best that Mr. X can say for his own proposal is that if for a long period of time we can prevent the Soviet power from winning, the Soviet power will eventually perish or "mellow" because it has been "frustrated." This is a dismal conclusion. . . .

Now the strength of the western world is great, and we may assume that its resourcefulness is considerable. Nevertheless there are weighty reasons for thinking that the kind of strength we have and the kind of resourcefulness we are capable of showing are peculiarly unsuited to operating a policy of containment.

How, for example, under the Constitution of the United States is Mr. X going to work out an arrangement by which the Department of State has the money and the military power always available in sufficient amounts to apply "counterforce" at constantly shifting points all over the world? Is he going to ask Congress for a blank check on the Treasury and for a blank authorization to use the armed forces? Not if the American constitutional system is to be maintained. Or is he going to ask for an appropriation and for authority each time the Russians "show signs of encroaching upon the interests of a peaceful and stable world"? If that is his plan for dealing with the maneuvers of a dictatorship, he is going to arrive at the points of encroachment with too little and he is going to arrive too late. The Russians, if they intend to encroach, will have encroached while Congress is getting ready to hold hearings.

A policy of shifts and maneuvers may be suited to the Soviet system of government, which, as Mr. X tells us, is animated by patient persistence. It is not suited to the American system of government. . . .

Thus Mr. X and the planners of policy in the State Department, and not supply and demand in the world market, must determine continually what portion of the commodities produced here may be sold in the United States, what portion is to be set aside for export, and then sold, lent, or given to this foreign country rather than to that one. The Department of State must be able to allocate the products of American industry and agriculture, to ration the goods allocated for export among the nations which are to contain the Soviet Union, and to discriminate among them, judging correctly and quickly how much each nation must be given, how much each nation can safely be squeezed, so that all shall be held in line to hold the line against the Russians. . . . [Mr. X] is proposing to meet the Soviet challenge on the ground which is most favorable to the Soviets, and with the very instruments, procedures, and weapons in which they have a manifest superiority. . . .

The policy of containment, which Mr. X recommends, demands the employment of American economic, political, and in the last analysis, American military power at "sectors" in the interior of Europe and Asia. This requires, as I have pointed out, ground forces, that is to say reserves of infantry, which we do not possess.

The United States cannot by its own military power contain the expansive pressure of the Russians "at every point where they show signs of encroaching." The United States cannot have ready "unalterable counterforce" consisting of American troops. Therefore, the counterforces which Mr. X requires have to be composed of Chinese, Afghans, Iranians, Turks, Kurds, Arabs, Greeks, Italians, Austrians, of anti-Soviet Poles, Czechoslovaks, Bulgars, Yugoslavs, Albanians, Hungarians, Finns and Germans.

The policy can be implemented only by recruiting, subsidizing and supporting a heterogeneous array of satellites, clients, dependents and puppets. The instrument of the policy of containment is therefore a coalition of disorganized, disunited, feeble or disorderly nations, tribes and factions around the perimeter of the Soviet Union. . . .

It would require, however, much the real name for it were disavowed, continual and complicated intervention by the United States in the affairs of all the members of the coalition which we were proposing to organize, to protect, to lead and to use. Our diplomatic agents abroad would have to have an almost unerring capacity to judge correctly and quickly which men and which parties were reliable containers. Here at home Congress and the people would have to stand ready to back their judgments as to who should be nominated, who should be subsidized, who should be white-washed, who should be seen through rose-colored spectacles, who should be made our clients and our allies. . . .

In the complicated contest over this great heterogeneous array of unstable states, the odds are heavily in favor of the Soviets. For if we are to succeed, we must organize our satellites as unified, orderly and reasonably contented nations. The Russians can defeat us by disorganizing states that are already disorganized, by disuniting peoples that are torn with civil strife, and by inciting their discontent which is already very great. . . .

These weak states are vulnerable. Yet the effort to defend them brings us no nearer to a decision or to a settlement of the main conflict. Worst of all, the effort to develop such an unnatural alliance of backward states must alienate the natural allies of the United States.

The natural allies of the United States are the nations of the Atlantic community: that is to say, the nations of western Europe and of the Americas. The Atlantic Ocean and the Mediterranean Sea, which is an arm of the Atlantic Ocean, unite them in a common strategic, economic and cultural system. The chief components of the Atlantic community are the British Commonwealth of nations, the Latin states on both sides of the Atlantic, the Low Countries and Switzerland, Scandinavia and the United States. . . .

By forcing us to expend our energies and our substance upon . . . dubious and unnatural allies on the perimeter of the Soviet Union, the effect of the policy is to neglect our natural allies in the Atlantic community, and to alienate them.

They are alienated also by the fact that they do not wish to become, like the nations of the perimeter, the clients of the United States in whose affairs we intervene, asking as the price of our support that they take the directives of their own policy from Washington. They are alienated above all by the prospect of war, which could break out by design or accident, by miscalculation or provocation, if at any of these constantly shifting geographical and political points the Russians or Americans became so deeply engaged that no retreat or compromise was possible. In this war their lands would be the battlefield. Their peoples would be divided by civil conflict. Their cities and their fields would be the bases and the bridgeheads in a total war which, because it would emerge into a general civil war, would be as indecisive as it was savage.

We may now ask why the official diagnosis of Soviet conduct, as disclosed by Mr. X's article, has led to such an unworkable policy for dealing with Russia. It is, I believe, because Mr. X has neglected even to mention the fact that the Soviet Union is the successor of the Russian Empire and that Stalin is not only the heir of Marx and of Lenin but of Peter the Great, and the Czars of all the Russias.

For reasons which I do not understand, Mr. X decided not to consider the men in the Kremlin as the rulers of the Russian State and Empire, and has limited his analysis to the interaction of "two forces": "the ideology inherited by the present Soviet leaders from the movement in which they had their political origin" and the "circumstances of the power which they have now exercised for nearly three decades in Russia". . . .

But with these two observations alone he cannot, and does not, explain the conduct of the Soviet government in this postwar era—that is to say its aims and claims to territory and to the sphere of influence which it dominates. The Soviet government has been run by Marxian revolutionists for thirty years; what has to be explained by a planner of American foreign policy is why in 1945 the Soviet government expanded its frontiers and its orbit, and what was the plan and pattern of its expansion. That can be done only by remembering that the Soviet government is a Russian government and that this Russian government has emerged victorious over Germany and Japan. . . .

The westward expansion of the Russian frontier and of the Russian sphere of influence, though always a Russian aim, was accomplished when, as, and because the Red Army defeated the German army and advanced to the center of Europe. It was the mighty power of the Red Army, not the ideology of Karl Marx, which enabled the Russian government to expand its frontiers. It is the pressure of that army far beyond the new frontiers which makes the will of the Kremlin irresistible within the Russian sphere of influence. It is the threat that the Red Army may advance still farther west—into Italy, into western Germany, into Scandinavia—that gives the Kremlin and the native communist parties of western Europe an abnormal and intolerable influence in the affairs of the European continent.

Therefore, the immediate and the decisive problem of our relations with the Soviet Union is whether, when, on what conditions the Red Army can be prevailed upon to evacuate Europe.

I am contending that the American diplomatic effort should be concentrated on the problem created by the armistice—which is on how the continent of Europe can be evacuated by the three non-European armies [Russian, American, and British] which are now inside Europe. This is the problem which will have to be solved if the independence of the European nations is to be restored. Without that there is no possibility of a tolerable peace. . . .

We may now examine a question which must be answered before the policy, which I contend is preferable to the Truman Doctrine, can be accepted with conviction. What about the communist parties which are also the instruments of Soviet power? If the Red Army withdrew behind the frontiers of the Soviet Union, the communist parties would remain—to put it bluntly, as a Soviet fifth column. They will be assisted, we may take it, by Soviet agents and by Soviet funds and Soviet contraband weapons and by Soviet propaganda and by Soviet diplomacy.

That is true. There will still be the problem of communism. Nevertheless, the heart of our problem is, I contend, the presence of the Red Army in Europe. The communist party in any country is the *fifth column*. It is, however, only a fifth column. There are the *other four columns*, and they are the Red Army. The policy which I suggest is designed to separate the first four columns from the fifth, to divide the Red Army from the Red International. For the Soviet power is most formidable where they are able to work together, that is to say, where the communist party has the support and protection of the Red Army. . . .

The evacuation of Europe can be accomplished only if we can negotiate, sign, and ratify a treaty of peace for Germany and for Austria to which the Soviet government is a party. For the peace treaties about eastern Europe, which is between Germany and Russia, cannot become effective until there are German and Austrian treaties. The Red Army will remain in eastern Europe as long as it remains in Germany and in Austria. . . .

In its approach to the German problem, which is crucial in a world settlement, we come upon the most dangerous and destructive consequences of what Mr. X calls a policy of firm containment and what the world knows as the Truman Doctrine. . . .

The underlying assumption, which is implicit though unavowed, has been that since Germany has lost the eastern provinces to the Russians and to a Russian satellite, Poland, German national feeling will naturally be directed against the Soviet Union. Historical experience and the logic of the situation indicate, I believe, that this is a profound miscalculation. For we are encouraging the Germans to want something—namely, national unity—which we cannot give them except by going to war with Russia. Germany cannot have unity, as all Germans must understand unity, except by recovering the lost provinces of eastern Germany. We would have to conquer Russia and Poland in order to restore the eastern provinces to Germany.

But Russia can return them to Germany whenever she decides that an alliance with Germany is a vital Russian interest. This can be done by performing another partition of Poland, an act which the men who signed the Molotov-Ribbentrop pact of 1939 [between Russia and Germany] could carry out if they deemed it expedient and necessary. . . .

The truncated area [of Germany] will have to be decentralized, not unified, and the German states which are in it will have to take their places within a larger European system and a European economy. Not German unity but European unity, not German self-sufficiency but European self-sufficiency, not a Germany to contain Russia but a Germany neutralized as between Russia and the west, not the Truman Doctrine but the Marshall Plan, purged of the Truman Doctrine, should be the aims of our German policy. . . .

If, nevertheless, the Soviet government will not negotiate an agreement, if the price of a settlement is impossibly high, if the ransom is deliberately set in terms which mean that Russia does not intend to evacuate Europe, the situation will be no more dangerous than it is today. But our energies will be concentrated, not dispersed all over the globe, and the real issues will be much clearer. . . .

We may now consider how we are to relate our role in the United Nations to our policy in the conflict with Russia. Mr. X does not deal with this question. But the State Department, in its attempt to operate under the Truman Doctrine, has shown where that doctrine would take us. It would take us to the destruction of the U.N.

The Charter and the organization of the United Nations are designed to maintain peace *after* a settlement of the Second World War has been arrived at. Until there is a settlement of that war, the United Nations does not come of age . . . .

[But] the policy of containment, as Mr. X has exposed it to the world, does not have as its objective a settlement of the conflict with Russia. It is therefore implicit in the policy that the U.N. has no future as a universal society, and that either the U.N. will be cast aside like the League of Nations, or it will be transformed into an anti-Soviet coalition. In either event the U.N. will have been destroyed. . . .

Mr. X has reached the conclusion that all we can do is to "contain" Russia until Russia changes, ceases to be our rival, and becomes our partner.

The conclusion is, it seems to me, quite unwarranted. . . .

The method by which diplomacy deals with a world where there are rival powers is to organize a balance of power which deprives the rivals, however lacking in intimacy and however unresponsive to common appeals, of a good prospect of successful aggression. That is what a diplomat means by the settlement of a conflict among rival powers. He does not mean that they will cease to be rivals. He does not mean that they will all be converted to thinking and wanting the same things. He means that, whatever they think, whatever they want, whatever their ideological purposes, the balance of power is such that they cannot afford to commit aggression. . . .

## 10   Dean Acheson: The Triumph of the Communists in China was beyond the Control of the United States ( 1949 )

*When Dean Acheson became Secretary of State in January 1949, he personified in his personal attitudes and in his policies the American belief that Europe must rank first on the list of Washington's diplomatic priorities. He had been in office less than ten months, however, when China came under the control of the Chinese Communists and Americans began turning more attention to Asian affairs. In this selection from a long State Department paper published in August 1949, Acheson justified the American decision not to intervene in order to save the Chiang Kai-shek government. The use of history in justifying American noninvolvement in this instance is important, and Acheson outlines the historical background with clarity and effect. The fall of China nevertheless was a turning point in American foreign policy since it convinced many Americans in Congress and in the Administration itself that the United States could not in the future allow similar Communist successes. Is there any indication of this turning point in the reading that follows? How do the views of the Secretary of State differ concerning the aiding of Greece and Turkey (as in the Truman Doctrine policy) and the aiding of China?*

---

. . . The interest of the people and the Government of the United States in China goes far back into our history. Despite the distance and broad differences in background which separate China and the United States, our friendship for that country has always been intensified by the religious, philanthropic and cultural ties which have united the two peoples, and has been attested by many acts of good will over the period of many years, including the use of the Boxer indemnity for the education of Chinese

SOURCE. U.S. Department of State, *U.S. Relations with China*, Washington, D.C.: Government Printing Office, 1949, pp. iii–xvii.

students, the abolition of extraterritoriality during the Second World War, and our extensive aid to China during and since the close of the war. The record shows that the United States has consistently maintained and still maintains those fundamental principles of our foreign policy toward China which include the doctrine of the Open Door, respect for the administrative and territorial integrity of China, and opposition to any foreign domination of China. . . .

Two factors have played a major role in shaping the destiny of modern China.

The population of China during the eighteenth and nineteenth centuries doubled, thereby creating an unbearable pressure upon the land. The first problem which every Chinese Government has had to face is that of feeding this population. So far none has succeeded. The Kuomintang [led by Chiang Kai-shek] attempted to solve it by putting many land-reform laws on the statute books. Some of these laws have failed, others have been ignored. In no small measure, the predicament in which the National Government finds itself today is due to its failure to provide China with enough to eat. A large part of the Chinese Communists' propaganda consists of promises that they will solve the land problem.

The second major factor which has shaped the pattern of contemporary China is the impact of the West and of Western ideas. For more than three thousand years the Chinese developed their own high culture and civilization, largely untouched by outside influences. Even when subjected to military conquest the Chinese always managed in the end to subdue and absorb the invader. It was natural therefore that they should come to look upon themselves as the center of the world and the highest expression of civilized mankind. Then in the middle of the nineteenth century the heretofore impervious wall of Chinese isolation was breached by the West. These outsiders brought with them aggressiveness, the unparalleled development of Western technology, and a high order of culture which had not accompanied previous foreign incursions into China. Partly because of these qualities and partly because of the decay of Manchu rule, the Westerners, instead of being absorbed by the Chinese, introduced new ideas which played an important part in stimulating ferment and unrest.

By the beginning of the twentieth century, the combined force of overpopulation and new ideas set in motion that chain of events which can be called the Chinese revolution. It is one of the most imposing revolutions in recorded history and its outcome and consequences are yet to be foreseen. Out of this revolutionary whirlpool emerged the Kuomintang, first under the leadership of Dr. Sun Yat-sen, and later Generalissimo Chiang Kai-shek, to assume the direction of the revolution. The leadership of the Kuomintang was not challenged until 1927 by the Chinese Communist party which had been organized in the early twenties under the ideological impetus of the Russian revolution. It should be remembered that Soviet doctrine and practice had a measurable effect upon the thinking and principles of Dr. Sun Yat-sen, particularly in terms of economics and party organization, and that the Kuomintang and the Chinese Communists cooperated until 1927 when the Third International demanded a predominant position in the Government and the army. It was this demand which precipitated the break between the two groups. To a large extent the history of the period between 1927 and 1937 can be written in terms of the struggle for power between the Kuomintang and the Chinese Communists, with the latter apparently fighting a losing battle. During this period the Kuomintang made considerable progress in its efforts to unify the country and to build up the nation's financial and economic strength. Somewhere during this decade, however, the Kuomintang began to lose the dynamism and revolutionary fervor which had created it, while in the Chinese Communists the fervor became fanaticism.

[In 1937 the Japanese began their attempt to conquer China proper. By the early 1940's, however, it became apparent that the Kuomintang and the Chinese Communists were as preoccupied with fighting each other for internal control as they were with fighting the Japanese.]

[By late 1945, United States policy] was inspired by the two objectives of bringing peace to China under conditions which would permit stable government and progress along democratic lines, and of assisting the National Government to establish its authority over as wide areas of China as possible. As the event proved, the first objective was unrealizable because neither side desired it to succeed: the Communists because they refused to accept conditions which would weaken their freedom to proceed with what remained consistently their aim, the communization of all China; the Nationalists because they cherished the illusion, in spite of repeated advice to the contrary from our military representatives, that they could destroy the Communists by force of arms.

The second objective of assisting the National Government, however, we pursued vigorously from 1945 to 1949. . . .

The reasons for the failures of the Chinese National Government appear in some detail in the attached record. They do not stem from any inadequacy of American aid. Our military observers on the spot have reported that the Nationalist armies did not lose a single battle during the crucial year of 1948 through lack of arms or ammunition. The fact was that the decay which our observers had detected in Chungking early in the war had fatally sapped the powers of resistance of the Kuomintang. Its leaders had proved incapable of meeting the crisis confronting them, its troops had lost the will to fight, and its Government had lost popular support. The Communists, on the other hand, through a ruthless discipline and fanatical zeal, attempted to sell themselves as guardians and liberators of the people. The Nationalist armies did not have to be defeated; they disintegrated. . . .

It has been urged that relatively small amounts of additional aid—military and economic—to the National Government would have enabled it to destroy communism in China. The most trustworthy military, economic, and political information available to our Government does not bear out this view.

A realistic appraisal of conditions in China, past and present, leads to the conclusion that the only alternative open to the United States was full-scale intervention in behalf of a Government which had lost the confidence of its own troops and its own people. Such intervention would have required the expenditure of even greater sums than have been fruitlessly spent thus far, the command of Nationalist armies by American officers, and the probable participation of American armed forces—land, sea, and air—in the resulting war. Intervention of such a scope and magnitude would have been resented by the mass of the Chinese people, would have diametrically reversed our historic policy, and would have been condemned by the American people. . . .

The unfortunate but inescapable fact is that the ominous result of the civil war in China was beyond the control of the government of the United States. . . . It was the product of internal Chinese forces, forces which this country tried to influence but could not. A decision was arrived at within China, if only a decision by default.

And now it is abundantly clear that we must face the situation as it exists in fact. . . . We continue to believe that, however tragic may be the immediate future of China and however ruthlessly a major portion of this great people may be exploited by a party in the interest of a foreign imperialism, ultimately the profound civilization and the democratic individualism of China will reassert themselves and she will throw off the foreign yoke. I consider that we should encourage all developments in China which now and in the future work toward this end.

In the immediate future, however, the implementation of our historic policy of friendship for China must be profoundly affected by current developments. It will necessarily be influenced by the degree to which the Chinese people come to recognize that the Communist regime serves not their interests but those of Soviet Russia and the manner in which, having become aware of the facts, they react to this foreign domination. One point, however, is clear. Should the Communist regime lend itself to the aims of Soviet Russian imperialism and attempt to engage in aggression against China's neighbors, we and the other members of the United Nations would be confronted by a situation violative of the principles of the United Nations Charter and threatening international peace and security.

Meanwhile our policy will continue to be based upon our own respect for the Charter, our friendship for China, and our traditional support for the Open Door and for China's independence and administrative and territorial integrity.

## 11     NSC–68: How to Prepare for an Indefinite Period of Tension and Danger (April, 1950)

*After the fall of China and the first explosion of a Russian atomic bomb in the autumn of 1949, President Truman ordered a top-secret review of American policies and tactics. By the early spring of 1950 (several months before the Korean War began), a committee of top Administration officials, who represented particularly the Defense and State Departments, had formulated a document that was to be known as NSC–68 (National Security Council paper No. 68). The paper accurately forecast the economic, political, military, and diplomatic policies that the nation must follow if it hoped to wage the Cold War successfully. Whether these policies would have been put into effect if the Korean War had not occurred of course, is speculative, but certainly that war allowed the Truman Administration to implement much of NSC–68 rapidly and forcefully. The results were to shape American foreign relations for the next decade and a half at least. The following selection is a paraphrase of this document, which remains classified. How does NSC–68 assess Soviet motives and how does this assessment differ from the Mr. "X" and Lippmann views (Readings 6 and 9)? Is NSC–68 a logical result of the Truman Doctrine (Reading 7)? How do the premises laid down in the early part of the document lead to the final selection of the fourth policy alternative as "inescapably the preferred one?" If these premises are mistaken, would the fourth policy, alternatively, remain preferable? What does this policy paper suggest the American position to be if revolutionary disturbances occur?*

---

Events since the end of World War II have created a new power relationship in the world which must be viewed not as a temporary distortion but as a long-range and fundamental realign-

SOURCE. From a paraphrase in Cabell Phillips, *The Truman Presidency* (New York, 1966), pp. 306–308; reprinted by permission of the Macmillan Company. Copyright 1966 by Cabell Phillips.

ment among nations. This has arisen out of two historical events: the Russian revolution and the growth of the Communist movement throughout the world; and the development of nuclear weapons with their capacity for unlimited destruction. The U.S. and the U.S.S.R. are the terminal poles of this new international axis.

Kremlin policy has three main objectives: (1) to preserve and to strengthen its position as the ideological and power center of the Communist world; (2) to extend and to consolidate that power by the acquisition of new satellites; and (3) to oppose and to weaken any competing system of power that threatens Communist world hegemony.

These objectives are inimical to American ideals, which are predicated on the concepts of freedom and dignity. . . .

It must be assumed that these concepts and objectives of American life will come under increasing attack. If they are to be protected, the nation must be determined, at whatever cost or sacrifice, to preserve at home and abroad those conditions of life in which these objectives can survive and prosper. We must seek to do this by peaceful means and with the cooperation of other like-minded peoples. But if peaceful means fail we must be willing and ready to fight.

Conceding the possibility of such a war, what are the relative capabilities of the U.S. and its probable allies, and the U.S.S.R. and its probable allies?

As a first consideration, Russia's progress in the development of atomic bombs probably means that an approximate stalemate in nuclear weapons will be reached by about 1954. The United States might extend its advantage for a few years longer if the hydrogen bomb should be perfected, but success in that effort is uncertain.

While the economic and productive capacity of the U.S.S.R. is markedly below that of the West, its potential for growth is great, and the Communist nations are striving more determinedly than the West to realize full potentials for growth.

In spite of these weaknesses, the Communist military capability for conventional, or nonatomic, warfare is now substantially superior to that of the West and is continuing to improve at a more rapid rate. This imbalance can be expected to continue for at least as long as it takes to achieve the economic rehabilitation of Western Europe and the full implementation of the NATO alliance.

Could the crisis between the two great powers be reduced through negotiation and particularly by mutual arms reduction? The prospects at present are poor, given the immutability of Soviet objectives and its advantage in military power. The West cannot abandon its efforts to negotiate, particularly to neutralize the threat of a nuclear holocaust, but it must act in the realization that Stalin respects the reality of force a great deal more than he does the abstraction of peace.

Based on these premises, an indefinite period of tension and danger is foreseen for the United States and for the West—a period that should be defined less as a short-term crisis than as a permanent and fundamental alteration in the shape of international relations. To meet this new condition, four possible lines of action are open to the United States:

1. It can continue on its present course of reduced defense budgets and limited military capabilities, but without reducing its commitments to free-world security.

2. It can abandon these commitments, maintain its military capabilities at the present level, and withdraw behind the shield of a "fortress America."

3. It can attempt through "preventive war" a quick, violent but possibly more favorable redress in the world balance of power.

4. It can strike out on a bold and massive program of rebuilding the West's defensive potential to surpass that of the Soviet world, and of meeting each fresh challenge promptly and unequivocally. Such a program must have the United States at its political and material center with other free nations in variable orbits around it. The strength of such an alliance should be insurmountable as long as each of its members remains strong.

This fourth alternative is inescapably the preferred one. Its fulfillment calls for the United States to take the lead in a rapid and substantial buildup in the defensive power of the West, beginning "at the center" and radiating outward. This means virtual abandonment by the United States of trying to distinguish between national and global security. It also means the end of subordinating security needs to the traditional budgeting restrictions; of asking, "How much security can we afford?" In other words, security must henceforth become the dominant element in the national budget, and other elements must be accommodated to it.

The wealth potential of the country is such that as much as 20 percent of the gross national product can be devoted to security without causing national bankruptcy. This new concept of the security needs of the nation calls for annual appropriations of the order of $50 billion, or not much below the former wartime levels.

# CHAPTER II
# TRANSITION (1950-1956)

**12**  *Harry S. Truman: The Commitment of American Forces in Korea—and Elsewhere ( June 27, 1950)*

*On June 25, North Korean forces crossed the 38th parallel to invade South Korea. This move climaxed five years of American-Russian sparring over a Korean settlement and followed several months of bitter political exchanges between the North and South Korean governments. The Soviet Union was the dominant outside power in North Korean affairs, as was the United States in those of South Korea. Stalin had aided the rebuilding of the armies in the north; although he maintained until his death in March 1953 that the Soviets had no responsibility in instigating the attack, the Truman Administration assumed that Russia was deeply involved. The American officials, indeed, saw the invasion as evidence that Stalin was now prepared to use military force to expand Communist power. Consequently, the President's announcement that he had ordered American forces to Korea indicated that the United States would bolster other threatened areas as well. Notice particularly the reference to Indochina. Later the American commitment would be labeled a United Nations force; what role does the United Nations play in this policy statement? Could the North Korean invasion be cited as evidence for the dire warnings issued earlier in the Mr. "X" article, the Truman Doctrine, and NSC–68 concerning Communist aggression?*

---

In Korea, the Government forces, which were armed to prevent border raids and to preserve internal security, were attacked by invading forces from North Korea. The Security Council of the United Nations called upon the invading troops to cease hostilities

SOURCE. U. S. Department of State, *American Foreign Policy, 1950–1955, Basic Documents*, Washington, D. C.: Government Printing Office, 1957, II, pp. 2539–2540.

and to withdraw to the 38th Parallel. This they have not done but, on the contrary, have pressed the attack. The Security Council called upon all members of the United Nations to render every assistance to the United Nations in the execution of this resolution. In these circumstances, I have ordered United States air and sea forces to give the Korean Government troops cover and support.

The attack upon Korea makes it plain beyond all doubt that communism has passed beyond the use of subversion to conquer independent nations and will now use armed invasion and war. It has defied the orders of the Security Council of the United Nations issued to preserve international peace and security. In these circumstances, the occupation of Formosa by Communist forces would be a direct threat to the security of the Pacific area and to United States forces performing their lawful and necessary functions in that area.

Accordingly, I have ordered the Seventh Fleet to prevent any attack upon Formosa. As a corollary of this action, I am calling upon the Chinese Government on Formosa to cease all air and sea operations against the mainland. The Seventh Fleet will see that this is done. The determination of the future status of Formosa must await the restoration of security in the Pacific, a peace settlement with Japan, or consideration by the United Nations.

I have also directed that United States forces in the Philippines be strengthened and that military assistance to the Philippine Government be accelerated.

I have similarly directed acceleration in the furnishing of military assistance to the forces of France and the Associated States in Indochina and the dispatch of a military mission to provide close working relations with those forces.

I know that all members of the United Nations will consider carefully the consequences of this latest aggression in Korea in defiance of the Charter of the United Nations. A return to the rule of force in international affairs would have far-reaching effects. The United States will continue to uphold the rule of law.

I have instructed Ambassador [Warren] Austin, as the representative of the United States to the Security Council, to report these steps to the Council.

## 13   Chinese Foreign Ministry: Why China Intervened in Korea (November 11, 1950)

*By mid-September 1950, the American and South Korean forces had turned back the North Korean invasion. The Truman Administration then made the critical decision to drive north of the 38th parallel into North Korea and then to the Yalu River (dividing Korea and China) in an attempt to reunify Korea. This decision was taken despite the Administration's assertions in June and July that the American effort aimed only at clearing South Korea north to the 38th. In early October, Communist China warned that it would not allow United Nations forces to encamp along the Yalu. Later that month, Chinese "volunteers" (as Peking called them) began moving into North Korea. By late November the Chinese forces had intervened in mass and were driving the American-South Korean forces back with heavy casualties on both sides. The next selection is one official Chinese version of why Peking decided to intervene in Korea. How do the Chinese believe that their interests coincide with the interests of the North Koreans? In the opinion of the Chinese Foreign Ministry what relationship exists between the Chinese Communist revolution and the war? How convincing is the Chinese recounting of the historical record?*

---

. . . Immediately after the beginning of its aggressive war in Korea, the United States sent its fleet into the waters of Taiwan (Formosa), which belongs to China. It then sent its air forces to invade the air space of north-east China and carried out bombings. The United Nations took under consideration a charge brought by the Chinese Government that the United States fleet had invaded the waters of Taiwan and is ready to discuss this charge. In the last three months numerous cases have been noted of United States aircraft violating the air borders of China, bombing Chinese

SOURCE. United Nations Document S/1902, November 15, 1950, pp. 2–4.

territory, killing Chinese civilians and destroying Chinese property. The full tale of the crimes committed in north-east China by the United States air forces which have invaded Korea is given below. Recently the number of air attacks has been increasing daily. These crimes committed by the United States armed forces, which are violating the territorial sovereignty of China and threatening its security, have alarmed the whole Chinese people. Righteously indignant, many Chinese citizens are expressing a desire to help the Korean people and resist American aggression. Facts have shown that the aim of United States aggression in Korea is not only Korea itself but also the extension of aggression to China. The question of the independent existence or the downfall of Korea has always been closely linked with the security of China. To help Korea and repel United States aggression means to protect our own homes and our own country. It is, therefore, completely natural for the Chinese people to be ready to help Korea and offer resistance to United States aggression. This natural desire of the Chinese people to help Korea and offer resistance to United States aggression has a whole series of precedents in world history, a fact which no one can deny. Everyone knows that in the eighteenth century the progressive people of France, led and inspired by Lafayette, gave similar voluntary assistance to the American people in their War of Independence. Before the Second World War democrats from all countries of the world, including Britishers and Americans, also helped by similar volunteer action the Spanish people in its civil war against Franco. The whole world admitted that those acts were lawful.

The spontaneous assistance of the Chinese people in Korea and their resistance to United States aggression has a firm moral foundation. The Chinese people will never forget how the Korean people magnanimously gave the Chinese people voluntary assistance in its revolutionary struggle. The Korean people took part not only in the Chinese war of national liberation, but also in the northern march of the Chinese people in 1925 to 1927, in the war against Japan from 1937 to 1945. Throughout the four stages of the Chinese people's revolution the Korean people always fought shoulder to shoulder with the Chinese people to overthrow imperialism and feudalism. Now that the bloodthirsty United States aggressors are exterminating Koreans, the Chinese are sharing their sufferings and, as must be perfectly obvious, cannot remain indifferent. . . .

The American aggressors have gone too far. After making a five-thousand-mile journey across the Pacific they invaded the territories of China and Korea. In the language of the American imperialists that is not aggression on their part, whereas the just struggle of the Chinese and Koreans in defence of their land and their people is aggression. The world knows who is right and who is wrong. . . .

The United States Government itself provoked the civil war in Korea; the United States Government itself unleashed a war of aggression against Korea; the United States itself invaded Taiwan, which belongs to China, bombed Chinese territory and threatened the security of China. From the outset the Central People's Government of the Chinese People's Republic denounced the war of aggression in Korea waged by the United States Government and demanded a peaceful decision of the Korean question. At the present time it likewise resolutely denounces the war of aggression in Korea carried on by the United States Government and calls for a peaceful settlement of the Korean question.

In order to achieve a peaceful settlement of the Korean question it is essential, above all, to withdraw all foreign troops from Korea. The Korean question can be solved only by the people of North and South Korea themselves; this is the only way in which the Korean problem can be solved peacefully. The Chinese people ardently loves peace but it will not be afraid to take action against aggressors and no aggressors can intimidate it. [Then follows the account of recent American flights over Chinese territory.]

## 14   The Great Debate: MacArthur versus Marshall on the Threats Posed by Communist China (May-June 1951)

*The intervention by Communist Chinese troops resulted in a stalemated war along the battle line of the 38th parallel by early 1951. The American commander, General Douglas MacArthur (1880–1964), urged President Truman to allow freer use of American military power, including the bombing of Chinese power plants and troop concentrations in Manchuria. When Truman refused, MacArthur made public his complaints in speeches and letters to prominent Congressmen. In April 1951, the President decided that the American commander would have to be recalled. The Joint Chiefs of Staff agreed with the President's decision, adding that MacArthur was beginning to lose the confidence of troops in the field. The General returned to a tumultuous homecoming. He especially was courted by many Americans who shared his frustrations in fighting a limited war against a Communist enemy. In the early summer of 1951, the United States Senate held a special investigation into the Administration's handling of the Korean War and, particularly, into the controversy that had arisen over MacArthur's recall. The General first gave his views and several Administration officials then presented the President's position. The most prominent of these officials was General George C. Marshall, Secretary of Defense and one of the most honored soldiers in the nation's history. How do Generals MacArthur and Marshall differ in their assessment of Communism and Communist motivations? How do the two men differ in their views on the comparative importance of Asia and Europe? Does this difference of views also imply a difference in handling revolutions in each area? Which man's views are more consistent with the attitudes expressed in the Mr. "X", Truman Doctrine, and NSC–68 documents?*

---

SENATOR MORSE [Wayne Morse, Republican of Oregon]: . . . At any time were you asked for a recommendation, or advice, by your superiors in line of command, as to whether or not we should push beyond the thirty-eighth parallel, and go all the way to the Yalu?

GENERAL MACARTHUR: The original mission that was assigned was to clear all of Korea.

SOURCE. U. S. Senate, Committee on Armed Services and Committee on Foreign Relations, *Military Situation in the Far East*, in five parts, Washington, D. C.: Government Printing Office, 1951, pp. 245, 20–21, 29–30, 258–261, 217, 141–143, 120, 172–173, 45, 324–325, 351, 593–594, 642–643, 659, and 672–673.

That original declaration of policy was supplemented, in October [1950], by the United Nations General Assembly.

The actual crossing of the thirty-eighth parallel was specifically authorized by the Secretary of Defense, to me, in a message, a personal message, which said that he did not—the Defense Department did not wish to in any way embarrass me tactically or strategically in my crossing of the thirty-eighth parallel. . . .

As far as I know, the crossing of that parallel had the most complete agreement by everybody that was concerned with it, except the enemy. . . .

THE CHAIRMAN [Richard Russell, Democrat of Georgia]: General, did your intelligence have any previous knowledge of the fact that the Chinese were crossing the boundaries in any considerable force, prior to the attack, and our reversals in North Korea, last December?

GENERAL MACARTHUR: We had knowledge that the Chinese Communists had collected large forces along the Yalu River. My own reconnaissance, you understand, was limited entirely to Korea; but the general information which was available, from China and other places, indicated large accumulations of troops.

The Red Chinese, at that time, were putting out, almost daily, statements that they were not intervening, that these were volunteers only.

About the middle of September our Secretary of State announced that he thought there was little chance, and no logic, in Chinese intervention.

In November, our Central Intelligence Agency, here, had said that they felt there was little chance of any major intervention on the part of the Chinese forces. . . .

THE CHAIRMAN: Well, now going back to the concentration on the other side of the Yalu—of course, you would not have advised that they be bombed until they had disclosed their hand, that they were coming into the war and thereby precipitate a contest between Red China and ourselves, would you, General? . . .

GENERAL MACARTHUR: When that formation of troops, that extraordinary groupment of troops—those are the troops that [had] threatened Formosa. When they were withdrawn up there, I would have warned China that, if she intervened, we would have regarded it as war and we would have bombed her and taken every possible step to prevent it. That is what I would have done, and it seems to me that is what common sense would have dictated should have been done.

THE CHAIRMAN: . . . . Do you know whether or not any such warning was given to the Red Chinese?

GENERAL MACARTHUR: None that I know of. . . .

SENATOR WILEY: [Alexander Wiley, Republican of Wisconsin]: You have indicated in your public addresses that there has been a failure to take certain needed political decisions in the Korean matter. Can you tell us what you think those decisions might well have been?

GENERAL MACARTHUR: I can tell you what I would have done.

SENATOR WILEY: Yes.

GENERAL MACARTHUR: I would have served—as soon as it became apparent that Red China was throwing the full might of its military force against our troops in Korea, I would have served warning on her that if she did not within a reasonable time discuss a cease-fire order, that the entire force of the United Nations would be ultilized to bring to an end the predatory attack of her forces on ours.

In other words, I would have supplied her with an ultimatum that she would either come and talk terms of a cease fire within a reasonable period of time or her actions in Korea would be regarded as a declaration of war against the nations engaged there and that those nations would take such steps as they felt necessary to bring the thing to a conclusion. That is what I would have done, and I would still do it, Senator. . . .

SENATOR SALTONSTALL [Leverett Saltonstall, Republican of Massachusetts]: . . . Now, on April 15, the Assistant Secretary of State, Dean Rusk, in a television and press broadcast, stated, in part—and this is the pertinent part of his speech, as I read it:

"What we are trying to do is to maintain peace and security without a general war. We are saying to the aggressors, "You will not be allowed to get away with your crime. You must stop it." At the same time, we are trying to prevent a general conflagration which would consume the very things we are now trying to defend. . . ."

GENERAL MACARTHUR: That policy, as you have read it, seems

to me to introduce a new concept into military operations—the concept of appeasement, the concept that when you use force, you can limit that force.

The concept that I have is that when you go into war, you have exhausted all other potentialities of bringing the disagreements to an end.

As I understand what you read, that we would apply to the military situation in Korea certain military appeasements—that is, that we would not use our Air Forces to their maximum extent, only to the limited area of that Korea [sic]; that we would not use our Navy, except along the border lines of Korea.

To me, that would mean that you would have a continued and indefinite extension of bloodshed, which would have been limitless—a limitless end. . . .

SENATOR MORSE: You say, General, that you are opposed to a limited war in Korea, but some are saying that, in effect, what you are really proposing is a limited war in China. Do you think that is a fair evaluation of your proposal?

GENERAL MACARTHUR: I do not, sir. I do not call it a fair evaluation of my concept in any way, shape, or manner. I said that we should put such pressure on Red China as would force her to stop her war in North Korea. . . .

SENATOR MORSE: Is it fair to say, General, if—I am sorry I have to talk in terms of so many "if's"—if, after whatever you considered to be a reasonable time for applying those pressures, the Chinese aggression continued, either because they are supplied with more and more material from Soviet Russia or with other assistance from Soviet Russia, or for whatever cause, would you then, in carrying out the principle that we must meet this resistance until we have a victory over it, say we would have to then enlarge our military operations against China?

GENERAL MACARTHUR: No, sir. I say and repeat that I believe the application of that force, continued long enough, would accomplish completely the purpose I have in mind. If the Chinese continued to resist, we would continue to apply those forces until the time would come when those forces would force her to cease her campaign in North Korea. . . .

SENATOR MORSE: As I understand your position, I respectfully point out that, however, as a people, in the event of the possibility that I referred to coming to pass, that we couldn't win an ultimate victory in the Korean War along the lines that you recommend, we as a people then have the right to make clear what we think ought to be done to end it; and on the basis of that assumption, I raise my question.

I mean to imply would it not be better to resort to stronger bombing methods, including atomic warfare, than to risk the lives of millions of American soldiers on the soil of China?

GENERAL MACARTHUR: The use of the atomic weapon would certainly represent a great reserve potential which we could exercise at the discretion of the Commander in Chief. . . .

SENATOR MCMAHON [Brien McMahon, Democrat of Connecticut]: I said yesterday you stated that communism is our enemy all over the world. Where is most of the military power located that is held by communism?

GENERAL MACARTHUR: Unquestionably in Soviet Russia.

SENATOR MCMAHON: . . . . If we adopted your plan for China, and if that plan resulted in a pacification of China and Korea, the military force that is possessed by communism would still be the maverick that would be running loose in the world, is that not correct, General?

GENERAL MACARTHUR: Yes. . . .

SENATOR FULBRIGHT [J. William Fulbright, Democrat of Arkansas]: There are very definite cleavages of opinion about Russia and what she may do in Europe. It does seem to me that if we become bogged down in China, if by chance it proved to be a little more difficult than you think, that then the thing would come about that you mentioned earlier in your testimony. One of the major things that might induce Russia to attack all out would be a relative increase in her strength, which would come about if we expended very large resources in Asia, and if perchance at the same time our budget was cut $20 billion as suggested by the Senator from Ohio [Robert Taft, Republican]. All those things might happen. . . .

General, during the winter we had a bill before this Congress in my committee. I happened to be delegated to handle it on the floor and it concerned aid to Yugoslavia. We voted some fifty-odd-millions to Yugoslavia in aid, transferring ECA supplies. Do you approve of that action?

GENERAL MACARTHUR: I never read the bill, Senator. . . . On such superficial presentation, I have said I would not give a professional opinion. The entire matter of the defense of Europe, the entire economics of Europe, the degree of communism, if you can put it that way, that exists in Serbia and Yugoslavia, the entire atmosphere, a conglomeration of things that you have been studying and the authorities here for months and perhaps years, I would not attempt in 15 minutes to give an authoritative statement.

I must have the facts. It would take time to get those facts. It has never been within the scope of my responsibility to study those matters. Other agencies of the Government do that. Other military leaders do those things. Ask them, Senator, not me.

I am glad to answer any question that falls within the scope of what I have studied, but I am not going to give a professional opinion, an international opinion, on such a major subject as that without being properly acquainted with the basis of fact. I have been 14 years in the Far East, Senator.

SENATOR FULBRIGHT: Well, I realize that. . . . You made a statement just before lunch that interests me. You said in answer to a question by the Senator from Connecticut that the enemy—and it is important, I think, that we try to identify the enemy—is communism.

GENERAL MACARTHUR: That is correct.

SENATOR FULBRIGHT: What is your concept of communism? I mean is this the communism of Marx and Engels, or is it the communism as practiced by the Kremlin, or just what do you mean by that?

GENERAL MACARTHUR: Communism has many various factors. The great threat in what is called present communism is the imperialistic tendency or the lust of power beyond their own geographical confines. It is their effort to enslave the individual to the concepts of the state. It is the establishment of autocracy that squeezes out every one of the freedoms which we value so greatly. . . .

SENATOR FULBRIGHT: I had not myself thought of our enemy as being communism; I thought of it as primarily being an imperialistic Russia. That is what interests me.

GENERAL MACARTHUR: In that concept, Senator, I disagree with you completely.

SENATOR FULBRIGHT: That is what I was trying to develop there.

GENERAL MACARTHUR: It happens to be that the Soviet is communistic; but, if you think that communism is limited to Russia, I would disagree with you completely and absolutely.

SENATOR FULBRIGHT: I did not say it was limited to Russia. I would say this: If the country that has no association whatever with Russia—in fact, is antagonistic to them—then I do not see why, such as in the case of Yugoslavia, it is not to our benefit to assist them. In other words, it seems to me the present insecurity of the world arises primarily from Russia's imperialism. To you, that is not so at all?

GENERAL MACARTHUR: I have expressed my belief, Senator, on that point. . . .

SENATOR LODGE [Henry Cabot Lodge, Republican of Massachusetts]: Judging from the mail that I get, though, there are millions of Americans who are perplexed by the relationship of the defense of America in the Far East with the defense of America in Europe. . . .

GENERAL MACARTHUR: I tried to cover that yesterday, Senator, and in my speech before the Congress. I believe the problem is a global one. I believe we should defend every place from communism. I believe we can. I believe we are able to. I have confidence in us.

I don't believe we should write off anything and accept the defeat that is involved in it. I don't believe we should breach our own line.

SENATOR LODGE: I am delighted to hear you say that. . . .

SENATOR STENNIS [John Stennis, Democrat of Mississippi]: Can we defend every place, world-wide, from communism with no better cooperation than we are getting now from the other free nations?

GENERAL MACARTHUR: My concept of course, Senator, was that we are opposing communism.

SENATOR STENNIS: Yes.

GENERAL MACARTHUR: That we shall assist wherever we can in that opposition. I did not mean to convey that the United States should defend every mile of the world that was threatened by attack or might be attacked, but that we should assist those that would resist it to the maximum of our capacity without destroying ourselves.

SENATOR STENNIS: Well, yes, I emphasize this present lack of co-operation. We are faced here with a terrible budget and we have a limitation of manpower, as you know, and we have got to make decisions some way here as to how far we can go.

In other words, I have said we must draw a line somewhere in the Pacific. I wouldn't begin to say where we draw it, but unless we get better cooperation, I do not believe we can go on a world-wide concept.

GENERAL MACARTHUR: I don't believe that you can reduce the problem of resisting Communist aggression by the simple process of drawing lines on the map and saying, "You shan't go beyond this line." I believe where the aggression shows its face, we should attempt to meet it. I believe that it has very definitely shown its face in Korea. That is where the main fighting is going on, and that therefore we should meet it there.

SENATOR STENNIS: But there is also involved in this—

GENERAL MACARTHUR: If it should spring up in some other area, the military possibilities of that area would determine what we could do in the way of assistance, and always, to answer the spirit of your question, we must rely largely upon the determination and purpose of that sector which is threatened to do its utmost to resist. In Korea, the South Koreans have gone to the maximum on that.

SENATOR STENNIS: And at the same time, though, how far we can go is also going to be determined by the cooperation we get from other major free nations, and it has not been forthcoming this time to your expectation or your desires, I am sure.

GENERAL MACARTHUR: I would hope that they would do more than they have, especially in Korea. . . .

SENATOR GREEN [Theodore Francis Green, Democrat of Rhode Island]: There is one other phase to the question which applies to both Korea and China, which you touched upon, and that is this: you have dealt with these questions in both countries on a purely military basis. But isn't our Government required to give consideration and decide upon it on both a military and a polit-

ical basis? Can you separate them so distinctly and say that a
military victory is a political victory?

GENERAL MACARTHUR: I think that it is quite impossible to draw
a line of differentiation and say this is a political and this is a
military situation. The American Government should have such
coordination so that the political and military are in coordination.

The general definition which for many decades has been accepted was that war was the ultimate process of politics; that
when all other political means failed, you then go to force; and
when you do that, the balance of control, the balance of concept, the main interest involved, the minute you reach the killing
stage, is the control of the military. A theater commander, in any
campaign, is not merely limited to the handling of his troops; he
commands that whole area politically, economically, and militarily. You have got to trust at that stage of the game when
politics fails, and the military takes over, you must trust the military, or otherwise you will have the system that the Soviet once
employed of the political commissar, who would run the military
as well as the politics of the country.

Now, the differentiation that exists between the political features and the military features, I am not able to discuss because I
have not been here in Washington. Others will be able to tell you
more about that than I, but I do unquestionably state that when
men become locked in battle, that there should be no artifice under the name of politics, which should handicap your own men,
decrease their chances for winning, and increase their losses.

* * *

SECRETARY MARSHALL [General George C. Marshall, Secretary
of Defense]: . . . Now, as to the basic differences of judgment
which exist between General MacArthur on the one hand, and
the Joint Chiefs of Staff, the Secretary of Defense, and the President, on the other hand.

Our objective in Korea continues to be the defeat of the aggression and the restoration of peace. We have persistently
sought to confine the conflict to Korea and to prevent its spreading into a third world war. In this effort, we stand allied with the
great majority of our fellow-members of the United Nations.
Our efforts have succeeded in thwarting the aggressors, in Korea,

and in stemming the tide of aggression in southeast Asia and elsewhere throughout the world. Our efforts in Korea have given us
some sorely needed time and impetus to accelerate the building
of our defenses and those of our allies against the threatened on-
slaught of Soviet imperialism.

General MacArthur, on the other hand, would have us, on our
own initiative, carry the conflict beyond Korea against the mainland of Communist China, both from the sea and from the air. He
would have us accept the risk involvement not only in an extension of the war with Red China, but in an all-out war with the
Soviet Union. He would have us do this even at the expense of
losing our allies and wrecking the coalition of free peoples
throughout the world. He would have us do this even though the
effect of such action might expose Western Europe to attack by
the millions of Soviet troops poised in Middle and Eastern Europe.

This fundamental divergence is one of judgment as to the
proper course of action to be followed by the United States.
This divergence arises from the inherent difference between the
position of a field commander, whose mission is limited to a particular area and a particular antagonist, and the position of the
Joint Chiefs of Staff, the Secretary of Defense, and the President,
who are responsible for the total security of the United States,
and who, to achieve and maintain this security, must weigh our
interests and objectives in one part of the globe with those in
other areas of the world so as to attain the best over-all balance.

It is their responsibility to determine where the main threat
to our security lies, where we must fight holding actions, and
where and how we must gain time to grow stronger. On the other
hand, the responsibilities and the courses of action assigned to a
theater commander necessarily apply to his own immediate area
of responsibility. It is completely understandable and, in fact,
at times commendable that a theater commander should become so
wholly wrapped up in his own aims and responsibilities that some
of the directives received by him from higher authority are not
those that he would have written for himself. There is nothing
new about this sort of thing in our military history. What is
new, and what has brought about the necessity for General Mac-
Arthur's removal, is the wholly unprecedented situation of a local
theater commander publicly expressing his displeasure at and his

disagreement with the foreign and military policy of the United States.

It became apparent that General MacArthur had grown so far out of sympathy with the established policies of the United States that there was grave doubt as to whether he could any longer be permitted to exercise the authority in making decisions that normal command functions would assign to a theater commander. In this situation, there was no other recourse but to relieve him. . . .

CHAIRMAN RUSSELL: Now, General, as a military man with distinguished service to your country over a long period of years, I would like to get your professional opinion as well as your views as Secretary of Defense as to whether or not the Chinese Reds can be driven out of Korea and Korea pacified without the implementing General MacArthur recommends?

SECRETARY MARSHALL: . . . . I should say that if the Chinese Communists continue in force in North Korea with the potential of additional reinforcements that might be made available, and with our situation where we visualize no considerable reinforcement of the United Nations army, that they could not be driven out of North Korea, and I have my own doubts as to whether the actions recommended by General MacArthur would bring the conflict to a victorious end. . . .

CHAIRMAN RUSSELL: Wait a minute, do you mean to say in your opinion there is doubt even if we do bomb them whether they could be driven from there?

SECRETARY MARSHALL: . . . . Yes, sir.

SENATOR CAIN: [Harry P. Cain, Republican of Washington]: . . . . What are your fundamental reasons for assuming that an aggression will not take place in Western Europe until we are better prepared to meet it, while seemingly you believe that Russia will enter the Korean conflict if we bomb and destroy miiltary installations possessed by the Red Chinese?

SECRETARY MARSHALL: In regard to Western Europe, first I go on the basis myself that Russia may step into the aggression at any moment. Also that that is no argument that we do not do our best to prepare for it even though it may take 2 or 3 years. . . .

Now I will try to be brief again in regard to the difference I think in the situation in the Far East, and it is this in the main:

that Russia possesses a very valuable ally in China. That you might say is a Russian protectorate in a sense, but one who is paying a great bill of human lives and other things in order to fulfill that role.

Now in view of their treaty [February, 1950] with the Chinese Communist regime or government, if it appears that they have failed to support that government in its fight in Korea, we have a very special situation because it affects every other satellite of the Soviet Government. . . .

SENATOR FULBRIGHT: . . . . You said a moment ago . . . that you regard our great opponent as Soviet Russia.

SECRETARY MARSHALL: Yes, sir.

SENATOR FULBRIGHT: You do not regard this struggle as a sort of modern ideological crusade against communism, I take it?

SECRETARY MARSHALL: When I said Soviet Russia and the Soviet Union, I was thinking in terms of the Communist government.

SENATOR FULBRIGHT: Well, that is true; they are communistic, with which I agree. I understand you to say that the enemy we are concerned about is Russia. It is the armies of Soviet Russia.

SECRETARY MARSHALL: That is correct, sir.

SENATOR FULBRIGHT: If those armies did not happen to be Communist, but were the old-fashioned imperialists of the Czars, you would still be concerned about them, wouldn't you?

SECRETARY MARSHALL: If they had shown the indications—

SENATOR FULBRIGHT: That is what I mean. . . . My only point is that you do not look upon this as sort of a crusade against communism everywhere and in any form; but it is because it is an aggressive force, and has taken on the power of the Russian state is what concerns you, is it not?

SECRETARY MARSHALL: Yes, Sir. . . .

SENATOR SPARKMAN [John Sparkman, Democrat of Alabama]: Secretary Marshall, as I understand, some of the basic differences in the opinions that you have stated here and the opinions of the Joint Chiefs of Staff, as you have given them and those entertained by General MacArthur, have to do with the ability of the Chinese to fight, the ability of the Soviets to come to her aid, and also as to the tie between Red China and Soviet Russia.

General MacArthur has stated on several different occasions

that while China, Red China, and Russia were associates or allies, and I believe he referred to their courses as being parallel, that he considered Red China as being independent and acting on her own.

Do you believe that Red China does act on her own or is she subject to direction and influence from Moscow?

SECRETARY MARSHALL: I have gone on the assumption that she was operating not in conjunction with but literally under the direction of the Soviet Union.

SENATOR GILLETTE [Guy M. Gillette, Democrat of Iowa]: Can any instance be named where the Soviet at any time, any place, or any circumstance, including Yugoslavia, threatened or intimated that she would risk total war with us and our war potential, including atomic-warfare development, if we took certain steps to quickly end the Korean conflict?

SECRETARY MARSHALL: How does that question include Yugoslavia?

SENATOR GILLETTE: We will eliminate Yugoslavia. . . .

SECRETARY MARSHALL: I think there have been implications but I don't recall any specific statement.

## 15   *Dwight D. Eisenhower: The Falling Domino and Southeast Asia ( April 7, 1954 )*

*General MacArthur's recall and the Administration's success in keeping the Korean conflict limited (non-atomic and limited to Korea itself) did not indicate any lessening of the American commitment to Asian affairs. On the contrary, after the fighting finally stopped in Korea in 1953, the State Department intensified its efforts to contain Communism in Asia as well as in Europe. Central to this policy was the firming up of the slipping French effort to regain some measure of colonial control in Indochina. The French confronted a growing nationalist revolt in the area, led by Ho Chi Minh's Vietnamese Communist regime. The United States first committed itself to help France subdue the Vietnamese as early as May 1950, before the Korean War broke out. That commitment was reaffirmed in President Truman's*

*announcement of June 27, 1950 (Reading 12). By 1954, the United
States believed that its interests were consistent with the French in-
terests in this area and, at a public press conference, President Dwight
D. Eisnhower (1890–    ) explained why Indochina seemed vital to
American security. How accurate is the comparison of a row of
falling dominoes with the situation in Southeast Asia, which the
President outlines in these remarks?*

---

ROBERT RICHARDS, Copley Press: Mr. President, would you mind
commenting on the strategic importance of Indochina to the free
world? I think there has been, across the country, some lack of
understanding on just what it means to us.

THE PRESIDENT: You have, of course, both the specific and the
general when you talk about such things.

First of all, you have the specific value of a locality in its production of materials that the world needs.

Then you have the possibility that many human beings pass
under a dictatorship that is inimical to the free world.

Finally, you have broader considerations that might follow what
you would call the "falling domino" principle. You have a row
of dominoes set up, you knock over the first one, and what will
happen to the last one is the certainty that it will go over very
quickly. So you could have a beginning of a disintegration that
would have the most profound influences.

Now, with respect to the first one, two of the items from this
particular area that the world uses are tin and tungsten. They are
very important. There are others, of course, the rubber plantations and so on.

Then with respect to more people passing under this domination, Asia, after all, has already lost some 450 million of its peoples
to the Communist dictatorship, and we simply can't afford greater
losses.

But when we come to the possible sequence of events, the loss
of Indochina, of Burma, of Thailand, of the Peninsula, and Indo-

SOURCE. *Public Papers of the Presidents . . . Dwight D. Eisenhower, 1954,*
Washington, D. C.: Government Printing Office, 1960, pp. 382-383.

nesia following, now you begin to talk about areas that not only multiply the disadvantages that you would suffer through loss of materials, sources of materials, but now you are talking really about millions and millions and millions of people.

Finally, the geographical position achieved thereby does many things. It turns the so-called island defensive chain of Japan, Formosa, of the Philippines and to the southward; it moves in to threaten Australia and New Zealand.

It takes away, in its economic aspects, that region that Japan must have as a trading area or Japan, in turn, will have only one place in the world to go—this is, toward the Communist areas in order to live.

So, the possible consequences of the loss are just incalculable to the free world.

## 16 *Final Declaration of the Geneva Conference on the Problem of Restoring Peace in Indochina (July 21, 1954)*

*The extent of American aid was not sufficient to prevent the French from suffering a decisive defeat at the hands of Ho Chi Minh's forces at the battle of Dienbienphu in April-June, 1954. Before that battle was decided, the French met with Communist and non-Communist Vietnamese political factions at Geneva, Switzerland. They were joined by the other powers involved in the Indochina area. With their defeat at Dienbienphu, and facing intensified domestic pressure to settle the conflict, the French government agreed to a "Final Declaration" which outlined the political future of the area. The United States participated but refused to sign the Final Declaration, partly because of American political influences and partly because the Eisenhower Administration wanted to maintain its freedom of action in Indochina. What are the critical agreements in paragraphs 6 and 7? What kind of political future is outlined herein for Vietnam?*

FINAL DECLARATION, dated the 21st of July, 1954, of the Geneva Conference on the problem of restoring peace in Indo-China, in which the representatives of Cambodia, the Democratic Republic of Viet-Nam, France, Laos, the People's Republic of China, the State of Viet-Nam, the Union of Soviet Socialist Republics, the United Kingdom, and the United States of America took part.

1. The Conference takes note of the agreements ending hostilities in Cambodia, Laos and Viet-Nam and organizing international control and the supervision of the execution of the provisions of these agreements.

2. The Conference expresses satisfaction at the ending of hostilities in Cambodia, Laos and Viet-Nam; the Conference expresses its conviction that the execution of the provisions set out in the present declaration and in the agreements on the cessation of hostilities will permit Cambodia, Laos and Viet-Nam henceforth to play their part, in full independence and sovereignty, in the peaceful community of nations.

3. The Conference takes note of the declarations made by the Governments of Cambodia and of Laos of their intention to adopt measures permitting all citizens to take their place in the national community. . . .

4. The Conference takes note of the clauses in the agreement on the cessation of hostilities in Viet-Nam prohibiting the introduction into Viet-Nam of foreign troops and military personnel as well as of all kinds of arms and munitions. The Conference also takes note of the declarations made by the Governments of Cambodia and Laos of their resolution not to request foreign aid, whether in war material, in personnel or in instructors except for the purpose of the effective defense of their territory and, in the case of Laos, to the extent defined by the agreements on the cessation of hostilities in Laos.

5. The Conference takes note of the clauses in the agreement on the cessation of hostilities in Viet-Nam to the effect that no military base under the control of a foreign State may be estab-

SOURCE. U. S. Department of State, *American Foreign Policy, 1950–1955, Basic Documents*, Washington, D. C.: Government Printing Office, 1957, I, pp. 785–787.

lished in the regrouping zones of the two parties, the latter having the obligation to see that the zones allotted to them shall not constitute part of any military alliance and shall not be utilized for the resumption of hostilities or in the service of an aggressive policy. The Conference also takes note of the declarations of the Governments of Cambodia and Laos to the effect that they will not enjoin in any agreement with other States if this agreement includes the obligation to participate in a military alliance not in conformity with the principles of the Charter of the United Nations or, in the case of Laos, with the principles of the agreement on the cessation of hostilities in Laos or, so long as their security is not threatened, the obligation to establish bases on Cambodian or Laotian territory for the military forces of foreign Powers.

6. The Conference recognizes that the essential purpose of the agreement relating to Viet-Nam is to settle military questions with a view to ending hostilities and that the military demarcation line is provisional and should not in any way be interpreted as constituting a political or territorial boundary. The Conference expresses its conviction that the execution of the provisions set out in the present declaration and in the agreement on the cessation of hostilities creates the necessary basis for the achievement in the near future of a political settlement in Viet-Nam.

7. The Conference declares that, so far as Viet-Nam is concerned, the settlement of political problems, effected on the basis of respect for the principles of independence, unity and territorial integrity, shall permit the Viet-Namese people to enjoy the fundamental freedoms, guaranteed by democratic institutions established as a result of free general elections by secret ballot. In order to ensure that sufficient progress in the restoration of peace has been made, and that all the necessary conditions obtain for free expression of the national will, general elections shall be held in July 1956, under the supervision of an international commission composed of representatives of the Member States of the International Supervisory Commission [comprised of Canada, India, and Poland] referred to in the agreement on the cessation of hostilities. Consultations will be held on this subject between the competent representative authorities of the two zones from 20 July 1955 onwards.

8. The provisions of the agreements on the cessation of hostili-

ties intended to ensure the protection of individuals and of property must be most strictly applied and must, in particular, allow everyone in Viet-Nam to decide freely in which zone he wishes to live.

9. The competent representative authorities of the Northern and Southern zones of Viet-Nam, as well as the authorities of Laos and Cambodia, must not permit any individual or collective reprisals against persons who have collaborated in any way with one of the parties during the war, or against members of such persons' families.

10. The Conference takes note of the declaration of the Government of the French Republic to the effect that it is ready to withdraw its troops from the territory of Cambodia, Laos and Viet-Nam, at the request of the governments concerned and within periods which shall be fixed by agreement between the parties except in the cases where, by agreement between the two parties, a certain number of French troops shall remain at specified points and for a specified time.

11. The Conference takes note of the declaration of the French Government to the effect that for the settlement of all the problems connected with the re-establishment and consolidation of peace in Cambodia, Laos and Viet-Nam, the French Government will proceed from the principle of respect for the independence and sovereignty, unity and territorial integrity of Cambodia, Laos and Viet-Nam.

12. In their relations with Cambodia, Laos and Viet-Nam, each member of the Geneva Conference undertakes to respect the sovereignty, the independence, the unity and the territorial integrity of the above mentioned states, and to refrain from any interference in their internal affairs.

13. The members of the Conference agree to consult one another on any question which may be referred to them by the International Supervisory Commission, in order to study such measures as may prove necessary to ensure that the agreements on the cessation of hostilities in Cambodia, Laos and Viet-Nam are respected.

## 17 American Unilateral Declaration on the Final Declaration of the Geneva Conference (July 21, 1954)

*Although refusing to sign the "Final Declaration" of the Geneva Conference (Reading 16), the United States did issue its own declaration. How does the American document differ substantively from the Final Declaration? What meaning do the phrases about "free elections" have in the context of the Indochinese situation of 1954? What commitments does the United States government undertake in this unilateral declaration?*

### STATEMENT BY UNDER SECRETARY OF STATE WALTER BEDELL SMITH

As I stated on July 18, my Government is not prepared to join in a declaration by the Conference such as is submitted. However, the United States makes this unilateral declaration of its position in these matters:

The Government of the United States being resolved to devote its efforts to the strengthening of peace in accordance with the principles and purposes of the United Nations takes note of the agreements concluded at Geneva on July 20 and 21, 1954 between (a) the Franco-Laotian Command and the Command of the Peoples Army of Viet-Nam; (b) the Royal Khmer Army Command and the Command of the Peoples Army of Viet-Nam; (c) Franco-Vietnamese Command and the Command of the Peoples Army of Viet-Nam and of paragraphs 1 to 12 inclusive of the declaration presented to the Geneva Conference on July 21, 1954 declares with regard to the aforesaid agreements and paragraphs that (i) it will refrain from the threat or the use of force to dis-

SOURCE. U. S. Department of State, *American Foreign Policy, 1950-1955, Basic Documents*, Washington, D. C.: Government Printing Office, 1957, I, pp. 787-788.

turb them, in accordance with Article 2 (4) of the Charter of the United Nations dealing with the obligation of members to refrain in their international relations from the threat or use of force; and (ii) it would view any renewal of the aggression in violation of the aforesaid agreements with grave concern and as seriously threatening international peace and security.

In connection with the statement in the declaration concerning free elections in Viet-Nam my Government wishes to make clear its position which it has expressed in a declaration made in Washington on June 29, 1954, as follows:

"In the case of nations now divided against their will, we shall continue to seek to achieve unity through free elections supervised by the United Nations to insure that they are conducted fairly."

With respect to the statement made by the representative of the State of Viet-Nam, the United States reiterates its traditional position that peoples are entitled to determine their own future and that it will not join in an arrangement which would hinder this. Nothing in its declaration just made is intended to or does indicate any departure from this traditional position.

We share the hope that the agreements will permit Cambodia, Laos and Viet-Nam to play their part, in full independence and sovereignty, in the peaceful community of nations, and will enable the peoples of that area to determine their own future.

## 18  *The United States Moves into South Vietnam (1954-1955)*

*Within four months after the Geneva Agreements, the United States began moving into the Indochinese political situation, in place of the departing French. In October 1954, President Eisenhower assured the South Vietnam President, Ngo Dinh Diem, of American support of the South Vietnamese government. Eleven days later, the United States announced that it was sending military advisors and other personnel to South Vietnam. Finally in June 1955, Secretary of*

*State John Foster Dulles announced that the United States agreed with South Vietnam that elections to reunify the country, as provided for in the Geneva Final Declaration, could not be held. How do the President and, particularly, the Secretary of State view the Geneva Final Declaration in these statements? What are the differences between the United States position, these three documents, and the American unilateral declaration at Geneva (Reading 17)?*

---

## (A) PRESIDENT DWIGHT EISENHOWER TO PRESIDENT NGO DINH DIEM, OCTOBER 23, 1954

Dear Mr. President: I have been following with great interest the course of developments in Viet-Nam, particularly since the conclusion of the conference at Geneva. The implications of the agreement concerning Viet-Nam have caused grave concern regarding the future of a country temporarily divided by an artificial military grouping, weakened by a long and exhausting war and faced with enemies without and by their subversive collaborators within.

Your recent requests for aid to assist in the formidable project of the movement of several hundred thousand loyal Vietnamese citizens away from areas which are passing under a *de facto* rule and political ideology which they abhor, are being fulfilled. I am glad that the United States is able to assist in this humanitarian effort.

We have been exploring ways and means to permit our aid to Viet-Nam to be more effective and to make a greater contribution to the welfare and stability of the Government of Viet-Nam. I am, accordingly, instructing the American Ambassador to Viet-Nam to examine with you in your capacity as Chief of Government, how an intelligent program of American aid given directly to your Government can serve to assist Viet-Nam in its present hour of trial, provided that your Government is prepared to give

SOURCE. U. S. Department of State, *American Foreign Policy 1950-1955, Basic Documents*, Washington, D. C.: Government Printing Office, 1957, II, pp. 2401–2404.

assurances as to the standards of performance it would be able to maintain in the event such aid were supplied.

The purpose of this offer is to assist the Government of Viet-Nam in developing and maintaining a strong, viable state, capable of resisting attempted subversion or aggression through military means. The Government of the United States expects that this aid will be met by performance on the part of the Government of Viet-Nam in undertaking needed reforms. It hopes that such aid, combined with your own continuing efforts, will contribute effectively toward an independent Viet-Nam endowed with a strong government. Such a government would, I hope, be so responsive to the nationalist aspirations of its people, so enlightened in purpose and effective in performance, that it will be respected both at home and abroad and discourage any who might wish to impose a foreign ideology on your free people.

## (B) WHITE HOUSE ANNOUNCEMENT ON AMERICAN MILITARY PERSONNEL GOING TO VIETNAM, NOVEMBER 3, 1954

The President on November 3 designated Gen. J. Lawton Collins as Special United States Representative in Viet-Nam with the personal rank of Ambassador, to undertake a diplomatic mission of limited duration. He will coordinate the operations of all U.S. agencies in that country. . . .

Since the conclusion of hostilities in Indochina, the U.S. Government has been particularly concerned over developments in Viet-Nam, a country ravaged by 8 years of war, artificially divided into armistice zones, and confronted by dangerous forces threatening its independence and security. . . .

## (C) SECRETARY OF STATE DULLES EXPLAINS WHY THE UNITED STATES AGREES WITH SOUTH VIETNAM THAT THE PROPOSED 1956 ELECTIONS SHOULD NOT BE HELD, JUNE 28, 1955

Neither the United States Government nor the Government of Viet-Nam is, of course, a party to the Geneva armistice agreements. We did not sign them, and the Government of Viet-Nam did not sign them and, indeed, protested against them. On the other hand, the United States believes, broadly speaking, in the unification of countries which have a historic unity, where the people are akin. We also believe that, if there are conditions of really free elections, there is no serious risk that the Communists would win.

The Communists have never yet won any free election. I don't think they ever will. Therefore, we are not afraid at all of elections, provided they are held under conditions of genuine freedom which the Geneva armistice agreement calls for. If those conditions can be provided we would be in favor of elections, because we believe that they would bring about the unification of the country under free government auspices.

## 19 Southeast Asia Collective Defense Treaty: The Basis of the Southeast Treaty Organization (SEATO), Signed in Manila (September 8, 1954)

*The United States supported its own unilateral moves into Southeast Asia in 1954 with a collective defense treaty signed by eight of the important nations that had interests in the area. In the mind of the Secretary of State, John Foster Dulles, this pact was an extension of the North Atlantic Treaty Organization, which had been formed in 1949 to provide a military umbrella over Western Europe. What is the significance of the "Understanding of the United States of America" paragraph near the end of the treaty? As a result of this paragraph, is the United States free to move against non-Communist revolutions in the area? What is significant about the nations present —and not present—among the signatories?*

The Parties to this Treaty,

Recognizing the sovereign equality of all the Parties,

Reiterating their faith in the purposes and principles set forth in the Charter of the United Nations and their desire to live in peace with all peoples and all governments,

Reaffirming that, in accordance with the Charter of the United

SOURCE. U. S. Department of State, *American Foreign Policy, 1950–1955, Basic Documents*, Washington, D. C.: Government Printing Office, 1957, I, pp. 912–916.

Nations, they uphold the principle of equal rights and self-determination of peoples, and declaring that they will earnestly strive by every peaceful means to promote self-government and to secure the independence of all countries whose peoples desire it and are able to undertake its responsibilities,

Desiring to strengthen the fabric of peace and freedom and to uphold the principles of democracy, individual liberty and the rule of law, and to promote the economic well-being and development of all peoples in the treaty area,

Intending to declare publicly and formally their sense of unity, so that any potential aggressor will appreciate that the Parties stand together in the area, and

Desiring further to coordinate their efforts for collective defense for the preservation of peace and security,

Therefore agree as follows:

*Article I.* The Parties undertake, as set forth in the Charter of the United Nations, to settle any international disputes in which they may be involved by peaceful means in such a manner that international peace and security and justice are not endangered, and to refrain in their international relations from the threat or use of force in any manner inconsistent with the purposes of the United Nations.

*Article II.* In order more effectively to achieve the objectives of this Treaty, the Parties, separately and jointly, by means of continuous and effective self-help and mutual aid will maintain and develop their individual and collective capacity to resist armed attack and to prevent and counter subversive activities directed from without against their territorial integrity and political stability.

*Article III.* The Parties undertake to strengthen their free institutions and to cooperate with one another in the further development of economic measures, including technical assistance, designed both to promote economic progress and social well-being and to further the individual and collective efforts of governments toward these ends.

*Article IV.* (1) Each Party recognizes that aggression by means of armed attack in the treaty area against any of the Parties or against any State or territory which the Parties by unanimous agreement may hereafter designate, would endanger its own peace and safety, and agrees that it will in that event act to meet the common danger in accordance with its constitutional processes. Measures taken under this paragraph shall be immediately reported to the Security Council of the United Nations.

(2) If, in the opinion of any of the Parties, the inviolability or the integrity of the territory or the sovereignty or political independence of any Party in the treaty area or of any other State or territory to which the provisions of paragraph 1 of this Article from time to time apply is threatened in any way other than by armed attack or is affected or threatened by any fact or situation which might endanger the peace of the area, the Parties shall consult immediately in order to agree on the measures which should be taken for the common defense.

(3) It is understood that no action on the territory of any State designated by unanimous agreement under paragraph 1 of this Article or on any territory so designated shall be taken except at the invitation or with the consent of the government concerned.

*Article V.* The Parties hereby establish a Council, on which each of them shall be represented, to consider matters concerning the implementation of this Treaty. . . .

*Article VII.* Any other State in a position to further the objectives of this Treaty and to contribute to the security of the area may, by unanimous agreement of the Parties, be invited to accede to this Treaty. . . .

*Article VIII.* As used in this Treaty, the "treaty area" is the general area of Southeast Asia, including also the entire territories of the Asian Parties, and the general area of the Southwest Pacific not including the Pacific area north of 21 degrees 30 minutes north latitude. The Parties may, by unanimous agreement, amend this Article to include within the treaty area the territory of any State acceding to this Treaty in accordance with Article VII or otherwise to change the treaty area. . . .

*Article X.* This Treaty shall remain in force indefinitely, but any Party may cease to be a Party one year after its notice of denunciation has been given to the Government of the Republic of the Philippines, which shall inform the Governments of the other Parties of the deposit of each notice of denunciation. . . .

*Understanding of the United States of America:* The United

States of America in executing the present Treaty does so with the understanding that its recognition of the effect of aggression and armed attack and its agreement with reference thereto in Article IV, paragraph 1, apply only to communist aggression but affirms that in the event of other aggression or armed attack it will consult under the provisions of Article IV, paragraph 2.

*Protocol to the Treaty*: The Parties to the Southeast Asia Collective Defense Treaty unanimously designate for the purposes of Article IV of the Treaty the States of Cambodia and Laos and the free territory under the jurisdiction of the State of Vietnam.

The Parties further agree that the above mentioned states and territory shall be eligible in respect of the economic measures contemplated by Article III.

This Protocol shall enter into force simultaneously with the coming into force of the Treaty. . . .

*Signatories: the United States, Australia, France, New Zealand, Pakistan, the Philippines, Thailand, the United Kingdom.*


**20**    *John Foster Dulles: SEATO Is a New Departure in American Foreign Policy (November 11, 1954)*

*Two months after negotiating the creation of the Southeast Asian Treaty Organization, Secretary of State John Foster Dulles (1888–1959) defended American participation in SEATO before the Senate Foreign Relations Committee. The Senate ultimately ratified the treaty overwhelmingly. How does the Secretary of State use the historical record to justify the creation of SEATO? How does he explain the apparent conflict between SEATO and the Final Declaration at Geneva? What is the significance of his remarks about subversion? How persuasive is Dulles in answering the questions of Senator Theodore Green (Democrat of Rhode Island)?*

SOURCE. United States Senate, Committee on Foreign Relations, 83rd Congress, 2nd Session, *Hearing . . . on The Southeast Asia Collective Defense Treaty . . .* , Washington, D. C.: Government Printing Office, 1954, Part 1.

SECRETARY DULLES: . . . This treaty, Mr. Chairman . . . represents a major further step in the evolution of our policy to try to create a solid collective-security system in the Western Pacific area. That is a well-established policy. It was the policy which existed under the preceding administration, and which has been carried on by the present administration. . . .

It turned out, naturally, that it was quite difficult to complete a southeast Asia pact while the war in Indochina was still active. Nations, I think on the whole, like to go into these pacts on the theory that they are deterrents to war rather than involvements in a war. Furthermore, the issues of the war going on in Indochina were not entirely clear. . . .

The making of those armistice agreements at Geneva did not, of course, end the need for a pact. The need for the collective security pact is indeed quite evident as a result of many evidences of continuing aggressive tendencies on the part of the Communists.

To name only a few of these things, I could mention the fact that there exists on Chinese Communist soil a so-called "free Thai" movement, which is designed to subvert and overthrow the Government of Thailand. In Vietnam the military forces in the portion that has been conceded to the Communists have been almost doubled since the Geneva armistice.

In northern Laos, two provinces are largely dominated by the Communists who are in revolt against or do not accept the authority of the Government of Laos.

In Singapore there is continuing concern as to the activities being conducted by the Communists as against the large Chinese population of Malaya. . . .

In the Province of Yunan, China, where there is no risk at all of any armed attack against China, there is nevertheless maintained a very substantial military force by the Red Chinese.

All of these facts, and others which I could adduce, indicate that there persists an aggressive intention on the part of the Chinese Communists which belies their protestations of a desire for peace.

Therefore, the need for this treaty exists irrespective of the Geneva armistice. . . .

Broadly speaking, the pattern of the treaty is similar to the other Pacific treaties which we have made, the Anzus Treaty, the Philippine Treaty, the Korean Treaty, and so forth. But there are differences.

The treaty area is defined not merely by the treaty itself, but by a protocol to the treaty which brings in Laos, Cambodia, and the free portion of Vietnam as treaty territory which, if attacked, would be under the protection of the treaty and which, we hope, the treaty will deter from being attacked.

Those nations themselves are not members of the Manila Pact. The reason is that the armistice provisions at Geneva at least raised a question in the minds of some of the parties to those agreements as to whether the Associated States could actually join such a pact. Nevertheless, those states welcomed the fact that the mantle of protection of the treaty was thrown around this area. This provision is one novel feature of the treaty.

A second novel feature of the treaty is the fact that more than any other of our security treaties it emphasizes the danger from subversion. It deals, of course, as other treaties have, and in the same formula, which I call the Monroe Doctrine formula, with an open armed attack, and we believe that what is said in that respect will constitute a deterrent against such an open armed attack.

I might say in this connection, departing somewhat from order of my presentation, that it is not the policy of the United States to attempt to deter attack in this area by building up a local force capable itself of defense against an all-out attack by the Chinese Communists if it should occur. We do not expect to duplicate in this area the pattern of the North Atlantic Treaty Organization and its significant standing forces. . . .

We believe that our posture in that area should be one of having mobile striking power, and the ability to use that against the sources of aggression if it occurs. We believe that is more effective than if we tried to pin down American forces at the many points around the circumference of the Communist world in that area.

It may very well be that other countries of the area will want to dedicate particular forces for the protection of the area under this treaty. But we made clear at Manila that it was not the intention of the United States to build up a large local force including, for example, United States ground troops for that area, but that we rely upon the deterrent power of our mobile striking force. . . .

Of course, the Communists are trying desperately to make the Asian peoples believe that if they have any association at all with western powers it means perpetuation of colonialism. They do that because they know that the Asian powers will be extremely weak unless they can enjoy collective security, which, to some measure, will involve the western nations, and if they can create that breach, then Asia can readily fall under their control and power. Such slogans as "Asia for the Asians," "Keep the West Out," are only slogans which are invented by people who want to exert a mastery over all of Asia, and who know they can only do it effectively if they can get the Asians themselves first to break wholly their ties with the West, and then become so weak that they automatically almost fall into the Communist camp.

Now, that is the great danger which we are combating, in that area, and it is the danger which we must be eternally vigilant to combat. . . .

SENATOR GREEN [Theodore Francis Green, Democrat of Rhode Island]: Is there not some provision in the treaty . . . that we join in putting down insurrections in these countries?

SECRETARY DULLES: No, sir. There is a provision that if there is a subversion, threatened subversion, of the political independence of any country, then we will consult together what to do about it.

SENATOR GREEN: That is subversion then.

SECRETARY DULLES: Yes, sir.

SENATOR GREEN: Well, isn't that another word for insurrection?

SECRETARY DULLES: I would think insurrection is a form of subversion, yes.

SENATOR GREEN: Then we are obliged to help put down a revolutionary movement.

SECRETARY DULLES: No. If there is a revolutionary movement in Vietnam or in Thailand, we would consult together as to what to do about it, because if that were a subversive movement that was in fact propagated by communism, it would be a very grave threat to us. But we have no undertaking to put it down; all we have is an undertaking to consult together as to what to do about it. . . .

SENATOR GREEN: . . . . I know that, generally, both in Asia and in South America there is a feeling that the United States' sympathies ought to be with the revolutionaries because we were a revolutionary government ourselves, and they regret that not only do we not take the part of the revolutionaries, but we take the part against them. What would be your comment on that?

SECRETARY DULLES: My comment on that, Senator, is that there are two kinds of revolutions. One is a truly indigenous revolution which reflects the will of the people, and we ourselves, who had our birth in revolution, naturally are sympathetic to the aspirations of the peoples.

On the other hand, communism has adopted revolution as one of its principal tools of expansion. It gains control of revolutionary movements, and certainly I do not think that we should go so far as to say that any revolutionary movement has the sympathy of the United States.

The Communists got control of China through a revolution. The fact that they used a revolution to do it does not prove that we are, therefore, sympathetic with the Chinese Communists—at least I do not think so.

SENATOR GREEN: On the other hand, we ought not to take the position that any uprising of peoples is necessarily subversive and communistic.

SECRETARY DULLES: That is quite correct.

SENATOR GREEN: They usually are a result of mixed motives.

SECRETARY DULLES: That is why, Senator, there is no obligation whatever in this treaty for any automatic action in the event of a subversive movement. If there is a subversive thing which seems dangerous, we sit together and talk about it, and then try to agree as to whether it calls for action.

SENATOR GREEN: Well, that is largely because the Communists are clever enough to identify themselves with any uprising; is it not?

SECRETARY DULLES: Well, they are extremely clever in getting control of the discontented movements in all of the countries.

SENATOR GREEN: Well, we certainly go to the other extreme and identify ourselves against any uprising or revolutionary movement.

SECRETARY DULLES: We do not try to do that, but we do try not to identify ourselves with revolutionary movements which are dominated and engineered by communism.

## 21  Hans J. Morgenthau: Our Policies in Asia Are Irrelevant (1956)

*Secretary of State Dulles' policies in Asia soon came under strong attack. One of the most trenchant criticisms was written by an eminent political scientist and former consultant to the Department of State, Hans J. Morgenthau (1904–    ). Morgenthau supported the policies of Kennan and Acheson in Europe during the mid-1940's but, after the Korean War began, he warned against American overcommitment in Asia. In this article, published in 1956, Morgenthau delineated the reasons why the United States could act more effectively in European than in Asian affairs. How convincing is his historical account which argues that American "policies in Asia are irrelevant?" How does his view of SEATO differ fundamentally from Dulles' view (Reading 20)? If Morgenthau's observations are correct, what should American policies be when the United States observes a revolution developing in an Asian nation?*

What ails American foreign policy today—and what has ailed it during the better part of the last half-century—is not primarily clumsiness in execution here, weakness in administration there, improvidence at another place—even though it is no stranger to these ailments either—but an all-pervading deficiency of under-

SOURCE. Hans J. Morgenthau, *The Impasse of American Foreign Policy*, Chicago: The University of Chicago Press, 1962, pp. 252–254, 257–258, 263–264, and 273–275. Reprinted by permission of The University of Chicago Press and Hans J. Morgenthau. Copyright 1962 by the University of Chicago.

standing. *The foreign policy of the United States is not based upon the threat that faces it and, hence, is not capable of countering this threat.* The uncertainties and blunders of many of our concrete moves have their roots in that basic misunderstanding.

The negative political effects of that deficiency of understanding are less obvious in Europe than they are in Asia, for the conflict in Europe can indeed be defined in good measure in strictly military and purely ideological terms. The military security of Western Europe is threatened by Russian imperialism, as is its intellectual and moral identity by the advance of communism. It is true that by placing these two issues in a political vacuum and divorcing them thereby from the concrete, specific interests of the individual nations of Western Europe, we have done more than has our enemy to jeopardize our position in Europe.

But it is in Asia that the weakness of our thinking on foreign policy becomes fully apparent, for here both the extremes of philosophic generalities and local military preparations completely miss the point. The ideological cannonade, as it were, soars far above the advancing enemy, and military pacts, far from stopping him, actually help him to advance. Nowhere in Asia, with the exception of Japan, is the conflict between communism and democracy relevant or even intelligible as a philosophic contest between tyranny and freedom, between the total state and the individual. Nowhere in Asia does either the Soviet Union or Communist China advance under the banner of Marxism, calling upon the masses to assume the historic role which Marx had assigned them. Instead, communism advances by identifying itself with the concerns and, more particularly, the grievances, of different groups. . . .

All educated Asians remember with awe or pride the past greatness of China as a culture and a state. Thus Communist China impresses the unceasing stream of visitors from all over Asia— estimated for 1955 at close to 100,000—not with Communist qualities of its philosophy and institutions, but with the restored dignity and power of a great nation. Similarly, the delegations, books, magazines, and movies which Communist China is sending all over Asia make their impact by identifying themselves not with Chinese communism but with the great tradition of Chinese culture. . . .

The relative lack of success of communism in certain parts of Asia, such as Cambodia, Thailand, and Hong Kong, is due to nothing else but the lack of grievances which communism could exploit. The three major reverses which communism has suffered in Asia are likewise the result not, as we have been led to believe, of a revolt against Communist philosophy and the Communist way of life, but of specific and thus far unique circumstances. First, the Chinese soldiers who refused to return to Communist China after they had been captured by United Nations forces in the Korean War were members of former units of the Nationalist army who had most recently been captured by the Communists and whom, for want of sufficient indoctrination, the Chinese Communists considered as expendable. Second, the overwhelming majority of the approximately 800,000 refugees who left the Communist part of Vietnam for the South are Catholics who had lived in the North in compact communities and left in a body under the leadership of their priests [in 1954 and 1955]; the balance is composed of the families of soldiers of the army of South Vietnam who happened to live north of the demarcation line. And third, the main bulk of the refugees who streamed into Hong Kong in 1949 and 1950 did so for the traditional economic reasons, and the small-scale reverse movement from Hong Kong to Communist China is motivated by similar considerations. . . .

Our policies in Asia are irrelevant to the political problems confronting us. At best, they are ineffective, as are our propaganda and economic policies. At worst, the political damage they do is out of all proportion to whatever intrinsic merits they may have. . . .

By allying ourselves with Thailand, we have alienated Burma, which is militarily and in view of the social and political dynamics of Asia infinitely more important than a stagnant country —bypassed by the Asian revolution—such as Thailand, which has been traditionally misgoverned to the satisfaction of its population. By allying ourselves with Pakistan, we have alienated India, which for identical reasons is infinitely more important than our ally. The Baghdad Pact, far from erecting a barrier against Russian penetration of the Middle East, has given Egypt and the other Arab countries hostile to Iraq the incentive and the pretext to come to terms with each other and with the Soviet Union. . . .

Yet while SEATO is militarily hollow and politically per-
nicious, it is more than a unilateral pronouncement of the Secretary of State of the United States. It is a solemn undertaking to
which the representatives of the member states have put their
signatures. This circumstance imposes upon the United States
additional liabilities, both economic and political. Our Asian allies
make no bones about their intention to use SEATO as an entering
wedge into the treasury of the United States. Since they are our
allies, they must have first claim upon American financial support.
As one of the most astute of our representatives in Asia put it to
me: "This is like the Community Chest. Two agencies acting in
concert can collect more than two agencies acting alone."

SEATO, thus having become an instrument of economic pressure, transforms itself in the hands of its Asian members into a
political weapon directed against the United States. Since whatever economic and political support these allies receive can never
be enough, they are in a position of threatening the United States
with looking for support elsewhere. . . .

It is impossible for the United States to square a policy of
implacable enmity to China with the first objective of its Asian
policy: the containment of Communist imperialism. For in the
way that this enmity forces China to the side of the Soviet Union,
even if other circumstances would not do so anyhow, the very
same enmity forces virtually all of Asia to the side of China. Our
enmity toward China becomes a hindrance to the attainment of
our objectives in Asia. Yet so strong is China's position that even
if we should recognize the Communist government of China and
extend the hand of friendship to it, we would only strengthen
those very factors which are responsible for China's strong position in Asia in the first place. Thus we are here faced with a condition which our policy must take into account but cannot change,
short of the destruction of the Communist government of
China. . . .

The West faces another disadvantage which it is not able to
change, at least in the short run: the Asian suspicion of Western
intentions. A Western nation coming to Asia comes branded
with the stigma of Western colonialism, no matter what its purposes and actions. The wall of hostility and suspicion which dis-
mayed General William Dean when he begged food and shelter

from the Koreans whom he had come to liberate and protect constitutes a barrier, insurmountable at least for the time being, to Western influence and policy in Asia.

The intentions and policies of Western nations are doubly suspect in Asia by virtue of their domestic politics. All of Asia is extremely sensitive to the issue of racial equality; and in its relations with the West, the aspiration to be free from contempt takes precedence over all other issues. Every case of racial discrimination in the United States takes on in Asia the aspects of a *cause célèbre*. One has to travel in Asia for some length of time, reading nothing but Asian newspapers, in order to realize to what extent the Asian picture of America is determined by the American attitude on racial equality. For days on end, the only news about America the reader will find deals with racial discrimination and racial violence. Since the elimination of racial discrimination in the United States will inevitably be slow, our policies suffer from a handicap which they, at least in the short run, cannot escape.

## 22   John Foster Dulles: Why the Arbenz Government Was Overthrown in Guatemala (June 30, 1954)

*Between 1944 and 1951, the small, impoverished Central American nation of Guatemala endured the first important social, economic, and political changes in its history. In 1951, a reform government led by Colonel Jacobo Arbenz Guzmán was duly elected to power and continued to change Guatemala by confiscating large amounts of foreign-held property, particularly the vast holdings of the American-controlled United Fruit Company. Through its great economic power, that company had been able to control Guatemala's political affairs until the late 1940's. After Arbenz seized the company's property in 1953, Secretary of State Dulles demanded payment. The Guatemalan president refused, in large part because his nation was too poor to carry out the needed reform program and at the same time indemnify the United Fruit Company. The State Department began to view the*

*Arbenz government as Communist-oriented and, in March 1954,
Dulles successfully moved that the Inter-American Conference of
21 nations indirectly condemn Guatemala's actions. In May, arms and
ammunition arrived in Guatemala from Czechoslovakia. With large
amounts of United States aid, a group of Guatemalan exiles attacked
and overthrew the Arbenz government on June 18. In a radio address
twelve days later, Secretary of State Dulles explained the American
view. In the light of his historical account, what does Dulles mean in
his last paragraph when he states that "the United States will continue
to support the just aspirations of the Guatemalan people?" In his
view, what threat did "Communism" pose in Guatemala?*

---

Tonight I should like to talk with you about Guatemala. It is
the scene of dramatic events. They expose the evil purpose of
the Kremlin to destroy the inter-American system, and they test
the ability of the American States to maintain the peaceful integrity of this hemisphere.

For several years international communism has been probing
here and there for nesting places in the Americas. It finally chose
Guatemala as a spot which it could turn into an official base from
which to breed subversion which would extend to other American
Republics.

This intrusion of Soviet despotism was, of course, a direct
challenge to our Monroe Doctrine, the first and most fundamental
of our foreign policies. . . .

In Guatemala, international communism had an initial success.
It began 10 years ago, when a revolution occurred in Guatemala.
The revolution was not without justification. But the Communists
seized on it, not as an opportunity for real reforms, but as a chance
to gain political power.

Communist agitators devoted themselves to infiltrating the
public and private organizations of Guatemala. They sent recruits
to Russia and other Communist countries for revolutionary train-

SOURCE. Radio and Television Address in United States Department of
State, *American Foreign Policy, 1950–1955, Basic Documents*, Washington,
D. C.: Government Printing Office, 1957, I, pp. 1311–1315.

ing and indoctrination in such institutions as the Lenin School at Moscow. Operating in the guise of "reformers" they organized the workers and peasants under Communist leadership. Having gained control of what they call "mass organizations," they moved on to take over the official press and radio of the Guatemalan Government. They dominated the social security organization and ran the agrarian reform program. Through the technique of the "popular front" they dictated to the Congress and the President.

The judiciary made one valiant attempt to protect its integrity and independence. But the Communists, using their control of the legislative body, caused the Supreme Court to be dissolved when it refused to give approval to a Communist-contrived law. [Jacobo Guzmán] Arbenz, who until this week was President of Guatemala, was openly manipulated by the leaders of communism. . . .

If world communism captures any American State, however small, a new and perilous front is established which will increase the danger to the entire free world and require even greater sacrifices from the American people.

This situation in Guatemala had become so dangerous that the American States could not ignore it. At Caracas last March the American States held their Tenth Inter-American Conference. They then adopted a momentous statement. They declared that "the domination or control of the political institutions of any American State by the international Communist movement . . . would constitute a threat to the sovereignty and political independence of the American States, endangering the peace of America."

There was only one American State that voted against this declaration. That State was Guatemala.

This Caracas declaration precipitated a dramatic chain of events. From their European base the Communist leaders moved rapidly to build up the military power of their agents in Guatemala. In May a large shipment of arms moved from behind the Iron Curtain into Guatemala. The shipment was sought to be secreted by false manifests and false clearances. Its ostensible destination was changed three times while en route. . . .

In the face of these events and in accordance with the spirit of the Caracas declaration, the nations of this hemisphere laid further plans to grapple with the danger. The Arbenz government responded with an effort to disrupt the inter-American system. Because it enjoyed the full support of Soviet Russia, which is on the Security Council, it tried to bring the matter before the Security Council. It did so without first referring the matter to the American regional organization as is called for both by the United Nations Charter itself and by the treaty creating the American organization.

The Foreign Minister of Guatemala openly connived in this matter with the Foreign Minister of the Soviet Union . . . . The Security Council at first voted overwhelmingly to refer the Guatemala matter to the Organization of American States. The vote was 10 to 1. But that one negative vote was a Soviet veto.

Then the Guatemalan Government, with Soviet backing, redoubled its efforts to supplant the American States system by Security Council jurisdiction. However, last Friday, the United Nations Security Council decided not to take up the Guatemalan matter but to leave it in the first instance to the American States themselves. . . .

Throughout the period I have outlined, the Guatemalan Government and Communist agents throughout the world have persistently attempted to obscure the real issue—that of Communist imperialism—by claiming that the United States is only interested in protecting American business. We regret that there have been disputes between the Guatemalan Government and the United Fruit Company. We have urged repeatedly that these disputes be submitted for settlement to an international tribunal or to international arbitration. That is the way to dispose of problems of this sort. But this issue is relatively unimportant. All who know the temper of the U.S. people and Government must realize that our overriding concern is that which, with others, we recorded at Caracas, namely, the endangering by international communism of the peace and security of this hemisphere.

The people of Guatemala have now been heard from. Despite the armaments piled up by the Arbenz government, it was unable to enlist the spiritual cooperation of the people.

Led by Colonel Castillo Armas, patriots arose in Guatemala to challenge the Communist leadership—and to change it. Thus, the situation is being cured by the Guatemalans themselves.

Last Sunday, President Arbenz of Guatemala resigned and seeks asylum. Others are following his example. . . .

The events of recent months and days add a new and glorious chapter to the already great tradition of the American States. . . .

In conclusion, let me assure the people of Guatemala. As peace and freedom are restored to that sister Republic, the Government of the United States will continue to support the just aspirations of the Guatemalan people. A prosperous and progressive Guatemala is vital to a healthy hemisphere. The United States pledges itself not merely to political opposition to communism but to help to alleviate conditions in Guatemala and elsewhere which might afford communism an opportunity to spread its tentacles throughout the hemisphere. Thus we shall seek in positive ways to make our Americas an example which will inspire men everywhere.

## 23   *Philip B. Taylor, Jr.: Why the Arbenz Government Was Overthrown in Guatemala (September 1956)*

*The American support for a counterrevolution in Guatemala in 1954 was both warmly applauded and widely condemned throughout the Western Hemisphere. The best critical account (written within months after the intervention) was published by Philip B. Taylor, Jr., then a member of the Political Science Department at the University of Michigan. Compare Secretary of State Dulles' use of history in the preceding reading with that of Professor Taylor. At what points do the accounts diverge?*

SOURCE. Philip B. Taylor, Jr., "The Guatemalan Affair—A Critique of U. S. Foreign Policy," in *The American Political Science Review*, Vol. L, September 1956, pp. 787-806. Copyright 1956 by The American Political Science Association. Reprinted by permission of The American Political Science Association and Philip B. Taylor, Jr.

. . . There is little doubt that communism got its start in Guatemala under [Juan José] Arévalo [who was elected for the 1945–1951 presidential term]; Arévalo's successor, Lt. Col. Arbenz, who served from March, 1951, until his ouster in July, 1954, was quite sympathetic to Communist activities, but under the best of contrary circumstances the ouster of Communists from their positions in the government would have been extremely difficult and would have stripped the government of its trained, though not necessarily efficient, bureaucrats. . . .

Among the exiles forced from Guatemala by the operations of the Arévalo-Arbenz government was Lt. Colonel Carlos Castillo Armas, who had been condemned to death for his implication in an unsuccessful attempt against the government in late 1950. Castillo had escaped in June, 1951, and had established himself in neighboring Honduras. By the end of May, 1954, he was openly active in the preparation of a force designed to invade Guatemala and overthrow its government. The Honduran government seems not to have undertaken to fulfill the customary obligation of nations in international law to prevent one's territory from being employed as a base of operations against a state with which diplomatic relations are currently maintained. On the other hand, the Guatemalan government had not been overly-correct in its relations with Honduras. A general strike had gradually developed in Honduras between February and May, 1954, in a situation in which there had never before been organized unions or even significant labor leadership. . . . [United States] Ambassador [John E.] Peurifoy later testified that probably at least $750,000 entered the country as aid to the strikers from Guatemala. It is quite likely that Honduras' hospitality to Castillo Armas was a means of redressing the record against Guatemalan intervention.

The Tenth Inter-American Conference met at Caracas, Venezuela in March, 1954. The United States had previously expressed its desire to have the conference record itself as being anti-Communist. . . .

It is significant that those who sprang to Dulles' support in the debates following the presentation of the [United States] resolution were not the democratic nations but the authoritarians, Venezuela, the Dominican Republic, Cuba, and Peru. Guatemala's Foreign Minister, Guillermo Toriello, denouncing the Dulles proposal as ". . . the internationalization of McCarthyism, the burning of books, and the imposition of stereotyped thought," received twice the ovation that Dulles did. The *New York Times* reporter Sydney Gruson later put it succinctly:

"Senor Toriello had said many nasty things about the United States that virtually all Latin Americans believe. They were willing to applaud him since it cost them nothing. But not many were willing to vote against the United States when they might have to get up later in the conference and ask for economic aid. In the committee vote, only Mexico, Uruguay, and Argentina sided with Guatemala. . . ."

Events in Guatemala leading to the civil war seem to have commenced with the State Department announcement on May 17, 1954, that a shipment of arms totaling 1,900 tons had arrived at Puerto Barrios, Guatemala. . . .

The United States employed the shipment to arouse sympathy for its subsequent anti-Arbenz actions. It was also employed as the basis for a nearly unprecedented request to the other members of the North Atlantic Treaty Organization that they grant the United States the privilege of searching their merchant ships on the high seas for arms shipments to Guatemala. The request was rejected by all of the nations to which requests were made.

On May 20, the United States concluded a Mutual Security Treaty with Honduras (a similar treaty had been signed with Nicaragua on April 23), and on May 24 it was announced that the United States Air Force was airlifting war materiel to the two nations. . . .

Col. Castillo Armas' troops entered Guatemalan territory from Honduras on June 19. A period of somewhat desultory fighting followed. Arbenz resigned on June 27 after an all-day conference with his military leaders, and the Army Chief of Staff, Col. Enrique Díaz, established a short-lived provisional government composed of three officers. One of these, Colonel Elfego Monzón, replaced Díaz on the 29th, after the direct intervention of Ambassador Peurifoy. Peurifoy and a Marine bodyguard, both armed, were present in the conference room at the time power changed hands. . . .

The conclusion that the United States played an important

part in the struggle in Guatemala seems inescapable. It cannot be shown that any of the arms airlifted to Honduras or Nicaragua ultimately appeared in the hands of the Castillo Armas forces. Rather, news reports indicate that the Castillo troops were armed with a hodge-podge of weapons, including even a few muzzle-loading rifles. . . . In fact, the military strength of Castillo was largely symbolic, and casualties and combats were few. The decision of the Guatemalan army not to seek battle with Castillo was really what toppled Arbenz. But it can be shown that the United States played a role in the United Nations which tended to deny to Guatemala the privileges apparently guaranteed it by its membership in that organization. At the same time vacillatory Guatemalan action made it difficult for the U.N. and the O.A.S. to do anything significant to prevent the success of the Castillo movement.

In response to the urgent request of the Guatemalan representative on June 19, the U.N. Security Council met on the call of its president, United States representative Henry Cabot Lodge, on June 20. Guatemalan representative Eduardo Castillo-Arriola asked immediate U.N. investigation of his charge that the fighting had begun with the invasion of his country by forces stationed in Honduras and Nicaragua and backed by "foreign monopolies" with the knowledge of the United States State Department. The two accused nations denied this, and a draft resolution was presented by Brazil and Colombia. The draft pointed to the availability of machinery under the O.A.S. [Organization of American States] for the possible settlement of the problem, provided that the Security Council would refer the problem to this machinery, and asked for immediate O.A.S. action to bring bloodshed to an end. The vote on the resolution was 10-1, the Soviet representative vetoing. . . .

The Council meeting [of June 25] voted to take no direct action until it had the opportunity to receive a report from the Peace Committee. The Guatemalan government, which prior to the second Council meeting had rejected O.A.S. Peace Committee investigation, now reconsidered and announced it would welcome it. The date was the afternoon of June 26. After confirming the Guatemalan change of attitude, the Committee on the 27th determined that it would send a five-member team to Guatemala, Honduras, and Nicaragua, starting the 28th.

At this juncture, it was announced that ten nations, including the United States, had requested a special meeting of the O.A.S. Council to consider the advisability of calling a meeting of the Organ of Consultation of the Rio Treaty [of 1947] under the terms of articles 6 and 11 of that treaty. The note had been presented to the O.A.S. Council chairman on June 26. Notwithstanding the June 27 resignation of Arbenz in favor of Enrique Diáz, the matter was pressed on the 28th by the United States. The meeting was voted unanimously, for Rio de Janeiro on July 7. . . .

It seems quite tenable to argue that the action was intended as a smoke-screen rather than as a sincere request. [American delegate Joseph C.] Dreier's statement acknowledged that governmental changes were proceeding in Guatemala, but argued that it was yet too early to know if the new government would be free of the Communist taint. Certainly events between June 16, when it had been anticipated generally that the United States would ask such a convocation, and June 28, had not heightened the dangers of Communist profit in Guatemala. If anything, the position of Arbenz would seem to have weakened during this period. Surely there can have been no real suspicion that the government attacked by Castillo Armas could continue to govern Guatemala for any length of time. The question why the United States should have requested the investigation after the horse had fled the stable, rather than before, seems almost rhetorical under the circumstances. Investigation, or the proposal of a real study of the situation, prior to the outbreak of fighting, would have been sincere. The action of the 28th was only an empty gesture. Events, of course, proceeded in the direction of Arbenz' ouster, and with the agreement of July 2 between Castillo Armas and Monzón, all rationale for the meeting disappeared.

The O.A.S. Council met in special session on July 2 to approve 18-1, with one abstention, the motion presented by Honduras and seconded by the United States that the July 7 meeting be postponed *sine die*. . . .

And, of course, the inspection team of the Peace Committee

did not reach its destination either. It was in Mexico City when the Castillo-Monzón negotiations opened, and it remained there. At the urgent request of the Monzón *junta*, it cancelled its trip at that point on July 2 and returned to Washington. The inaction of the U.N. Security Council and of the Inter-American Peace Committee (as agent for the O.A.S.) had combined with the successful operations of Castillo Armas to overthrow the Arbenz government. . . .

The shocked conscience of the world was probably represented best in the British House of Commons on July 14, 1954, by Clement Attlee, head of the Labor party, in foreign affairs debate:

"The fact is that this was a plain act of aggression, and one cannot take one line on aggression in Asia and another line in Central America. I confess that I was rather shocked at the joy and approval of the American Secretary of State on the success of this *putsch*.

. . . we cannot pass this off as just a Central American squabble, of which there are so many. There was a principle involved and that principle was the responsibility of the United Nations. I think it was a mistake in these circumstances to try to hand over to a regional body. We might also have talk of handing over to a regional body in other parts of the world [China] and I do not think we would like the results very much. Therefore, I am afraid that Guatemala has left a rather unpleasant taste in one's mouth because, to illustrate the theme I was putting, it seems in some instances that the acceptance of the principles of the United Nations is subordinated to a hatred of Communism. . . ."

[The] entire situation leads to the conclusion that the United States failed to give evidence of faith in the processes of the United Nations; that it dragged its feet regarding effective O.A.S. action beyond the point of reason; that it was intimately involved in a situation of subversion of a constitutional government; and that it did not at any time undertake to make the record clear to the people either of the United States or of Latin America. . . .

# CHAPTER III CASTRO AND THE DOMINICAN REPUBLIC (1959-1965)

### 24  *Fidel Castro: Cuba Is No Longer an American Colony (October 1960)*

*After driving Spain from Cuba in a three-month war in 1898, the United States gave the Cubans political autonomy but, until 1959, controlled the island's economic and foreign policies. By so doing, Washington officials also were able to keep domestic Cuban politics consistent with American desires. After gaining power through force, Fulgencio Batista ruled Cuba from 1952 through 1958 with the aid of dictatorial methods, an American-trained and supplied army, and even the quiet support of the small Cuban Communist Party. On January 1, 1959, a young former Cuban lawyer, Fidel Castro, culminated a three-year guerilla campaign in the interior by successfully marching into the capital of Havana. Castro had succeeded largely because of peasant support and despite considerable opposition, through mid-1958, of the Communists and the labor movement in the urban areas. From the beginning, the American response to Castro was decidedly cool. No important economic aid program could be worked out with the new government and, consequently, Castro undertook a wide-ranging agrarian reform program financed in part by the property of American-controlled firms in Cuba which he seized. He also turned increasingly to factions within the Communist Party for help in imposing political discipline and in formulating reform programs which (he hoped) would free Cubans from foreign, and particularly American, economic controls. For the first time the United States confronted a realized, radical revolution in this hemisphere. The American response was unsuccessful in controlling or in*

127

*coming to terms with this revolution. By mid-1960, diplomatic ties were breaking. In October 1960, Castro presented his view to the United Nations. Why does he so sharply separate economic development from social development? Most important, how important to him is his use of history to justify the Cuban revolution? Is he correct in asserting that by doing away with "the desire of some to despoil others," mankind "will have done away forever with the philosophy of war?"*

As far as the world is concerned [Prime Minister Castro] said, the problem of Cuba had come to a head in the last two years, and as such it was a new problem. Before that, the world had few reasons for knowing that his country existed; for many it was an offshoot—in reality, a colony—of the United States.

He traced the history of Cuba and referred to the law passed by the United States Congress at the time of the American military occupation of Cuba during the war with Spain, which, he claimed, said that the Constitution of Cuba—which was then being drafted—must have a rider under which the United States would be granted the right to intervene in Cuba's political affairs and to lease certain parts of the country for naval bases or for their coal deposits. In other words, the right to intervene and to lease naval bases was imposed by force by the legislative body of another country, since Cuban senators were clearly told that if they did not accept, the occupation forces would not be withdrawn. . . .

Mr. Castro traced some of the conditions which he said the successful revolution in Cuba had uncovered. Public services, he alleged, all belonged to United States monopolies and a major portion of the banking business, importing business, oil refineries, sugar production, the lion's share of arable land and the most important industries in all fields in Cuba belonged to North American companies. The balance of payments from 1950 to 1960 was favorable to the United States by one billion dollars.

What the Revolutionary Government had wanted to do was to

SOURCE. Summary of a Speech to the United Nations, *United Nations Review*, Vol. VII, November 1960, pp. 46–48.

devote itself to the settling of its own problems at home; to carry out a program for the betterment of its people. But when the Revolutionary Government began to pass laws to overcome the advantages obtained by the monopolies, difficulties arose. Then "we began to be called communists; then we began to be painted red," he said.

The first unfriendly act perpetrated by the Government of the United States, he said, was to throw open its doors to a gang of murderers, bloodthirsty criminals who had murdered hundreds of defenceless peasants, who had never tired of torturing prisoners for many, many years, who had killed right and left. These hordes were received by the United States with open arms. . . .

He also criticized and blamed the United States Government for the fact that bombs were dropped on the sugar fields of Cuba before the harvest was in, and he accused the United States Government for allowing the planes which dropped the bombs to leave United States territory.

But, he said, aerial incursions finally stopped. Then came economic aggression. It was said that agrarian reform would cause chaos in agricultural production. That was not the case. Had it been so, the United States would not have had to carry on its economic aggression. They could have trusted in the Revolutionary Government's ruining the country. Fortunately that did not happen. Cuba needed new markets for its products. Therefore it signed a trade treaty with the Soviet Union to sell it a million tons of sugar and to purchase a certain amount of Russian products. Surely no one could say that was incorrect.

What could Cuba do? Go to the United Nations and denounce this economic aggression? The United Nations has power to deal with these matters; but it sought an investigation to be carried out by the Organization of American States. As a result, the United States was not condemned. No, the Soviet Union was condemned. All the Soviet Union had said was that if there was military aggression against Cuba, it would support the victims with rockets. Since when was the support of a weak country, conditioned on attack by a powerful country, regarded as interference. If there were no possibility that Cuba would be attacked, then there was no possibility that there would be Soviet support.

"We, the small countries," he added, "do not as yet feel too secure about the preservation of our rights. That is why, when we decide to be free, we know full well that we become free at our own risk."

The Cuban revolution, he continued, was changing. What was yesterday a land of misery, a land of illiterates, was gradually becoming one of the most enlightened, advanced and developed lands of the continent. Developing this theme, he gave figures about the building of schools, housing, and industries, told of the success of plans for conservation of natural resources, medical plans and other advances since the revolution.

In view of the tremendous reality of underdevelopment, the United States Government, at Bogotá, had come out with a plan for economic development, but he criticized it, saying that the governments of Latin America were being offered not the resources for economic development but resources for social development: houses for people who have no work, schools to which children could not go, and hospitals that would be unnecessary if there were enough food to eat. Cuba was not included in this proposed assistance, but they were not going to get angry about that because the Cubans were solving their own problems.

The Government of Cuba, he said, had always been ready to discuss its problems with the Government of the United States, but the latter had not been willing to do so. He quoted notes which had been addressed to the United States in January and February last, and a reply which said that the United States could not accept the conditions for negotiation laid down in those notes. The Government and the people of Cuba, he said, were much concerned "at the aggressive turn in American policy regarding Cuba" and denounced the efforts of the United States to promote "the organization of subversive movements against the Revolutionary Government of Cuba." . . .

The Case of Cuba, continued Mr. Castro, was the case of all the underdeveloped colonial countries and the problems he had described in relation to Cuba applied perfectly well to the whole of Latin America, where, he alleged, the economic resources were controlled by the North American monopolies. There is a United Nations report, he said, which explains how even private capital, instead of going to the countries which need it most for setting up basic industries, is preferably being channeled to the more industrialized countries. The development of Latin America, he added, would have to be achieved through public investment, planned and granted unconditionally without any political strings attached. In this, the problems of Latin America were like the problems of Africa and Asia. . . .

The Prime Minister praised the speech of Mr. Khrushchev and especially called attention to the fact that the Soviet leader had stated that the Soviet Union has no colonies and no investments in any country. Wars, he said, since the beginning of humanity, have emerged for one reason and one reason alone—the desire of some to despoil others. Do away with this, he said, and you will have done away forever with the philosophy of war.

Mr. Castro went on to comment on the speech made before the General Assembly by President Eisenhower. He quoted Mr. Eisenhower as saying that in the developing areas we must seek to promote peaceful change, as well as to assist economic and social progress. To do this the international community must be able to manifest its presence through United Nations observers or forces. "In other words," said Mr. Castro, "the United States is trying to carry out a revolution in the world. The Government of the United States proposes to use United Nations forces to avoid revolutions and changes. . . . He (the President of the United States) proposes to the countries that are receiving technical assistance that he is ready to give them more assistance for the formation of this United Nations emergency force." The Cuban delegation would not agree with that emergency force. . . .

## 25    United States Department of State: The Rationale for the Bay of Pigs Invasion (April 3, 1961)

*Having failed to control the Cuban revolution, the United States secretly began to prepare an army of Cuban exiles for an invasion of the island. Washington officials hoped that the invasion would trigger a rebellion by the Cuban people who, so American intelligence reports asserted, disliked Castro and his reform program. The plans were laid by the outgoing Eisenhower Administration and were adopted, with*

*all too-little questioning, by the newly-elected Chief Executive, John
F. Kennedy (1917–1963). The supposed success in Guatemala eight
years before clearly influenced the decision to try the same tactics
on Castro. Moreover, during the presidential campaign of 1960, Kennedy had called for increased pressure on Castro and for aid to Cuban
exile organizations. Two weeks before the invasion occurred, the
Kennedy Administration published a long statement that was to serve
as a rationale for the invasion. Notice, once again, how a view of
historical events provides the main basis for justifying the invasion.
Does this statement imply a crucial difference between Cuban Communism and "the Soviet line on international affairs?"*

---

The present situation in Cuba confronts the Western Hemisphere and the inter-American system with a grave and urgent
challenge.

This challenge does not result from the fact that the [Fidel]
Castro government in Cuba was established by revolution. The
hemisphere rejoiced at the overthrow of the [Fulgencio] Batista
tyranny, looked with sympathy on the new regime, and welcomed
its promises of political freedom and social justice for the Cuban
people. The challenge results from the fact that the leaders of the
revolutionary regime betrayed their own revolution, delivered
that revolution into the hands of powers alien to the hemisphere
and transformed it into an instrument employed with calculated
effect to suppress the rekindled hopes of the Cuban people for
democracy and to intervene in the internal affairs of other American Republics.

What began as a movement to enlarge Cuban democracy and
freedom has been perverted, in short, into a mechanism for the
destruction of free institutions in Cuba, for the seizure by international communism of a base and bridgehead in the Americas,
and for the disruption of the inter-American system.

It is the considered judgment of the Government of the United

States of America that the Castro regime in Cuba offers a clear and present danger to the authentic and autonomous revolution of the Americas—to the whole hope of spreading political liberty, economic development, and social progress through all the republics of the hemisphere.

## THE BETRAYAL OF THE CUBAN REVOLUTION

The character of the Batista regime in Cuba made a violent popular reaction almost inevitable. The rapacity of the leadership, the corruption of the government, the brutality of the police, the regime's indifference to the needs of the people for education, medical care, housing, for social justice and economic opportunity—all these, in Cuba as elsewhere, constituted an open invitation to revolution.

When word arrived from the Sierra Maestra of the revolutionary movement headed by Dr. Fidel Castro Ruz, the people of the hemisphere watched its progress with feeling and with hope. The Cuban Revolution could not, however, have succeeded on the basis of guerrilla action alone. It succeeded because of the rejection of the regime by thousands of civilians behind the lines—a rejection which undermined the morale of the superior military forces of Batista and caused them to collapse from within. This response of the Cuban people was not just to the cruelty and oppression of the Batista government but to the clear and moving declarations repeatedly made by Dr. Castro concerning his plans and purposes of post-revolutionary Cuba.

As early as 1953 Dr. Castro promised that the first revolutionary law would proclaim the Constitution of 1940 as "the supreme law of the land." In this and subsequent statements Dr. Castro promised "absolute guarantee of freedom of information, both of newspapers and radio, and of all the individual and political rights guaranteed by the Constitution," and a provisional government that "will hold general elections . . . at the end of one year under the norms of the Constitution of 1940 and the Electoral Code of 1943 and will deliver the power immediately to the candidate elected." Dr. Castro, in short, promised a free and democratic Cuba dedicated to social and economic justice. It was to assure these goals that the Rebel Army maintained itself in the hills, that the Cuban people turned against Batista, and that all elements of the revolution in the end supported the 26th of July Movement. It was because of the belief in the honesty of Dr. Castro's purposes that the accession of his regime to power on January 1, 1959, was followed within a single week by its acceptance in the hemisphere—a recognition freely accorded by nearly all the American Republics, including the United States.

For a moment the Castro regime seemed determined to make good on at least its social promises. The positive programs initiated in the first months of the Castro regime—the schools built, the medical clinics established, the new housing, the early projects of land reform, the opening up of beaches and resorts to the people, the elimination of graft in government—were impressive in their conception; no future Cuban government can expect to turn its back on such objectives. But so far as the expressed political aims of the revolution were concerned, the record of the Castro regime has been a record of the steady and consistent betrayal of Dr. Castro's prerevolutionary promises; and the result has been to corrupt the social achievements and make them the means, not of liberation, but of bondage.

The history of the Castro Revolution has been the history of the calculated destruction of the free-spirited Rebel Army and its supersession as the main military instrumentality of the regime by the new state militia. It has been the history of the calculated destruction of the 26th of July Movement and its supersession as the main political instrumentality of the regime by the Communist Party *(Partido Socialista Popular)*. It has been the history of the disillusion, persecution, imprisonment, exile, and execution of men and women who supported Dr. Castro—in many cases fought by his side—and thereafter doomed themselves by trying to make his regime live up to his own promises. . . .

. . . . In place of the democratic spontaneity of the Cuban Revolution, Dr. Castro placed his confidence in the ruthless discipline of the Cuban Communist Party. Today that party is the *only* political party permitted to operate in Cuba. Today its members and those responsive to its influence dominate the government of Cuba, the commissions of economic planning, the labor front, the press, the educational system, and all the agencies of national power.

The Cuban Communist Party has had a long and intricate history. For years it had a working arrangement with the Batista government; indeed, Batista in 1943 appointed to his cabinet the first avowed Communist ever to serve in any cabinet of any American Republic. Later Batista and the Communists fell out. But the Communists were at first slow to grasp the potentialities of the Castro movement. When Castro first went to the hills, the Cuban Communist Party dismissed him as "bourgeois" and "putschist." Only when they saw that he had a chance of winning did they try to take over his movement.

Their initial opposition was quickly forgiven. Dr. Castro's brother, Major Raul Castro, had himself been active in the international Communist student movement and had made his pilgrimage to the Communist world. Moreover, Major Ernesto (Che) Guevara, a dominating influence on Dr. Castro, was a professional revolutionary from Argentina who had worked with Communists in Guatemala and Mexico. Through Raul Castro and Guevara, the Communists, though unable to gain control either of the 26th of July Movement or of the Rebel Army, won ready access to Dr. Castro himself. What was perhaps even more important, the Communist Party could promise Castro not only a clear-cut program but a tough organization to put that program into execution. . . .

On one issue after another, the Castro regime has signified its unquestioning acceptance of the Soviet line on international affairs. After the termination of diplomatic relations with the United States, the Cuban Government turned over its diplomatic and consular representation to the Embassy of Czechoslovakia in Washington. In the United Nations, Cuba votes with the Communist bloc on virtually all major issues. . . .

It is important to understand the detail and the magnitude of this process of takeover. Since the middle of 1960, more than 30,000 tons of arms with an estimated value of $50 million have poured from beyond the Iron Curtain into Cuba in an ever-rising flood. The 8-hour military parade through Habana and the military maneuvers in January 1961 displayed Soviet JS-2 51-ton tanks, Soviet SU-100 assault guns, Soviet 85 mm. field guns, Soviet 122 mm. field guns. Except for motorized equipment, the Cuban armed forces have been reequipped by the Soviet bloc and are now dependent on the bloc for the maintenance of their armed power. Soviet and Czech military advisers and technicians have accompanied the flow of arms. And the Castro regime has sent Cubans to Czechoslovakia and the Soviet Union for training as jet pilots, ground maintenance crews, and artillerymen.

As a consequence of Soviet military aid, Cuba has today, except for the United States, the largest ground forces in the hemisphere—at least ten times as large as the military forces maintained by previous Cuban Governments, including that of Batista. Estimates of the size of the Cuban military establishment range from 250,000 to 400,000. On the basis of the lower figure, one out of every 30 Cubans is today in the armed forces as against one out of 50 in the Soviet Union and one out of 60 in the United States.

Soviet domination of economic relations has proceeded with similar speed and comprehensiveness. A series of trade and financial agreements has integrated the Cuban economy with that of the Communist world. The extent of Cuban economic dependence on the Communist world is shown by the fact that approximately 75 percent of its trade is now tied up in barter arrangements with Iron Curtain countries. The artificiality of this development is suggested by the fact that at the beginning of 1960 only 2 percent of Cuba's total foreign trade was with the Communist bloc. The Soviet Union, East Germany, Czechoslovakia, and Poland have permanent technical assistance missions in Cuba; and a Communist Chinese delegation will soon arrive in pursuance of the Cuban-Chinese agreement of December 1960. According to Major Guevara, 2,700 Cubans will be receiving technical training in bloc countries in 1961.

The same process is visible in the field of cultural relations. . . .

The transformation of Cuba into a Soviet satellite is, from the viewpoint of the Cuban leaders, not an end but a beginning. Dr. Castro's fondest dream is a continent-wide upheaval which would reconstruct all Latin America on the model of Cuba. "We promise," he said on July 26, 1960, "to continue making the nation the example that can convert the Cordillera of the Andes into the

Sierra Maestra of the hemisphere." "If they want to accuse us of wanting a revolution in all America," he added later, "let them accuse us."

Under Castro, Cuba has already become a base and staging area for revolutionary activity throughout the continent. In prosecuting the war against the hemisphere, Cuban embassies in Latin American countries work in close collaboration with Iron Curtain diplomatic missions and with the Soviet intelligence services. In addition, Cuban expressions of fealty to the Communist world have provided the Soviet Government a long-sought pretext for threats of direct interventions of its own in the Western Hemisphere. "We shall do everything to support Cuba in her struggle," Prime Minister Khrushchev said on July 9, 1960, ". . . Speaking figuratively, in case of necessity, Soviet artillerymen can support with rocket fire the Cuban people if aggressive forces in the Pentagon dare to start intervention against Cuba."

As Dr. Castro's alliance with international communism has grown closer, his determination to export revolution to other American Republics—a determination now affirmed, now denied —has become more fervent. The Declaration of Habana of September 2, 1960, was an open attack on the Organization of American States. Cuban intervention, though couched in terms designed to appeal to Latin American aspirations for freedom and justice, has shown its readiness to do anything necessary to extend the power of *Fidelismo*. . . .

No one contends that the Organization of American States is a perfect institution. But it does represent the collective purpose of the American Republics to work together for democracy, economic development, and peace. The OAS has established the machinery to guarantee the safety and integrity of every American Republic, to preserve the principle of nonintervention by any American State in the internal or external affairs of the other American States, and to assure each nation the right to develop its cultural, political, and economic life freely and naturally, respecting the rights of the individual and the principles of universal morality.

The Organization of American States is the expression of the moral and political unity of the Western Hemisphere. In rejecting the OAS, the Castro regime has rejected the hemisphere and has established itself as the outpost in the Americas for forces determined to wreck the inter-American system. Under Castro, Cuba has become the agency to destroy the Bolivarian vision of the Americas as the greatest region in the world, "greatest not so much by virtue of her area and wealth, as by her freedom and glory."

## 26    Robert Scheer and Maurice Zeitlin: The "White Paper" on Cuba: A Reply

*The invasion of Cuba at the Bay of Pigs turned into tragedy. Contrary to American intelligence reports, the Cuban people did not rebel against Castro, and the Cuban army all but wiped out the invasion forces. At several critical moments, President Kennedy refused to commit American troops or planes to carry through the invasion. The debacle began a long, vigorous debate within the United States on the question of why American policy toward Castro had become so bankrupt. Such discussion usually began with an interpretation of American-Cuban relations through 1960 and continued with an analysis of the Administration's statement of April 3, 1961 (Reading 25). One of the most cogent criticisms was penned by Robert Scheer, a widely-read "New Left" journalist, and Maurice Zeitlin, a respected sociologist and an expert on Cuban society. Notice particularly how these two authors dispute the Administration's use of history in its April 3 statement. In Scheer's and Zeitlin's view, what is the most important factor in explaining American fear and hatred of the Cuban revolution? How do they view the relationships between Cuban Communism and Soviet foreign policy, and how does their view differ from the Administration's view, exemplified in the April 3 statement?*

---

SOURCE. Robert Scheer and Maurice Zeitlin, "Cuba and the White Paper," *New University Thought*, I (Summer 1961), pp. 44–55. Copyright 1961, New University Thought Publishing Company. Reprinted with revisions by permission of *New University Thought* and the authors.

The State Department, on April 3, issued a pamphlet denouncing the Revolutionary Government of Cuba. The pamphlet or "White Paper," written by Arthur Schlesinger Jr. in close consultation with President Kennedy, showed only that the Kennedy Administration was continuing the tragic policy of the Eisenhower Administration which led to the present situation. It is paradoxical, indeed, that the eminent historian who wrote the pamphlet should ignore history—the history of the past two years which makes it clear that U.S. policies were largely responsible for whatever Soviet and Communist influence and anti-democratic tendencies there are in Cuba today.

Nowhere in the pamphlet does he mention the basic reason for U.S. opposition to the Revolution—that the reforms of the Revolutionary Government hurt private American business interests. Except for a slight ripple over the trials, relations between the governments of Cuba and the U.S. were cordial until Cuba promulgated the Agrarian Reform Law on May 13, 1959 and wrote it into law on June 3. One week after the Law's enactment, the U.S. sent an official note of protest. *The Wall Street Journal* (June 24, 1959) pointed out:

"Cuba's new Agrarian Reform Law, which will expropriate large landholdings and divide them up among landless Cuban country folk, has crystalized American opposition here [Cuba] to Prime Minister Castro."

It was also the Agrarian Reform Law, as the same issue of *The Wall Street Journal* pointed out, which first provoked serious accusations of Communism in Cuba by American investors who would be hurt by the Law's implementation:

"This revolution may be like a watermelon. The more they slice it, the redder it gets.

So says an American businessman, one of a growing number of American residents here who are becoming increasingly disenchanted with the policies of Fidel Castro's revolutionary government. . . .

"The harsh American appraisal here of Mr. Castro may be clouded by self-interest, it can be argued. But even though it is difficult to ascertain the truth or falsity of American charges that Mr. Castro flirts with Communism, the very fact that the accusations are being made is important. For the accusers are men who help manage $800 million of American investments in Cuba."

These accusations of Communism were clearly inspired by the intended reforms of the Revolutionary Government and had no basis in reality. They coincided with similar charges by Admiral Burke and Senators Keating and Mundt who said that Cuba was over-run with Communists.

Yet at that very moment, the revolutionary leaders, including Castro himself, were clashing openly with the Communists. Six months later, the Communists were thoroughly defeated in the National Labor elections, and excluded from positions on the Cuban Confederation of Labor (CTC) executive. The CTC was headed by David Salvador until April 1960—a man whom the State Department now recognizes as an anti-Communist since he has been imprisoned in Cuba. In November 1959, Deputy CIA Director, General C. P. Cabell, testified before the Senate Internal Security Committee that there was no Communist influence in the Revolutionary Government and that the 26th of July Movement and the Communists were hostile to each other.

## THE ORIGIN OF U.S. HOSTILITY

As the provisions of the Agrarian Reform Law were implemented, and other reforms adversely affected private American investments in Cuba, the U.S. government became increasingly hostile, and its notes of protest more frequent. The first quasi-diplomatic break in U.S.-Cuba relations occurred in September 1959 when the U.S. recalled Ambassador Bonsal to Washington so as to "underscore" U.S. displeasure over the Agrarian Reform Law, the "intervention" of the Cuban Telephone Company ("intervention" is the assumption by the government of the management functions of an enterprise while the profits continue to flow to the stockholders), and the reduction in rates of the Cuban Electric Company. The U.S. recalled Bonsal to Washington because the Revolutionary Government refused to modify Cuba's economic program.

At the root of the deterioration of relations lay the expropriating of U.S. sugar properties. The U.S. government repeated in almost every one of its notes, that while it did not oppose Cuba's right to expropriate, it demanded that expropriation "be accompanied by prompt, adequate and effective compensation." The U.S. never made clear what that meant. The Cubans took it to mean "cash payment." This was impossible. As late as December 1959, the U.S. Embassy reported Cuban reserves at $49.4 million, and that did not include the huge backlog of debts. Because of the economic situation inherited from the Batista regime, Cuba had *no choice* but to offer bonds rather than cash as payment for the expropriated properties.

But the core of the Revolution was the agrarian reform; it could not be impeded to satisfy the American sugar companies which owned at least 40% of Cuba's sugar production. The establishment of the cooperatives would permit the Cubans to diversify their agriculture and to industrialize the country, to facilitate the elimination of unemployment and illiteracy and to bring health and welfare facilities to the rural areas. Had the U.S. government recognized the imperative necessity of the reforms, and offered Cuba financial aid, the break in relations could easily have been avoided.

Castro came to the U.S. in April 1959 as a guest, not of our government, but of the Press Club. He received no offers of economic aid from the U.S., although to secure such aid was a major purpose of his visit. He brought three economic advisers to the U. S. who conferred with officials of the International Economic Development Bank, but were told that aid would be forthcoming only if Cuba pursued conservative fiscal policies, admittedly leading to increased unemployment and higher prices. Castro also asked the U.S. for a larger sugar import quota but was turned down. His position at that time was neutralist but pro-Western and anti-Communist. U.S. economic aid would have made compensation possible; the agrarian reform could have—so to speak—been financed by the U.S. government; American investors would not have had to be hurt; and relations could have developed on the basis of friendship and equality. This refusal of aid, and subsequent moves of the U.S., however, led to the break in relations and hastened changed attitudes among the revolutionaries.

The first major seizure of American-owned properties occurred in the fall of 1959 and early 1960. Unfortunately, when the business community sought sanctions against Cuba and did so in the name of Freedom vs. Communism, our government adopted that policy. The cut in the Cuban sugar was undoubtedly intended to hurt the Revolutionary Government and force it to halt its reforms and was pushed through by U.S. private investors in Cuba. The authoritative sugar industry publication, *Sugar*, in January 1960 described the forces behind the coming cut in the quota.

"Desires and demands of almost every sugar supplying area for a larger share of the U.S. market rose to a fever pitch with the coming of the Fidel Castro government in Cuba. Disappointed last year by Congress' refusal to take any action, these applicants are redoubling their efforts. . . . The would-be expansionists have also gained strong aid from sources which never figured in sugar legislation. American investors in oil, cattle, banking, and other enterprises in Cuba are angered at the confiscations under Castro. They feel reprisals are in order."

## FREEDOM AND THE SUGAR QUOTA

Scarcely a month later, the U.S. government determined to cut Cuba's sugar quota. The *New York Times* reported on February 5, 1960:

"It was learned that the Administration had decided to ask Congress for the authority to cut the sugar quota of any foreign country when this was necessary in the national interest, *and to use language blunt enough to make plain to Premier Castro why it was seeking this authority*." (Italics added.)

The U.S. government decided to ask for power to cut the Cuban sugar quota (and, as we shall see below, began planning the Cuban government's overthrow) when not one of its subsequent rationalizations for opposition to the Revolution had any basis in fact.

There was no Communist influence in the Revolutionary Government and the labor unions were under anti-Communist leadership. Cuba had a free and vehement opposition press—and had one until many months later. *The Wall Street Journal* (January 27, 1960) had only a few days earlier reported that 90% of the Cuban people supported the Revolutionary Government. Cuba did not yet have any official relations with the Soviet Bloc (excepting a November sugar deal similar to those made under Batista). She could not be correctly charged with "export of revolution" or its encouragement. She had (on the very day of the announced intention of the U.S. to get power to cut the quota) accepted a Brazilian offer to mediate the dispute with the U.S. (The U.S. rebuffed this offer because, as Secretary of State Herter said, the U.S. "did not feel there was any need for mediation.") Cuba had made other almost desperate attempts at conciliation with the U.S. Cuba's President Osvaldo Dorticos himself asked for negotiations and cordial relations. In short, not one of the present reasons given by the U.S. for opposing the Revolution, had any basis then. Cuba was as free as any country in the "free world"; non-Communist; conciliatory. Nevertheless, the U.S. was already seeking to hurt the Cuban economy.

The U.S. refusal to negotiate and its clear intention to cut the Cuban sugar quota were sufficient reason alone to make Cuba seek new markets for the sugar on which the entire Cuban economy depended.

In addition, Cuba's monetary reserves were extremely low and she faced a surplus stock of one and a half million tons of sugar. She had tried to increase sales in other markets, notably Japan, but her most obvious potential market lay in the Soviet Bloc. The other sugar consuming countries were in no position to ease the burden of Cuba's sugar surplus—their consumption was relatively inelastic and their supply assured. The Soviet Union and China, on the other hand, were increasing domestic consumption of sugar. And Cuba would be able to get necessary goods from

the Soviet Union which she could not get elsewhere because of
the low state of her [monetary] reserves. As *The Wall Street
Journal* (February 5, 1960) pointed out:

"European and U.S. credit sources are cracking down on Cuba
and the Cubans have no other place to go than to Russia. . . .
Russia will probably extend credit or barter because she is aggressively seeking markets."

When the Cuba-Soviet trade agreement was signed, *The Wall
Street Journal* (February 15, 1960) reported that the terms of the
agreement were not significantly different from those under
which Batista had traded with the Soviets to the amount of $200
million in the four years before the Revolution. The *Journal* also
pointed out that:

"The agreement says specifically that Russia will trade heavy
machinery to the Cubans. The island nation needs tractors, farm
equipment and industrial machinery which it has been unable to
purchase on credit terms from American companies."

## THE INCREASE IN SOVIET TRADE

The fact is that not only was this initial Soviet-Cuba trade
agreement necessary for economic reasons, but the subsequent
policies of the U.S. made it imperative for Cuba to rely on Soviet
economic trade and aid. After the Cuban agreement with the
Soviets, Cuba continued to try to negotiate differences with the
U.S. She asked only that, as the *New York Times* (February 24,
1960) reported, "the United States must undertake not to enact
*during the negotiations* a Sugar Act unacceptable to Cuba." The
U.S. answered on February 29, that it could not "accept the conditions for the negotiations."

"The Government of the United States must remain free, in
the exercise of its own sovereignty, to take what steps it deems
necessary, fully consistent with its international obligations, in
the defense of the legitimate rights and interests of its people.
The Government of the United States believes that these rights

and interests have been adversely affected by the unilateral acts of the Government of Cuba."

This meant quite clearly that the U.S. intended to go ahead with its plans to cut the Cuban sugar quota.

Leaving aside for the moment other crucial aspects of U.S. policy, three actions stand out as forcing the Cubans increasingly to depend on the Soviet Union: the refusal of the oil companies to refine Soviet crude oil, the cut in the sugar quota and the economic embargo.

Cuba was able to buy oil from the Soviet Union in return for sugar. The [American] oil companies demanded cash and would not extend further credit. By May 1960, Cuba owed them $50 million in unpaid accounts. She hardly had that much in her reserves. The Soviet oil was therefore both necessary and desirable for Cuba. It was generally understood that the oil companies would refine the Soviet crude oil, as *The Wall Street Journal* reported as late as May 24, 1960. Their subsequent refusal was a calculated move to precipitate a crisis which would justify a cut in the sugar quota so as to create difficulties for the Revolution. This intention to precipitate a crisis was, as *The Wall Street Journal* (June 13, 1960) reported, a reflection of the "tough line" of the U.S. The companies believed that the Cubans would not be able to operate the refineries and that the economy would come to a halt. The alternative was, of course, that the Soviets would supply the technicians and equipment and Cuba would have to rely on them in general.

When the oil companies refused to refine the Soviet crude oil, they were seized and intervened. This was followed by the cut in the Cuban sugar quota, which, of course, had long been planned. These U.S. attempts to hurt the Cuban economy and to force the revolutionaries to halt their program—together with the later economic embargo—gave the Soviets whatever influence they now have in Cuba. The economic embargo imposed in October which prevented U.S. firms from exporting goods to Cuba (with the exception of medical supplies) merely completed the chain of events, making it virtually necessary for Cuba to rely on the Soviet Bloc.

Not one of these critical U.S. actions is mentioned in the Schlesinger-Kennedy pamphlet. But if anyone is to be correctly accused, as the U.S. now accuses Cuba in that pamphlet, of "delivery of the revolution to the Sino-Soviet Bloc," it is our government. Other actions such as the clear countenancing of counterrevolutionary invasions of Cuba from our shores, the embargo on arms to allow the Revolution to protect itself, the Retalhuleau base in Guatemala, the Presidential campaign rhetoric, and so on, all contributed to the Cuban turn to the Soviets for political as well as economic aid.

The very same actions which necessitated Soviet economic aid, also led to the radicalization of the Cuban economy and the nationalization of U.S. industry in Cuba. . . .

. . . . The Schlesinger-Kennedy pamphlet presents little or no reliable evidence to buttress its assertions. How can we intelligently evaluate U.S. foreign policy if not only the mass media but our own government misinforms and deludes us?

When the Revolutionary Government called its invasion alerts, it was ridiculed. When the Revolutionary Government charged the U.S. was planning aggression and financing a base in Retalhuleau, Guatemala, the charge was first hushed-up then denied. When the invasion occurred, it was rationalized as necessary in a world of power politics. Morality was out of place. But what is the reply to the most damaging disclosure? Since May, 1960 U.S. agents had been training Cuban counterrevolutionaries in "the complex camps on Guatemala's Pacific Coast" (Tad Szulc, *New York Times*, April 20, 1961)—and the order to plan the overthrow of the Revolutionary Government was given as early as March! Former President Eisenhower acknowledged two months after the invasion that

". . . while President, he had directed that measures be taken to help organize, train and equip Cuban refugees so they could act at the proper time. . . .

"The former President said *he gave the order* for the organization, training and equipping of the Cuban refugees *on March 17, 1960.*" (*New York Times*, June 13, 1961, italics added.)

The U.S. was planning to overthrow an exceedingly popular

non-Communist nationalist government because of the revolution's adverse impact on U.S. private business interests in Cuba.

Cuba is an American tragedy. It is the tragedy of intellectuals who have succumbed to the new liberal *realpolitik*, and it is the tragedy of our country's betrayed and fallen ideals—of its commitment to democracy and the self-determination of peoples.

## 27    John F. Kennedy: The Soviets Are Building Nuclear Missile Sites in Cuba (October 22, 1962)

*The Bay of Pigs invasion and an increased economic interdependence led to close political and military relationships between Cuba and the Soviet Union. Throughout the summer of 1962, rumors spread that the Soviets were placing missiles in Cuba, but they were discounted by the Kennedy Administration and by many others on the grounds that the emplacements were for defensive, not offensive (ground-to-ground, long-range) missiles. However, in mid-October 1962, high-flying American reconnaissance planes spotted Soviet-built offensive missiles being moved into place. On October 22, President Kennedy told the American people in a nationwide television and radio address about the missiles, warning that the Soviets must remove them or face American counteraction. The world was on the brink of nuclear war. How does President Kennedy justify historically the American position in this crisis? What is the difference between the Administration's view of Cuba in the President's address, and the view shown in the April 3, 1961 statement made on the eve of the Bay of Pigs? (Reading 25.)*

Good evening, my fellow citizens. This Government, as promised, has maintained the closest surveillance of the Soviet military

SOURCE. *Department of State Bulletin*, Vol. XLVII, November 12, 1962, pp. 715–720.

buildup on the island of Cuba. Within the past week unmistakable evidence has established the fact that a series of offensive missile sites is now in preparation on that imprisoned island. The purpose of these bases can be none other than to provide a nuclear strike capability against the Western Hemisphere.

Upon receiving the first preliminary hard information of this nature last Tuesday morning [October 16] at 9:00 a.m., I directed that our surveillance be stepped up. . . .

The characteristics of these new missile sites indicate two distinct types of installations. Several of them include medium-range ballistic missiles capable of carrying a nuclear warhead for a distance of more than 1,000 nautical miles. Each of these missiles, in short, is capable of striking Washington, D.C., the Panama Canal, Cape Canaveral, Mexico City, or any other city in the southeastern part of the United States, in Central America, or in the Caribbean area.

Additional sites not yet completed appear to be designed for intermediate-range ballistic missiles capable of traveling more than twice as far—and thus capable of striking most of the major cities in the Western Hemisphere. . . .

This urgent transformation of Cuba into an important strategic base—by the presence of these large, long-range, and clearly offensive weapons of sudden mass destruction—constitutes an explicit threat to the peace and security of all the Americas, in flagrant and deliberate defiance of the Rio Pact of 1947, the traditions of this nation and hemisphere, the Joint Resolution of the 87th Congress, the Charter of the United Nations, and my own public warnings to the Soviets on September 4 and 13.

This action also contradicts the repeated assurances of Soviet spokesmen, both publicly and privately delivered, that the arms buildup in Cuba would retain its original defensive character and that the Soviet Union had no need or desire to station strategic missiles on the territory of any other nation. . . .

Neither the United States of America nor the world community of nations can tolerate deliberate deception and offensive threats on the part of any nation, large or small. We no longer live in a world where only the actual firing of weapons represents a sufficient challenge to a nation's security to constitute maximum peril. Nuclear weapons are so destructive and ballistic missiles are so swift that any substantially increased possibility of their use or any sudden change in their deployment may well be regarded as a definite threat to peace.

For many years both the Soviet Union and the United States, recognizing this fact, have deployed strategic nuclear weapons with great care, never upsetting the precarious *status quo* which insured that these weapons would not be used in the absence of some vital challenge. Our own strategic missiles have never been transferred to the territory of any other nation under a cloak of secrecy and deception; and our history, unlike that of the Soviets since the end of World War II, demonstrates that we have no desire to dominate or conquer any other nation or impose our system upon its people. Nevertheless, American citizens have become adjusted to living daily on the bull's eye of Soviet missiles located inside the U.S.S.R. or in submarines.

In that sense missiles in Cuba add to an already clear and present danger—although it should be noted the nations of Latin America have never previously been subjected to a potential nuclear threat. . . .

Acting, therefore, in the defense of our own security and of the entire Western Hemisphere, and under the authority entrusted to me by the Constitution as endorsed by the resolution of the Congress, I have directed that the following *initial* steps be taken immediately:

*First:* To halt this offensive buildup, a strict quarantine on all offensive military equipment under shipment to Cuba is being initiated. All ships of any kind bound for Cuba from whatever nation or port will, if found to contain cargoes of offensive weapons, be turned back. This quarantine will be extended, if needed, to other types of cargo and carriers. We are not at this time, however, denying the necessities of life as the Soviets attempted to do in their Berlin blockade of 1948.

*Second*: I have directed the continued and increased close surveillance of Cuba and its military buildup. The Foreign Ministers of the OAS [Organization of American States] in their communique of October 3 rejected secrecy on such matters in this hemisphere. Should these offensive military preparations continue, thus increasing the threat to the hemisphere, further action will be justified. I have directed the Armed Forces to prepare for any eventualities; and I trust that, in the interest of both the Cuban people and the Soviet technicians at the sites, the hazards to all concerned of continuing this threat will be recognized.

*Third*: It shall be the policy of this nation to regard any nuclear missile launched from Cuba against any nation in the Western Hemisphere as an attack by the Soviet Union on the United States, requiring a full retaliatory response upon the Soviet Union.

*Fourth*: As a necessary military precaution I have reinforced our base at Guantanamo, evacuated today the dependents of our personnel there, and ordered additional military units to be on a standby alert basis.

*Fifth*: We are calling tonight for an immediate meeting of the Organ of Consultation, under the Organization of American States. . . . Our other allies around the world have also been alerted.

*Sixth*: Under the Charter of the United Nations, we are asking tonight that an emergency meeting of the Security Council be convoked without delay to take action against this latest Soviet threat to world peace. Our resolution will call for the prompt dismantling and withdrawal of all offensive weapons in Cuba, under the supervision of U.N. observers, before the quarantine can be lifted.

*Seventh and finally*: I call upon Chairman Khrushchev to halt and eliminate this clandestine, reckless, and provocative threat to world peace and to stable relations between our two nations. I call upon him further to abandon this course of world domination and to join in an historic effort to end the perilous arms race and transform the history of man. He has an opportunity now to move the world back from the abyss of destruction—by returning to his Government's own words that it had no need to station missiles outside its own territory, and withdrawing these weapons from Cuba—by refraining from any action which will widen or deepen the present crisis—and then by participating in a search for peaceful and permanent solutions. . . .

Finally, I want to say a few words to the captive people of Cuba, to whom this speech is being directly carried by special radio facilities. I speak to you as a friend, as one who knows of your deep attachment to your fatherland, as one who shares your aspirations for liberty and justice for all. And I have watched and the American people have watched with deep sorrow how your nationalist revolution was betrayed and how your fatherland fell under foreign domination. How your leaders are no longer Cuban leaders inspired by Cuban ideals. They are puppets and agents of an international conspiracy which has turned Cuba against your friends and neighbors in the Americas—and turned it into the first Latin American country to become a target for nuclear war, the first Latin American country to have these weapons on its soil.

These new weapons are not in your interest. They contribute nothing to your peace and well-being. They can only undermine it. But this country has no wish to cause you to suffer or to impose any system upon you. We know that your lives and land are being used as pawns by those who deny you freedom.

Many times in the past the Cuban people have risen to throw out tyrants who destroyed their liberty. And I have no doubt that most Cubans today look forward to the time when they will be truly free—free from foreign domination, free to choose their own leaders, free to select their own system, free to own their own land, free to speak and write and worship without fear or degradation. And then shall Cuba be welcomed back to the society of free nations and to the associations of this hemisphere.

My fellow citizens, let no one doubt that this is a difficult and dangerous effort on which we have set out. No one can foresee precisely what course it will take or what costs or casualties will be incurred. Many months of sacrifice and self-discipline lie ahead—months in which both our patience and our will will be tested, months in which many threats and denunciations will keep us aware of our dangers. But the greatest danger of all would be to do nothing. . . .

## 28 Khrushchev-Kennedy Correspondence on the Missile Crisis (October 1962)

*After President Kennedy's speech to the nation (Reading 27), the United States placed a naval blockade around Cuba in order to prevent any Soviet ship carrying missiles or missile-fuel from reaching the island. When Soviet ships approached the blockade, they first stopped in the water and then turned around and headed back across the Atlantic. The Soviets nevertheless refused to remove those missiles already emplaced in Cuba. By October 27, the United States was preparing a bombing strike on the missile-sites, an action that no doubt would have meant the death of Soviet technicians and would have led to an even deeper crisis. But, on October 27, Soviet Premier Nikita Khrushchev wrote one in a series of letters that he sent to President Kennedy during this tense week, justifying the Russian position and then opening slightly the possibility of a negotiated settlement. President Kennedy replied that "the key elements" of Khrushchev's proposals were acceptable. The crisis abated. What does President Kennedy deliberately overlook in Premier Khrushchev's letter in order to obtain a settlement satisfactory to the United States? Looking at American-Cuban relations in the 1959–1962 period, what are the historical lessons to be learned from this experience?*

---

### KHRUSHCHEV TO KENNEDY, OCTOBER 27

Dear Mr. President: It is with great satisfaction that I studied your reply to Mr. U Thant [Secretary-General of the United Nations] on the adoption of measures in order to avoid contact by our ships and thus avoid irreparable fatal consequences. This reasonable step on your part persuades me that you are showing

SOURCE. *Department of State Bulletin*, Vol. XLVII, November 1962, pp. 741-746.

solicitude for the preservation of peace, and I note this with satisfaction. . . .

Our purpose has been and is to help Cuba, and no one can challenge the humanity of our motives aimed at allowing Cuba to live peacefully and develop as its people desire. You want to relieve your country from danger and this is understandable. However, Cuba also wants this. All countries want to relieve themselves from danger. But how can we, the Soviet Union and our government, assess your actions which, in effect, mean that you have surrounded the Soviet Union with military bases, surrounded our allies with military bases, set up military bases literally around our country, and stationed your rocket weapons at them? This is no secret. High-placed American officials demonstratively declare this. Your rockets are stationed in Britain and in Italy and pointed at us. Your rockets are stationed in Turkey.

You are worried over Cuba. You say that it worries you because it lies at a distance of 90 miles across the sea from the shores of the United States. However, Turkey lies next to us. Our sentinels are pacing up and down and watching each other. Do you believe that you have the right to demand security for your country and the removal of such weapons that you qualify as offensive, while not recognizing this right for us?

You have stationed devastating rocket weapons, which you call offensive, in Turkey literally right next to us. How then does recognition of our equal military possibilities tally with such unequal relations between our great states? This does not tally at all. . . .

This is why I make this proposal: We agree to remove those weapons from Cuba which you regard as offensive weapons. We agree to do this and to state this commitment in the United Nations. Your representatives will make a statement to the effect that the United States, on its part, bearing in mind the anxiety and concern of the Soviet state, will evacuate its analogous weapons from Turkey. Let us reach an understanding on what time you and we need to put this into effect. . . .

We, having assumed this commitment in order to give satisfaction and hope to the peoples of Cuba and Turkey and to increase their confidence in their security, will make a statement in the Security Council to the effect that the Soviet Government gives a solemn pledge to respect the integrity of the frontiers and the sovereignty of Turkey, not to intervene in its domestic affairs. . . .

The U.S. Government will make the same statement in the Security Council with regard to Cuba. . . .

Why would I like to achieve this? Because the entire world is now agitated and expects reasonable actions from us. . . . I attach a great importance to such understanding because it might be a good beginning and, specifically, facilitate a nuclear test ban agreement. The problem of tests could be solved simultaneously, not linking one with the other, because they are different problems. However, it is important to reach an understanding to both these problems in order to make a good gift to the people, to let them rejoice in the news that a nuclear test ban agreement has also been reached and thus there will be no further contamination of the atmosphere. Your and our positions on this issue are very close. . . .

## KENNEDY TO KHRUSHCHEV, OCTOBER 27

. . . The first thing that needs to be done . . . is for work to cease on offensive missile bases in Cuba and for all weapons systems in Cuba capable of offensive use to be rendered inoperable, under effective United Nations arrangements. . . .

As I read your letter, the key elements of your proposals—which seem generally acceptable as I understand them—are as follows:

(1) You would agree to remove these weapons systems from Cuba under appropriate United Nations observation and supervision; and undertake, with suitable safeguards, to halt the further introduction of such weapons systems into Cuba.

(2) We, on our part, would agree—upon the establishment of adequate arrangements through the United Nations to ensure the carrying out and continuation of these commitments—(a) to remove promptly the quarantine measures now in effect and (b) to give assurances against an invasion of Cuba. I am confident that other nations of the Western Hemisphere would be prepared to do likewise. . . .

I would like to say again that the United States is very much interested in reducing tensions and halting the arms race; and if your letter signifies that you are prepared to discuss a detente affecting NATO and the Warsaw Pact, we are quite prepared to consider with our allies any useful proposals. . . .

## 29   *John Gerassi: Castro's Continuing Attractiveness* (*January 1963*[1])

*The Kennedy Administration's success in removing the missiles from Cuba without having to use a military strike (or a nuclear exchange) led some to believe that the United States had scored a decisive victory over Castro. John Gerassi, a long-time and knowledgeable observer of Latin American affairs, argued that any such conclusion was wrong. How do Gerassi's approach and use of the historical record differ from the ones found in the American statement of April 3, 1961 (Reading 25), and from President Kennedy's analysis on October 22, 1962 (Reading 27) of Cuba's recent history? Which document do you find more helpful as a basis for long-range American policy-making in regard to Cuba—the April 3, 1961 analysis or Gerassi's description?*

---

A front-page headline in a Washington, D.C. newspaper last week read: *Castro Battles for His Political Life.* In my opinion, whether he wins or loses that battle, what he represents has scored victories in the rest of Latin America which will not soon

[1] Mr. Gerassi has requested that the following note be added to this article: "Since 1964, I have repeatedly visited Cuba and am now convinced that the Revolution is genuinely humanistic, that Latin American nationalists agree, and that, therefore, they are now pro-Castro."

SOURCE. John Gerassi, "Castroism's Appeal," in *The New Republic*, Vol. 148, No. 2, January 12, 1963, pp. 13–15. Copyright 1963 by Harrison-Blaine of New Jersey, Inc. Reprinted by permission of *The New Republic* and John Gerassi.

be forgotten. While it is true that most Latin Americans are disappointed with the Cuban leader, this has been so ever since he delivered his "Marxist-Leninist" speech in December, 1961. And while it is true that many Latin American Nationalists, who are the leaders of whatever revolutions are forthcoming, publicly condemned Castro for allowing Cuba to become a Soviet base, they still believe he could not have done otherwise. Paradoxical as it may seem, the Nationalists are both anti-Castro and Castroite. If we fail to distinguish between the man and idea, we have not begun to understand the true state of affairs in Latin America.

First of all, out of 200 million Latin Americans, according to figures compiled by the Economic Commission for Latin America, no less than 120 million never drink potable water and 1,000 children die every day from lack of water. The average daily calorie intake is 1,200. Fifty-two percent of the population get no more than 500 calories a day (the US average is 3,100). In 1961 alone, one million died from starvation or lack of proper foods. One-third of Latin Americans live in slums, without heat, light, garbage disposal systems or medical attention. Seventy percent are illiterate.

Not counting Bolivia or Cuba, where land reform is well under way, but counting Mexico, where meaningful land reform stopped in 1940, 1.2 percent of the people own 71.6 percent of the arable land. (In the US about 80 percent of the farmers own their own land.) Just under 25 percent of the corporations in Latin America (*Sociedades Anonimas*) are controlled by less than 8,000 individuals and foreign (mostly US) firms and earn 74 percent of the total income. In these circumstances, very little will be accomplished by putting the "ins" out and the "outs" in, because both, usually called the Liberals and the Conservatives, are bent upon keeping the present structure intact.

Part of the Latin American's need for self-respect—and it is fundamental need—can be satisfied only by material progress. The other, truer condition for self-respect is their feeling that their governments say and do what is good for *their* countries. I don't know of one would-be-proud Latin American, for example, who thinks it is good for his country not to trade with the Soviet bloc just because the US would prefer it that way—when the US itself so trades. Every Chilean knows, to pursue the point, that

Chile does not sell its copper to Russia because the US, declaring copper a strategic raw material, does not want it to; but he also knows a few years ago England resold Chilean copper to the Soviet bloc—and as reported in all Chilean newspapers and by the AP [Associated Press]—with US acquiescence.

National pride and self-confidence do not require that Latin America must become an enemy of the US, any more than England became an enemy when it recognized Communist China. Its leaders must be able, however, to adopt policies independent of the US. In modern history, Latin America has had only five truly popular regimes: Peron in Argentina, Vargas in Brazil, the MNR in Bolivia, Cardenas in Mexico and Castro (at least until 1961) in Cuba. Most were demagogic, corrupt and dictatorial, but they were popular because they had the air—no matter what the US thought—of independence. Except in Bolivia where US interests were small, these regimes nationalized US corporations, and were therefore more or less opposed by the Administration in Washington.

Again and again, one is told that Latin America's industrialization is dependent upon foreign capital. That is not so. Were the governments to take over the private banks, freeze all big accounts, and nationalize the major native-owned industries and large landed estates, they would have more capital at their disposal than is now being invested by foreign corporations. Local oligarchs ship more than $1 billion ($1.5 billion according to the consensus of Latin American Finance Ministries) every year to foreign (mostly Swiss or US) banks, while foreign investment in Latin America has not topped $1 billion in any year since 1953.

Major corporations' press agentry to the contrary, more money leaves Latin America in profits than enters in investment. US investment in Latin America brings home more, proportionally, than US investment anywhere else in the world. . . . US private investment in Western Europe in 1958 totaled $422 million, its remitted income was $325 million; in Latin America that year, $317 million was invested and $653 million taken out. These are the official figures; millions of dollars more are lost to Latin America in other ways.

For example, in Venezuela, though both oil production and taxes have been going up steadily over the last few years and the retail prices on gasoline, kerosene, diesel oil, heating oil, asphalt or lubricants have not gone down, Venezuelan revenue from oil taxes has actually been declining: 2,938 million bolivars in 1958; 2,724 million in 1959; 2,631 million in 1960. How is this possible? It is possible because Venezuela taxes *profits*. The big oil corporations (US and British-Dutch) claim lower profits, though they produce more. How do they do it? They claim this lower profit by charging themselves higher shipping rates; their ships' profits are *not* taxed by Venezuela. By hiking tanker costs charged against their Venezuelan subsidiaries but paid by shipping lines registered in Panama, Liberia or wherever shipping taxes are lowest, they reduce their taxable profits. This is one main reason why so many private US ships fly non-US flags.

There are other ways of taking profits out of Latin America. In Peru, US mines take off from their taxable income as much as 17 percent for depletion and 49 percent for depreciation. In effect, reserves (depreciation) and depletion are profits not taken out of the country and not taxed—but they are profits nonetheless. . . .

Another method of sending home unofficial profits is through loans made by a subsidiary in Latin America to the parent organization in the US, which then defaults payment. The state of Rio Grande do Sul in Brazil accused IT&T's [International Telephone and Telegraph] subsidiary there, the *Companhia Telefonica Nacional*, of doing just that. It pointed out that though IT&T owned 370,308 of CTN's 374,970 shares, the latter had loaned the former 1,270,443,930.60 cruzeiros (about $3 million) while claiming that the reason it could not improve service (the state has 6 million inhabitants, only 28,648 phones, compared to, say Minneapolis, with 650,000 people and 200,000 phones) was because it was losing money. One final point: the huge sums that US corporations supposedly invest in Latin America are huge on paper only. Most US firms simply deposit the "investment" in US banks, take out the equivalent in local currency in Latin America from the banks' branches, thus do not help alleviate the area's dollar shortage.

Even if US and other foreign capital played by Queensbury rules in Latin America, the type of industrialization it would foster would not necessarily be beneficial to the area. Unregulated development in underdeveloped countries seems to increase social injustice, not lessen it. . . .

What if the industrialization of Latin America *were* possible only with foreign capital? Still, in my judgment major foreign corporations must be nationalized. The reasons for that are psychological, but that does not make them any the less real. Can a Latin American feel proud of his country when so much of its energy, its minerals, its major export production, its phones and trains, its cars and TVs are foreign-owned or made? In Latin America, 85 percent of steel mills and hydroelectric plants, 40 percent of transportation systems, 95 percent of mining, and 30 percent of all other industries are US-owned. If you add up all the corporations, farms, services, etc., that together produce the annual $600 billion Gross National Product of Latin America, 40 percent of these corporations, farms, services, etc., are owned 51 percent or more by US corporations. Not only has private US investment brought little social progress, it has exacerbated envy.

Castro crushed Cuba's oligarchy and upper middle class which, as in other un-independent countries, not only controlled the state machinery, the press and the army behind the rulers (in this case, Batista), but also encouraged its business partners, the US corporations, to tighten their grip on the country's economy. In Cuba, American business owned 60 percent of absolutely everything, from sugar to lipstick. To Cubans, it seemed well worth going without luxuries, even necessities, to smash this control. Everywhere in Latin America, the Nationalist is willing to make the same sacrifice. That is why Castroism, if not Castro, still has a ringing appeal throughout the hemisphere. . . .

To all Nationalists, even to the 50,000 Latin American technicians who went to Cuba in 1959 to help out and who left in 1961 when Communist Chief Carlos Rafael Rodriguez took command of the economy, Castro's Revolution unfortunately remains the only example of the kind of restructuring Latin America needs. A Chilean technician who had worked 18 months in Cuba put it thus: "Castro may have disillusioned us, and I for one left Cuba a very bitter man, but his Revolution also gave us back the right to our dignity. Now we have to earn it. We will."

## 30 *Lyndon B. Johnson: The Johnson Doctrine; Why the United States Intervened in the Dominican Republic (May 2, 1965)*

*Perhaps the most interesting aspect of Castro's revolution was that, although American officials argued that this situation was an isolated one and that other Latin Americans would not follow such a pattern because Castro had (in President Kennedy's words) used Cuban lives and land "as pawns" while denying Cubans "freedom," the same officials were extremely fearful that similar revolutions, in fact, would occur in Latin America. This fear was best demonstrated in the Dominican Republic intervention of April-May 1965. Four years before, the long-time dictator of the Dominican Republic, Rafael Trujillo, had been gunned down by some of his fellow countrymen. Four years of political and economic uncertainty followed. In 1963, the legally-elected government of Juan Bosch was overthrown by army officers supported by conservative elements from the church and the business community in the country. The army government rapidly lost favor until, in early 1965, its only trustworthy friend was the United States government. Pro-Bosch forces moved to overthrow the army regime on April 24, 1965. The Lyndon Johnson Administration proceeded to send American Marines into the Dominican Republic to forestall what American officials feared would be the beginning of another Castro-type revolution. In a speech of May 2, President Johnson (1908–) justified the American action and then announced the so-called "Johnson Doctrine": "The American nations cannot, must not, and will not permit the establishment of another Communist government in the Western Hemisphere." What are the similarities and the differences between this statement and that of April 3, 1961 which justified the Bay of Pigs invasion (Reading 25)? Most important, how do you reconcile the Johnson Doctrine with the President's statement in this address that "neither we nor any other nation in this hemisphere can or should take it upon itself to ever interfere with the affairs of your country or any other country?"*

. . . In the dark mist of conflict and violence, revolution and confusion, it is not easy to find clear and unclouded truths. But certain things are clear. And they require equally clear action. To understand, I think it is necessary to begin with the events of 8 or 9 days ago.

Last week our observers warned of an approaching political storm in the Dominican Republic. I immediately asked our Ambassador to return to Washington at once so that we might discuss the situation and might plan a course of conduct. But events soon outran our hopes for peace.

Saturday, April 24th—8 days ago—while Ambassador [W. Tapley] Bennett [U.S. Ambassador to the Dominican Republic] was conferring with the highest officials of your Government, revolution erupted in the Dominican Republic. Elements of the military forces of that country overthrew their government. However, the rebels themselves were divided. Some wanted to restore former President Juan Bosch. Others opposed his restoration. President Bosch, elected after the fall of Trujillo and his assassination, had been driven from office by an earlier revolution in the Dominican Republic.

Those who opposed Mr. Bosch's return formed a military committee in an effort to control that country. The others took to the street and they began to lead a revolt on behalf of President Bosch. Control and effective government dissolved in conflict and confusion.

Meanwhile the United States was making a constant effort to restore peace. From Saturday afternoon onward, our embassy urged a cease-fire, and I and all the officials of the American Government worked with every weapon at our command to achieve it.

On Tuesday the situation of turmoil was presented to the peace committee of the Organization of American States. . . .

Meanwhile, all this time, from Saturday to Wednesday, the danger was mounting. Even though we were deeply saddened by bloodshed and violence in a close and friendly neighbor, we had no desire to interfere in the affairs of a sister republic.

SOURCE. *Public Papers of the Presidents . . . Lyndon B. Johnson, 1965,* Washington, D.C.: Government Printing Office, 1966, I, pp. 469-474.

On Wednesday afternoon, there was no longer any choice for the man who is your President. I was sitting in my little office reviewing the world situation with Secretary [of State Dean] Rusk, Secretary [of Defense Robert] McNamara, and Mr. McGeorge Bundy [Special Assistant to the President]. Shortly after 3 o'clock I received a cable from our Ambassador and he said that things were in danger, he had been informed that the chief of police and the governmental authorities could no longer protect us. We immediately started the necessary conference calls to be prepared.

At 5:14, almost 2 hours later, we received a cable that was labeled "critic," a word that is reserved for only the most urgent and immediate matters of national security.

The cable reported that Dominican law enforcement and military officials had informed our embassy that the situation was completely out of control and that the police and the Government could no longer give any guarantee concerning the safety of Americans or of any foreign nationals.

Ambassador Bennett, who is one of our most experienced Foreign Service officers, went on in that cable to say that only an immediate landing of American forces could safeguard and protect the lives of thousands of Americans and thousands of other citizens of some 30 other countries. Ambassador Bennett urged your President to order an immediate landing.

In this situation hesitation and vacillation could mean death for many of our people, as well as many of the citizens of other lands.

I thought that we could not and we did not hesitate. Our forces, American forces, were ordered in immediately to protect American lives. They have done that. They have attacked no one, and although some of our servicemen gave their lives, not a single American civilian and the civilian of any other nation, as a result of this protection, lost their lives. . . .

Meanwhile, the revolutionary movement took a tragic turn. Communist leaders, many of them trained in Cuba, seeing a chance to increase disorder, to gain a foothold, joined the revolution. They took increasing control. And what began as a popular democratic revolution, committed to democracy and social justice, very shortly moved and was taken over and really seized and placed into the hands of a band of Communist conspirators.

Many of the original leaders of the rebellion, the followers of President Bosch, took refuge in foreign embassies because they had been superseded by other evil forces, and the Secretary General of the rebel government, Martínez Francisco, appealed for a cease-fire. But he was ignored. The revolution was now in other and dangerous hands.

When these new and ominous developments emerged, the OAS [Organization of American States] met again and it met at the request of the United States. I am glad to say that they responded wisely and decisively. A five-nation OAS team is now in the Dominican Republic acting to achieve a cease-fire to ensure the safety of innocent people, to restore normal conditions, and to open a path to democratic process.

That is the situation now.

I plead, therefore, with every person and every country in this hemisphere that would choose to do so, to contact their ambassador and the Dominican Republic directly and to get firsthand evidence of the horrors and the hardship, the violence and the terror, and the international conspiracy from which U.S. servicemen have rescued the people of more than 30 nations from that war-torn island.

Earlier today I ordered two additional battalions—2,000 extra men—to proceed immediately to the Dominican Republic. . . .

The American nations cannot, must not, and will not permit the establishment of another Communist government in the Western Hemisphere. This was the unanimous view of all the American nations when, in January 1962, they declared, and I quote: "The principles of communism are incompatible with the principles of the inter-American system."

This is what our beloved President John F. Kennedy meant when, less than a week before his death, he told us: "We in this hemisphere must also use every resource at our command to prevent the establishment of another Cuba in this hemisphere."

This is and this will be the common action and the common purpose of the democratic forces of the hemisphere. For the danger is also a common danger, and the principles are common principles. . . .

We know that many who are now in revolt do not seek a Communist tyranny. We think it is tragic indeed that their high motives have been misused by a small band of conspirators who receive their directions from abroad.

To those who fight only for liberty and justice and progress I want to join with the Organization of American States in saying, in appealing to you tonight, to lay down your arms, and to assure you there is nothing to fear. The road is open for you to share in building a Dominican democracy and we in America are ready and anxious and willing to help you. Your courage and your dedication are qualities which your country and all the hemisphere need for the future. You are needed to help shape that future. And neither we nor any other nation in this hemisphere can or should take it upon itself to ever interfere with the affairs of your country or any other country.

We believe that change comes and we are glad it does, and it should come through peaceful process. But revolution in any country is a matter for that country to deal with. It becomes a matter calling for hemispheric action only—repeat—*only* when the object is the establishment of a communistic dictatorship.

Let me also make clear tonight that we support no single man or any single group of men in the Dominican Republic. Our goal is a simple one. We are there to save the lives of our citizens and to save the lives of all people. Our goal, in keeping with the great principles of the inter-American system, is to help prevent another Communist state in this hemisphere. And we would like to do this without bloodshed or without large-scale fighting.

The form and the nature of a free Dominican government, I assure you, is solely a matter for the Dominican people, but we do know what kind of government we hope to see in the Dominican Republic. For that is carefully spelled out in the treaties and the agreements which make up the fabric of the entire inter-American system. It is expressed, time and time again, in the words of our statesmen and in the values and hopes which bind us all together.

We hope to see a government freely chosen by the will of all the people.

We hope to see a government dedicated to social justice for every single citizen.

We hope to see a government working, every hour of every day, to feeding the hungry, to educating the ignorant, to healing the sick—a government whose only concern is the progress and the elevation and the welfare of all the people. . . .

And before I leave you, my fellow Americans, I want to say this personal word: I know that no American serviceman wants to kill anyone. I know that no American President wants to give an order which brings shooting and casualties and death. I want you to know and I want the world to know that as long as I am President of this country, we are going to defend ourselves. We will defend our soldiers against attackers. We will honor our treaties. We will keep our commitments. We will defend our Nation against all those who seek to destroy not only the United States but every free country of this hemisphere. We do not want to bury anyone as I have said so many times before. But we do not intend to be buried.

## 31  J. William Fulbright: Intervention in Santo Domingo; We Are Much Closer to Being the Most Unrevolutionary Nation on Earth (September 15, 1965)

*Until 1964, Senator J. William Fulbright (1905–    ), Democrat from Arkansas, had been a staunch supporter of American foreign policies. As Chairman of the powerful Senate Foreign Relations Committee, he particularly emphasized the need for close American ties with Western Europe. However, by early 1965, the policies of Dulles, Kennedy, and Johnson in the newly emerging areas of the world (Latin America, Asia, Africa) had driven Fulbright into opposition. His committee conducted a wide-ranging investigation of the American intervention in the Dominican Republic. On September 15, 1965, Senator Fulbright spoke in the Senate, attacking that intervention and raising fundamental questions about the entire set of assumptions that guided American foreign policy as it confronted revolutionary situations. The differences between the President and*

*the Senator regarding factual information is obvious; but how does*
*Fulbright's approach and main assumptions about the causes and course*
*of revolutions in Latin America differ from President Johnson's state-*
*ment of May 2, 1965 (Reading 30)? Also, compare Senator Fulbright's*
*analysis of American views toward revolutions with Tocqueville's*
*(Reading 5), written more than 125 years before. Would you call*
*Senator Fulbright's views "conservative" or "radical"? Why?*

---

U.S. policy in the Dominican crisis was characterized initially by overtimidity and subsequently by overreaction. Throughout the whole affair, it has also been characterized by a lack of candor. . . .

Another theme that emerges from the Dominican crisis is the occurrence of a striking change in U.S. policy toward the Dominican Republic and the possibility—not a certainty, because the signs are ambiguous, but only the possibility—of a major change as well in the general Latin American policies of the United States. Obviously, an important change in the official outlook on Dominican affairs occurred between September 1963, when the United States was vigorously opposed to the overthrow of Juan Bosch [then the President of Santo Domingo], and April 1965, when the United States was either unenthusiastic or actually opposed to his return. . . .

We simply cannot have it both ways; we must choose between the Alliance for Progress and a foredoomed effort to sustain the status quo in Latin America. The choice which we are to make is the principal unanswered question arising out of the unhappy events to the Dominican Republic and, indeed, the principal unanswered question for the future of our relations with Latin America.

It is not surprising that we Americans are not drawn toward the uncouth revolutionaries of the non-Communist left. We are not, as we like to claim in Fourth of July speeches, the most truly revolutionary nation on earth; we are, on the contrary, much

SOURCE. *Congressional Record*, 89th Congress, 2nd Session, September 15, 1965.

closer to being the most unrevolutionary nation on earth. We are sober and satisfied and comfortable and rich; our institutions are stable and old and even venerable, and our Revolution of 1776, for that matter, was not much of an upheaval compared to the French and Russian revolutions and to current and impending revolutions in Latin America, Asia, and Africa.

Our heritage of stability and conservatism is a great blessing, but it also has the effect of limiting our understanding of the character of social revolution and sometimes as well of the injustices which spawn them. Our understanding of revolutions and their causes is imperfect not because of any failures of mind or character but because of our good fortune since the Civil War in never having experienced sustained social injustice without hope of legal or more or less peaceful remedy. We are called upon, therefore, to give our understanding and our sympathy and support to movements which are alien to our experience and jarring to our preferences and prejudices. . . .

The Foreign Relations Committee's study of the Dominican crisis leads me to draw certain specific conclusions regarding American policy in the Dominican Republic and also suggests some broader considerations regarding relations between the United States and Latin America. My specific conclusions regarding the crisis in Santo Domingo are as follows:

*First.* The United States intervened forcibly in the Dominican Republic in the last week of April 1965 not primarily to save American lives, as was then contended, but to prevent the victory of a revolutionary movement which was judged to be Communist-dominated. The decision to land thousands of marines on April 28 was based primarily on the fear of "another Cuba" in Santo Domingo.

*Second.* This fear was based on fragmentary and inadequate evidence. There is no doubt that Communists participated in the Dominican revolution on the rebel side, probably to a greater extent after than before the landing of U.S. marines on April 28, but just as it cannot be proved that the Communists would not have taken over the revolution neither can it be proved that they would have. There is little basis in the evidence offered the committee for the assertion that the rebels were Communist-dominated or certain to become so; on the contrary, the evidence suggests a chaotic situation in which no single faction was dominant at the outset and in which everybody, including the United States, had opportunities to influence the shape and course of the rebellion.

*Third*. The United States let pass its best opportunities to influence the course of events. The best opportunities were on April 25, when Juan Bosch's party, the PRD, requested a "United States presence," and on April 27, when the rebels, believing themselves defeated, requested United States mediation for a negotiated settlement. Both requests were rejected, in the first instance for reasons that are not entirely clear but probably because of United States hostility to the PRD, in the second instance because the U.S. Government anticipated and desired a victory of the anti-rebel forces.

*Fourth*. U.S. policy toward the Dominican Republic shifted markedly to the right between September 1963 and April 1965. In 1963, the United States strongly supported Bosch and the PRD as enlightened reformers; in 1965 the United States opposed their return to power on the unsubstantiated ground that a Bosch or PRD government would certainly, or almost certainly, become Communist dominated. Thus the United States turned its back on social revolution in Santo Domingo and associated itself with a corrupt and reactionary military oligarchy.

*Fifth*. U.S. policy was marred by a lack of candor and by misinformation. The former is illustrated by official assertions that U. S. military intervention was primarily for the purpose of saving American lives; the latter is illustrated by exaggerated reports of massacres and atrocities by the rebels—reports which no one has been able to verify. . . . A sober examination of such evidence as is available indicates that the Imbert junta was guilty of at least as many atrocities as the rebels.

*Sixth*. Responsibility for the failure of American policy in Santo Domingo lies primarily with those who advised the President. In the critical days between April 25 and April 28, these officials sent the President exaggerated reports of the danger of a Communist takeover in Santo Domingo and, on the basis of these, recommended U.S. massive military intervention. It is not at all difficult to understand why, on the basis of such advice, the President made the decisions that he made.

*Seventh.* Underlying the bad advice and unwise actions of the United States was the fear of another Cuba. The specter of a second Communist state in the Western Hemisphere—and its probable repercussions within the United States and possible effects on the careers of those who might be held responsible—seems to have been the most important single factor in distorting the judgment of otherwise sensible and competent men. . . .

Many North Americans seem to believe that, while the United States does indeed participate in Latin American affairs from time to time, sometimes by force, it is done, with the best of intentions, usually indeed to protect the Latin Americans from intervention by somebody else, and therefore cannot really be considered intervention. The trouble with this point of view is that it is not shared by our neighbors to the south. Most of them do think they need protection from the United States, and the history of the Monroe Doctrine and the "Roosevelt corollary" suggests that their fears are not entirely without foundation. "Good intentions" are not a very sound basis for judging the fulfillment of contractual obligations. Just about everybody, including the Communists, believes in his own "good intentions". . . .

The standard on which [Latin Americans] rely most heavily is the principle of nonintervention; however obsolete it may seem to certain U.S. officials, it remains vital and pertinent in Latin America. When we violate it, we are not overriding the mere letter of the law; we are violating what to Latin Americans is its vital heart and core.

The inter-American system is rooted in an implicit contract between the Latin American countries and the United States. In return for our promise not to interfere in their internal affairs they have accepted a role as members of our "sphere" and to support, or at least not to obstruct, our global policies. In the Dominican Republic we violated our part of the bargain; it remains to be seen whether Latin Americans will now feel free to violate theirs.

In the eyes of educated, energetic, and patriotic young Latin Americans—which is to say, the generation that will make or break the Alliance for Progress—the United States committed a worse offense in the Dominican Republic than just intervention; it intervened against social revolution and in support, at least temporarily, of a corrupt, reactionary military oligarchy. . . . The tragedy of Santo Domingo is that a policy that purported to defeat communism in the short run is more likely to have the effect of promoting it in the long run.

# CHAPTER IV
# VIETNAM AND CHINA (1961-1967)

**32**  *United States Department of State:*
  *The Present Danger in Vietnam*
  *(November 1961)*

  *The American commitment to South Vietnam during the mid-1950's
  (Readings 15 to 20) was not only inherited but expanded by the Administration of President John F. Kennedy. In late 1961, after a
  thorough investigation and discussions by top United States officials,
  the President decided to increase the number of American military
  advisers and supplies in order to quell an insurgent movement against
  the government of Ngo Dinh Diem. This revolt had begun in 1958
  within South Vietnam as a protest against Diem's failure to carry
  through reforms. By 1961, the North Vietnamese Communist government of Ho Chi Minh was sending men and supplies southward to
  aid the insurgents. The rationale for increased American help to the
  Diem government was given by the United States Department of
  State in November, 1961. What is the main point of the State Department's argument, and what are the historical precedents for that
  argument?*

---

## THE PRESENT DANGER

  The Communist program to take over South Viet-Nam has
moved into a new and more dangerous phase. Political and propa-

SOURCE. U.S. Department of State, *A Threat to the Peace. .* , Washington, D.C.: Government Printing Office, Part I, pp. 49–53.

ganda activity has been stepped up. More important, the Viet
Cong have advanced from relatively small actions and hit-and-run
tactics, common to the early phase of a guerrilla-type operation,
to the employment of larger units and more sophisticated strategy.

At first concerned only with gathering enough rice and other
food supplies to meet their own needs, the Viet Cong this year
sought through a variety of techniques to choke off the flow
of food to Saigon and thereby to deal the Government of the
Republic of Viet-Nam [RVN] a mortal economic blow. They
were aided by nature in the form of floods, the most serious in
decades, in the southern delta.

In the military field a series of carefully planned and well-
executed moves by the RVN military forces in the delta region
caused heavy casualties among the Viet Cong and set back their
timetable. But they retaliated with a number of major attacks
in the North and in the central highlands. For the first time, Viet
Cong units of 500 to 1,000 or more troops were thrown into
action at a number of points. . . .

Control over the Lao corridor by friendly Pathet Lao troops
has permitted the Viet Cong to move with impunity along the
infiltration trails in that area into South Viet-Nam. A Soviet
airlift has provided large stocks of military supplies to Tchepone,
only 20 miles from the South Viet-Nam border.

Junk traffic from North Viet-Nam to the South increased
during the summer. In June, for example, South Vietnamese
patrols seized 21 boats from the North with 100 Viet Cong
aboard. Given the Government's shortage of adequate equipment
and trained personnel to counter this kind of activity, it must be
assumed that many more Viet Cong junks were able to complete
their missions.

That the Viet Cong have stepped up their efforts to win control
in the South is evident. However, this development did not come
as a surprise to officials in the RVN Government. The acceleration had been accurately forecast in a number of documents
captured from the Viet Cong earlier in the year. One of the most
detailed and specific of these documents was seized on May 12
at Hat Dich in Phuoc Tuy Province.

The document bears the title "Military Plan of the Provincial
Party Committee at Baria." (Baria is the former name of Phuoc

Tuy.) It described in minute detail plans for building up the Viet Cong guerrilla force in the region. It set as the party's goal recruitment of at least 36,000 "volunteers" for guerrilla action in Baria. . . .

## CONCLUSIONS

It is impossible to look at South Viet-Nam today without recognizing the clear and present danger of Communist conquest. The people of South Viet-Nam and their friends in other countries must look soberly at this problem and at the likely consequences should the Viet Cong succeed.

For the people of South Viet-Nam the meaning of a Communist victory is obvious. They would join their compatriots in the North within the Communist orbit. They would take their place alongside the North Koreans, the Tibetans, the Hungarians, the East Germans, and others in the conformity of an "order" ruled by Moscow and Peiping.

Those who had opposed the Viet Cong would swiftly be eliminated. "Land for the tillers" would become "land for the state." Promises of "autonomy" for minority peoples would be forgotten except by the disillusioned highland tribes themselves. Absolute political control would rest with the Communist Party. In short, the pattern of Communist domination and dictatorship would be imposed over the entire country, and 14 million able and energetic people would find themselves in the "socialist camp."

For Viet-Nam's neighbors the consequences of a Communist victory in all Viet-Nam would be far-reaching. It would doubtless seal the fate of Laos, where the Communists already control about half the country. Cambodia's precarious neutrality would be subjected to heavy and steadily increasing pressure. Thailand, too, would have to expect to see the tactics used in Laos and in Viet-Nam directed against her.

The present balance of forces between independent and Communist states in Asia would be tipped perilously if Viet-Nam, Cambodia, and Laos fell under Communist domination. What then would be the prospects for Thailand and Burma, for Pakistan and India, for Malaya and Indonesia?

If the Viet Cong effort proves successful in Viet-Nam, other states with Communist neighbors are likely to be exposed to similar covert and overt methods of aggression. It is not logical to expect that the Communists will abandon techniques that prove successful. Conversely, failure in Viet-Nam might prove an important deterrent to repetition elsewhere.

The responsibility for meeting and overcoming the Viet Cong threat falls primarily on the people of South Viet-Nam and on their Government. Their stake is by far the largest of all those involved. It is their country, their lives, their future that are most directly in danger.

The Republic of Viet-Nam must cope with aggression that almost daily increases in intensity and scope. As units of larger size have moved in from the North, the nature of the war in South Viet-Nam has changed from one of an almost entirely guerrilla character toward one with the proportions of conventional warfare. The size of engagements fought recently testifies to the accelerated pace of Viet Cong infiltration. . . .

North Viet-Nam, in guiding and supporting the Viet Cong effort, has had the full backing of Moscow, Peiping, and the rest of the Communist world. It is too much to expect that the people of South Viet-Nam would be able to oppose this massive threat without outside support. The United States and other friendly countries have already contributed much to the cause of strengthening South Viet-Nam's military and economic programs. In the face of heightened efforts by the Viet Cong, more assistance may be needed. The problem here is to work out cooperatively the kind of assistance program that is likely to prove most effective in meeting the present danger.

The world community itself bears some responsibility toward the people of South Viet-Nam. It is not enough for other non-Communist states to point to their own serious problems and to shrug their shoulders and ask: "What can *we* do?" We can all do much. . . .

One need not accept the word of others. Any friendly government can send in its own observers to see for themselves. It can consult closely with those on or near the scene who know most about what has been happening in Viet-Nam. Free men could, if they would, force a halt to such things as infiltration through

Laos and the use of neighboring territories as "safe" bases for Viet Cong operations.

Viet-Nam is not an isolated problem. The tactics used there have been used before. They will be used again, particularly if they prove successful. A government or a people who now think that "Viet-Nam is so far away from us" may well discover that they are the South Vietnamese of tomorrow. Then they may wish they had done more now. But then it will be late, very late, perhaps too late!

## 33  *John F. Kennedy: The United States Should Not Withdraw (September 9, 1963)*

*By the autumn of 1963, American troops in Vietnam were no longer mere advisers but were bearing the brunt of the fighting. United States interests, pride, and prestige were now fully involved with the South Vietnamese side of the Indochinese warfare that had begun more than a decade before. As the American involvement deepened and no end to the fighting seemed to be in sight, a few critical voices arose to question the Administration's policies. The criticism increased when it became apparent that the Diem government was independent enough not to follow American advice, but was not strong enough to pull the South Vietnamese people together for a concerted effort against the insurgents. How does President Kennedy explain this dilemma in the following interview? How does President Kennedy's view of the "domino theory" differ from President Eisenhower's (Reading 15)?*

*On November 1, a South Vietnamese military group, acting with the implicit if not explicit permission of the United States, overthrew Diem. Within 24 hours Diem was shot, and South Vietnam entered into a period of political instability that severely hurt the American-South Vietnamese war effort.*

MR. [CHET] HUNTLEY: Mr. President, in respect to our difficulties in South Viet-Nam, could it be that our Government tends
occasionally to get locked into a policy or an attitude and then
finds it difficult to alter or shift that policy?

THE PRESIDENT: Yes, that is true. I think in the case of South
Viet-Nam we have been dealing with a government which is in
control, has been in control for 10 years. In addition, we have felt
for the last 2 years that the struggle against the Communists was
going better. Since June, however, the difficulties with the
Buddhists, we have been concerned about a deterioration, particularly in the Saigon area, which hasn't been felt greatly in the
outlying areas but may spread. So we are faced with the problem
of wanting to protect the area against the Communists. On the
other hand, we have to deal with the government there. That
produces a kind of ambivalence in our efforts which exposes us
to some criticism. We are using our influence to persuade the
government there to take those steps which will win back support.
That takes some time and we must be patient, we must persist.

MR. HUNTLEY: Are we likely to reduce our aid to South Viet-
Nam now?

THE PRESIDENT: I don't think we think that would be helpful
at this time. If you reduce your aid, it is possible you could have
some effect upon the government structure there. On the other
hand, you might have a situation which could bring about a
collapse. Strongly in our mind is what happened in the case of
China at the end of World War II, where China was lost, a weak
government became increasingly unable to control events. We
don't want that.

MR. [DAVID] BRINKLEY: Mr. President, have you had any reason
to doubt this so-called "domino theory," that if South Viet-Nam
falls, the rest of southeast Asia will go behind it?

THE PRESIDENT: No, I believe it. I believe it. I think that the
struggle is close enough. China is so large, looms so high just
beyond the frontiers, that if South Viet-Nam went, it would not
only give them an improved geographic position for a guerrilla
assault on Malaya, but would also give the impression that the

SOURCE. *Public Papers of the Presidents . . . John F. Kennedy, 1963*,
Washington, D.C.: Government Printing Office, 1964, pp. 658–660.

wave of the future in southeast Asia was China and the Communists. So I believe it. . . .

MR. BRINKLEY: With so much of our prestige, money, so on, committed in South Viet-Nam, why can't we exercise a little more influence there, Mr. President?

THE PRESIDENT: We have some influence. We have some influence, and we are attempting to carry it out. I think we don't— we can't expect these countries to do every thing the way we want to do them. They have their own interest, their own personalities, their own tradition. We can't make everyone in our image, and there are a good many people who don't want to go in our image. In addition, we have ancient struggles between countries. In the case of India and Pakistan, we would like to have them settle Kashmir. That is our view of the best way to defend the subcontinent against communism. But that struggle between India and Pakistan is more important to a good many people in that area than the struggle against the Communists. We would like to have Cambodia, Thailand, and South Viet-Nam all in harmony, but there are ancient differences there. We can't make the world over, but we can influence the world. The fact of the matter is that with the assistance of the United States, SEATO, southeast Asia and indeed all of Asia has been maintained independent against a powerful force, the Chinese Communists. What I am concerned about is that Americans will get impatient and say because they don't like events in southeast Asia or they don't like the government in Saigon, that we should withdraw. That only makes it easy for the Communists. I think we should stay. We should use our influence in as effective a way as we can, but we should not withdraw.

## 34    Debate on the "Gulf of Tonkin Resolution" (August 1964)

*Three weeks after Diem's death, President Kennedy was assassinated in Dallas, Texas. President Lyndon Johnson carried on the Kennedy policies in Vietnam, enlarging the American commitment, and, in*

*August 1964, carrying out the first heavy bombing raids on North Vietnam. These raids were in retaliation for North Vietnamese attacks on American ships in the Gulf of Tonkin, the body of water that washes the eastern shore of North Vietnam. President Johnson used the Gulf of Tonkin episode as an opportunity to ask Congress for a resolution "expressing the support of the Congress for all necessary action to protect our Armed Forces and to assist nations covered by the SEATO Treaty." This resolution was passed overwhelmingly. However, some critics questioned whether the American ships had been attacked as the Administration claimed; four years later this point was still unclear. Others, including Senator Wayne Morse (1900–    ), argued that a crucial point of procedure was at stake. How important is procedure in policy-making such as this? Which statement, President Johnson's or Senator Morse's, is better supported by a coherent and full historical argument?*

---

THE PRESIDING OFFICER: The message from the President of the United States will be read. . . .

*To the Congress of the United States:*

Last night I announced to the American people that the North Vietnamese regime had conducted further deliberate attacks against U.S. naval vessels operating in international waters, and that I had therefore directed air action against gunboats and supporting facilities used in these hostile operations. This air action has now been carried out with substantial damage to the boats and facilities. Two U.S. aircraft were lost in the action.

After consultation with the leaders of both parties in the Congress, I further announced a decision to ask the Congress for a resolution expressing the unity and determination of the United States in supporting freedom and in protecting peace in southeast Asia.

These latest actions of the North Vietnamese regime have given a new and grave turn to the already serious situation in southeast Asia. Our commitments in that area are well known to the Con-

SOURCE. *Congressional Record, Senate,* 88th Congress, 2nd Session, August 5-August 7, 1964, pp. 18132, 18134–18135, 18443–18444, 18409.

gress. They were first made in 1954 by President Eisenhower. They were further defined in the Southeast Asia Collective Defense Treaty approved by the Senate in February 1955.

This treaty with its accompanying protocol obligates the United States and other members to act in accordance with their constitutional processes to meet Communist aggression against any of the parties or protocol states.

Our policy in southeast Asia has been consistent and unchanged since 1954. I summarized it on June 2 in four simple propositions:

1. America keeps her word. Here as elsewhere, we must and shall honor our commitments.

2. The issue is the future of southeast Asia as a whole. A threat to any nation in that region is a threat to all, and a threat to us.

3. Our purpose is peace. We have no military, political, or territorial ambitions in the area.

4. This is not just a jungle war, but a struggle for freedom on every front of human activity. Our military and economic assistance to South Vietnam and Laos in particular has the purpose of helping these countries to repel aggression and strengthen their independence.

The threat to the free nations of southeast Asia has long been clear. The North Vietnamese regime has constantly sought to take over South Vietnam and Laos. This Communist regime has violated the Geneva accords for Vietnam. It has systematically conducted a campaign of subversion, which includes the direction, training, and supply of personnel and arms for the conduct of guerrilla warfare in South Vietnamese territory. In Laos, the North Vietnamese regime has maintained military forces, used Laotian territory for infiltration into South Vietnam, and most recently carried out combat operations—all in direct violation of the Geneva Agreements of 1962.

In recent months, the actions of the North Vietnamese regime have become steadily more threatening. In May, following new acts of Communist aggression in Laos, the United States undertook reconnaissance flights over Laotian territory at the request of the Government of Laos. These flights had the essential mission of determining the situation in territory where Communist forces were preventing inspection by the International Control Commission. When the Communists attacked these aircraft, I responded by furnishing escort fighters with instructions to fire when fired upon. Thus, these latest North Vietnamese attacks on our naval vessels are not the first direct attack on Armed Forces of the United States. . . .

As I have repeatedly made clear, the United States intends no rashness, and seeks no wider war. We must make it clear to all that the United States is united in its determination to bring about the end of Communist subversion and aggression in the area. We seek the full and effective restoration of the international agreements signed in Geneva in 1954, with respect to South Vietnam, and again at Geneva in 1962, with respect to Laos.

I recommend a resolution expressing the support of the Congress for all necessary action to protect our Armed Forces and to assist nations covered by the SEATO Treaty. At the same time, I assure the Congress that we shall continue readily to explore any avenues of political solution that will effectively guarantee the removal of Communist subversion and the preservation of the independence of the nations of the area.

The resolution could well be based upon similar resolutions enacted by the Congress in the past—to meet the threat to Formosa in 1955, to meet the threat to the Middle East in 1957, and to meet the threat in Cuba in 1962. It could state in the simplest terms the resolve and support of the Congress for action to deal appropriately with attacks against our Armed Forces and to defend freedom and preserve peace in southeast Asia in accordance with the obligations of the United States under the Southeast Asia Treaty. I urge the Congress to enact such a resolution promptly and thus to give convincing evidence to the aggressive Communist nations, and to the world as a whole, that our policy in southeast Asia will be carried forward—and that the peace and security of the area will be preserved.

The events of this week would in any event have made the message of a congressional resolution essential. But there is an additional reason for doing so at a time when we are entering on 3 months of political campaigning. Hostile nations must understand that in such a period the United States will continue to protect its national interests, and that in these matters there is no division among us.

LYNDON B. JOHNSON

MR. MORSE [Wayne Morse, Democrat of Oregon]: . . . The incident that has inspired the joint resolution we have just heard read is as much the doing of the United States as it is the doing of North Vietnam. For 10 years, the role of the United States in South Vietnam has been that of a provocateur, every bit as much as North Vietnam has been a provocateur. For 10 years, the United States, in South Vietnam, has violated the Geneva agreement of 1954. For 10 years, our military policies in South Vietnam have sought to impose a military solution upon a political and economic problem. . . .

Our extensive military aid to South Vietnam was a violation of the Geneva accords in the first instance. Our sending troops into South Vietnam, even under the semantic camouflage of designation as military advisers, was a violation of the Geneva accords. In fact, both of those two counts were also a clear violation of the spirit and intent of the peaceful purposes of the United Nations Charter itself. . . .

In a very recent incident which was the forerunner to the attacks on American destroyers in the Tonkin Bay, it is known that South Vietnamese naval vessels bombarded two North Vietnamese islands within 3 to 5 or 6 miles of the main coast of North Vietnam. Of course, the national waters of North Vietnam extend, according to our international claims, 3 miles seaward from the eastern extremity of those islands and 12 miles seaward under national water boundary claims of North Vietnam. While the South Vietnamese vessels were attacking the North Vietnamese islands, the newspapers tell us that U.S. vessels of war were patrolling Tonkin Bay, presumably some 6 to 11 miles off the shore of North Vietnam.

Was the U.S. Navy standing guard while vessels of South Vietnam shelled North Vietnam? That is the clear implication of the incident.

In regard to international waters, a subject which is one of the highly disputed and still unsettled questions of international law, I believe that the position of the United States is the sounder position. I believe that the 3-mile limit has the better support under international law principles. But we have neighbors to the south of us in Latin America who do not accept that principle and insist on a 12-mile limit—in one instance, as I recall, a longer limit. . . .

The U.S. Government knew that the matter of national and international waters was a controversial issue in Tonkin Bay. The United States also knew that the South Vietnamese vessels planned to bomb, and did bomb, two North Vietnamese islands within 3 to 6 miles of the coast of North Vietnam. Yet, these war vessels of the United States were in the vicinity of that bombing, some miles removed.

Can anyone question that even their presence was a matter of great moral value to South Vietnam? Or the propaganda value to the military totalitarian tyrant and despot who rules South Vietnam as an American puppet—General Khanh, who is really, when all is said and done, the leader whom we have put in charge of an American protectorate called South Vietnam.

It should be unnecessary to point out either to the Senate or to the American people what the position of the United States and its people would be if the tables were reversed and Soviet warships or submarines were to patrol 5 to 11 miles at sea while Cuban naval vessels bombarded Key West. . . .

The American people will quickly lose their liberty if you do not stop feeding the trend toward Government by executive supremacy. In my opinion, the joint resolution would do just exactly that. It would give to the President of the United States an authority which, in my judgment, he does not need, by any stretch of the imagination. He has inherent power to react, in the self-defense of this Republic, in the event of an immediate attack.

It is particularly essential that we continue to require a President of the United States to conform to article I, section 8, of the Constitution, in regard to making war, and that we continue to hold any President—I care not who he is—under the strictest restraint with regard to the making of war.

We have entered an era of civilization in which an unconstitutional act of war on the part of a President of the United States can lead to nuclear war and the end of this Republic, no matter how sincere a President may be in his intentions in respect to exercising the power to make war. . . .

I have heard sincere colleagues on the floor of the Senate—

and I respect them—differ with me in regard to the effect of the joint resolution. There are also colleagues on the other side of the issue who have come to me and said, as did one who discussed it with me this morning, "Wayne, there is no doubt as to the effect of the resolution that you are pointing out, and that you pointed out in [the Formosa Resolution] in 1955. It bothered me in 1955; but we have every reason to count on the fact that the President of the United States will not abuse the power."

I do not think he would deliberately abuse the power, but he could most sincerely exercise the power in a manner that would result in great damage to this Republic.

There is an elementary rule of law which states that when we come to deal with procedural matters, if a procedure is subject to abuse we had better change the procedure. . . . We should never forget that our substantive rights are never any better, and can never be any better, than our procedural rights. Our procedural rights determine our substantive rights. There are no substantive rights unless there are procedures for implementing them. . . .

MR. COOPER [John Sherman Cooper, Republican of Kentucky]: My first question goes to the first section of the resolution—the operative part which, as the chairman [J. William Fulbright, Democrat of Arkansas, Chairman of the Foreign Relations Committee] has said, applies to any armed attack or any aggression directed against the forces of the United States.

MR. FULBRIGHT: That is correct.

MR. COOPER: In that case, of course, we confirm the power that the President now has to defend our forces against an immediate attack.

MR. FULBRIGHT: The Senator is a very distinguished lawyer, and I therefore hesitate to engage in a discussion with him on the separation of powers and the powers of the President. We are not giving to the President any powers he has under the Constitution as Commander in Chief. We are in effect approving of his use of the powers that he has. That is the way I feel about it. . . .

MR. COOPER: The second section of the resolution goes, as the Senator said, to steps the President might take concerning the parties to the Southeast Asia Collective Defense Treaty and the countries under the protocol—which are, of course, Laos,

Cambodia, and South Vietnam. The Senator will remember that the SEATO Treaty, in article IV, provides that in the event an armed attack is made upon a party to the Southeast Asia Collective Defense Treaty, or upon one of the protocol states such as South Vietnam, the parties to the treaty, one of whom is the United States, would then take such action as might be appropriate, after resorting to their constitutional processes. I assume that would mean, in the case of the United States, that Congress would be asked to grant the authority to act.

Does the Senator consider that in enacting this resolution we are satisfying that requirement of article IV of the Southeast Asia Collective Defense Treaty? In other words, are we now giving the President advance authority to take whatever action he may deem necessary respecting South Vietnam and its defense, or with respect to the defense of any other country included in the treaty?

MR. FULBRIGHT: I think that is correct.

MR. COOPER: Then, looking ahead, if the President decided that it was necessary to use such force as could lead into war, we will give that authority by this resolution?

MR. FULBRIGHT: That is the way I would interpret it. If a situation later developed in which we thought the approval should be withdrawn, it could be withdrawn by concurrent resolution.

The result was announced—yeas 88, nays 2. . . . So the joint resolution was passed as follows:

> Whereas naval units of the Communist regime in Vietnam, in violation of the principles of the Charter of the United Nations and of international law, have deliberately and repeatedly attacked United States naval vessels lawfully present in international waters, and have thereby created a serious threat to international peace; and
>
> Whereas these attacks are part of a deliberate and systematic campaign of aggression that the Communist regime in North Vietnam has been waging against its neighbors and the nations joined with them in the collective defense of their freedom; and
>
> Whereas the United States is assisting the peoples of southeast Asia to protect their freedom and has no territorial, military or political ambitions in that area, but desires only that these peoples

should be left in peace to work out their own destinies in their own way: Now, therefore, be it

*Resolved by the Senate and House of Representatives of the United States of America in Congress assembled,* That the Congress approves and supports the determination of the President, as Commander in Chief, to take all necessary measures to repel any armed attack against the forces of the United States and to prevent further aggression.

*Section 2.* The United States regards as vital to its national interest and to world peace the maintenance of international peace and security in southeast Asia. Consonant with the Constitution of the United States and the Charter of the United Nations and in accordance with its obligations under the Southeast Asia Collective Defense Treaty, the United States is, therefore, prepared, as the President determines, to take all necessary steps, including the use of armed force, to assist any member or protocol state of the Southeast Asia Collective Defense Treaty requesting assistance in defense of its freedom.

*Section 3.* This resolution shall expire when the President shall determine that the peace and security of the area is reasonably assured by international conditions created by action of the United Nations or otherwise, except that it may be terminated earlier by concurrent resolution of the Congress.

## 35  *Lyndon B. Johnson: Why Must We Take This Painful Road? (April 7, 1965)*

*The growing American commitment to Vietnam was matched by rising opposition to the war within the United States. On April 7, 1965, President Johnson presented perhaps his best defense of the American effort. A central portion of the argument emphasized the need to contain "the deepening shadow of Communist China." In which particulars does President Johnson's statement compare and contrast with the Mr. "X" article (Reading 6) which first detailed the policy of containment? How do Walter Lippmann's criticisms of the original containment thesis (Reading 9) apply to President Johnson's statement of 18 years later?*

Tonight Americans and Asians are dying for a world where each people may choose its own path to change.

This is the principle for which our ancestors fought in the valleys of Pennsylvania. It is the principle for which our sons fight tonight in the jungles of Viet-Nam.

Viet-Nam is far away from this quiet campus. We have no territory there, nor do we seek any. The war is dirty and brutal and difficult. And some 400 young men, born into an America that is bursting with opportunity and promise, have ended their lives on Viet-Nam's steaming soil.

Why must we take this painful road?

Why must this Nation hazard its ease, and its interest, and its power for the sake of a people so far away?

We fight because we must fight if we are to live in a world where every country can shape its own destiny. And only in such a world will our own freedom be finally secure.

This kind of world will never be built by bombs or bullets. Yet the infirmities of man are such that force must often precede reason, and the waste of war, the works of peace.

We wish that this were not so. But we must deal with the world as it is, if it is ever to be as we wish.

The world as it is in Asia is not a serene or peaceful place.

The first reality is that North Viet-Nam has attacked the independent nation of South Viet-Nam. Its object is total conquest.

Of course, some of the people of South Viet-Nam are participating in attack on their own government. But trained men and supplies, orders and arms, flow in a constant stream from north to south. This support is the heartbeat of the war.

And it is a war of unparalleled brutality. Simple farmers are the targets of assassination and kidnapping. Women and children are strangled in the night because their men are loyal to their government. And helpless villages are ravaged by sneak attacks. Large-scale raids are conducted on towns, and terror strikes in the heart of cities.

The confused nature of this conflict cannot mask the fact that it is the new face of an old enemy.

SOURCE. *Public Papers of the Presidents . . . Lyndon B. Johnson, 1965*, Washington, D.C.: Government Printing Office, 1966, I, pp. 394–399.

Over this war—and all Asia—is another reality: the deepening shadow of Communist China. The rulers in Hanoi are urged on by Peking. This is a regime which has destroyed freedom in Tibet, which has attacked India, and has been condemned by the United Nations for aggression in Korea. It is a nation which is helping the forces of violence in almost every continent. The contest in Viet-Nam is part of a wider pattern of aggressive purposes.

Why are these realities our concern? Why are we in South Viet-Nam?

*We are there because we have a promise to keep.* Since 1954 every American President has offered support to the people of South Viet-Nam. We have helped to build, and we have helped to defend. Thus, over many years, we have made a national pledge to help South Viet-Nam defend its independence.

And I intend to keep that promise.

To dishonor that pledge, to abandon this small and brave nation to its enemies, and to the terror that must follow, would be an unforgivable wrong.

*We are also there to strengthen world order.* Around the globe, from Berlin to Thailand, are people whose well-being rests, in part, on the belief that they can count on us if they are attacked. To leave Viet-Nam to its fate would shake the confidence of all these people in the value of an American commitment and in the value of America's word. The result would be increased unrest and instability, and even wider war.

*We are also there because there are great stakes in the balance.* Let no one think for a moment that retreat from Viet-Nam would bring an end to conflict. The battle would be renewed in one country and then another. The central lesson of our time is that the appetite of aggression is never satisfied. To withdraw from one battlefield means only to prepare for the next. We must say in southeast Asia—as we did in Europe—in the words of the Bible: "Hitherto shalt thou come, but no further."

There are those who say that all our effort there will be futile —that China's power is such that it is bound to dominate all southeast Asia. But there is no end to that argument until all of the nations of Asia are swallowed up.

There are those who wonder why we have a responsibility there. Well, we have it there for the same reason that we have a responsibility for the defense of Europe. World War II was fought in both Europe and Asia, and when it ended we found ourselves with continued responsibility for the defense of freedom.

Our objective is the independence of South Viet-Nam, and its freedom from attack. We want nothing for ourselves—only that the people of South Viet-Nam be allowed to guide their own country in their own way.

We will do everything necessary to reach that objective. And we will do only what is absolutely necessary.

In recent months attacks on South Viet-Nam were stepped up. Thus, it became necessary for us to increase our response and to make attacks by air. This is not a change of purpose. It is a change in what we believe that purpose requires.

We do this in order to slow down aggression.

We do this to increase the confidence of the brave people of South Viet-Nam who have bravely borne this brutal battle for so many years with so many casualties.

And we do this to convince the leaders of North Viet-Nam— and all who seek to share their conquest—of a very simple fact:

We will not be defeated.

We will not grow tired.

We will not withdraw, either openly or under the cloak of a meaningless agreement.

We know that air attacks alone will not accomplish all of these purposes. But it is our best and prayerful judgment that they are a necessary part of the surest road to peace. . . .

Because we fight for values and we fight for principles, rather than territory or colonies, our patience and our determination are unending.

Once this is clear, then it should also be clear that the only path for reasonable men is the path of peaceful settlement.

Such peace demands an independent South Viet-Nam—securely guaranteed and able to shape its own relationships to all others— free from outside interference—tied to no alliance—a military base for no other country.

These are the essentials of any final settlement.

We will never be second in the search for such a peaceful settlement in Viet-Nam.

There may be many ways to this kind of peace: in discussion

or negotiation with the governments concerned; in large groups or in small ones; in the reaffirmation of old agreements or their strengthening with new ones.

We have stated this position over and over again, fifty times and more, to friend and foe alike. And we remain ready, with this purpose, for unconditional discussions. . . .

These countries of southeast Asia are homes for millions of impoverished people. Each day these people rise at dawn and struggle through until the night to wrestle existence from the soil. They are often wracked by disease, plagued by hunger, and death comes at the early age of 40.

Stability and peace do not come easily in such a land. Neither independence nor human dignity will ever be won, though, by arms alone. It also requires the work of peace. The American people have helped generously in times past in these works. Now there must be a much more massive effort to improve the life of man in that conflict-torn corner of our world.

The first step is for the countries of southeast Asia to associate themselves in a greatly expanded cooperative effort for development. We would hope that North Viet-Nam would take its place in the common effort just as soon as peaceful cooperation is possible.

The United Nations is already actively engaged in development in this area. As far back as 1961 I conferred with our authorities in Viet-Nam in connection with their work there. And I would hope tonight that the Secretary General of the United Nations could use the prestige of his great office, and his deep knowledge of Asia, to initiate, as soon as possible, with the countries of that area, a plan for cooperation in increased development.

For our part I will ask the Congress to join in a billion dollar American investment in this effort as soon as it is underway.

And I would hope that all other industrialized countries, including the Soviet Union, will join in this effort to replace despair with hope, and terror with progress. . . .

I also intend to expand and speed up a program to make available our farm surpluses to assist in feeding and clothing the needy in Asia. We should not allow people to go hungry and wear rags while our own warehouses overflow with an abundance of wheat and corn, rice and cotton.

So I will very shortly name a special team of outstanding, patriotic, distinguished Americans to inaugurate our participation in these programs. This team will be headed by Mr. Eugene Black, the very able former President of the World Bank.

In areas that are still ripped by conflict, of course, development will not be easy. Peace will be necessary for final success. But we cannot and must not wait for peace to begin this job. . . .

We often say how impressive power is. But I do not find it impressive at all. The guns and the bombs, the rockets and the warships, are all symbols of human failure. They are necessary symbols. They protect what we cherish. But they are witness to human folly.

A dam built across a great river is impressive.

In the countryside where I was born, and where I live, I have seen the night illuminated, and the kitchens warmed, and the homes heated, where once the cheerless night and the ceaseless cold held sway. And all this happened because electricity came to our area along the humming wires of the REA Electrification of the countryside—yes, that, too, is impressive. . . .

Every night before I turn out the lights to sleep I ask myself this question: Have I done everything that I can do to unite this country? Have I done everything I can to help unite the world, to try to bring peace and hope to all the peoples of the world? Have I done enough?

Ask yourselves that question in your homes—and in this hall tonight. Have we, each of us, all done all we could? Have we done enough?

We may well be living in the time foretold many years ago when it was said: "I call heaven and earth to record this day against you, that I have set before you life and death, blessing and cursing: therefore choose life, that both thou and thy seed may live."

This generation of the world must choose: destroy or build, kill or aid, hate or understand.

We can do all these things on a scale never dreamed of before. *Well, we will choose life.* In so doing we will prevail over the enemies within man, and over the natural enemies of all mankind.

**36**  *Premier Pham Van Dong: Hanoi's Position
for Negotiations (April 13, 1965)*

*Within a week after President Johnson's speech (Reading 35), the
North Vietnamese government (speaking through Premier Pham Van
Dong) laid down its own demands for a peace settlement. How does
this statement answer specific points of President Johnson's speech
of April 7?*

The unswerving policy of the DRV Government is to respect
strictly the 1954 Geneva agreements on Vietnam and to implement correctly their basic provisions as embodied in the following
points:

1.  Recognition of the basic national rights of the Vietnamese
people—peace, independence, sovereignty, unity, and territorial
integrity. According to the Geneva agreements, the U.S. Government must withdraw from South Vietnam U.S. troops, military
personnel, and weapons of all kinds, dismantle all U.S. military
bases there, and cancel its military alliance with South Vietnam.
It must end its policy of intervention and aggression in South
Vietnam. According to the Geneva agreements, the U.S. Government must stop its acts of war against North Vietnam and completely cease all encroachments on the territory and sovereignty
of the DRV.

2.  Pending the peaceful reunification of Vietnam, while Viet-
nam is still temporarily divided into two zones the military provisions of the 1954 Geneva agreements on Vietnam must be
strictly respected. The two zones must refrain from entering into
any military alliance with foreign countries and there must be no

foreign military bases, troops, or military personnel in their respective territory.

3. The internal affairs of South Vietnam must be settled by the South Vietnamese people themselves in accordance with the program of the NFLSV without any foreign interference.

4. The peaceful reunification of Vietnam is to be settled by the Vietnamese people in both zones, without any foreign interference.

This stand of the DRV Government unquestionably enjoys the approval and support of all peace and justice-loving governments and peoples in the world. The government of the DRV is of the view that the stand expounded here is the basis for the soundest political settlement of the Vietnam problem.

If this basis is recognized, favorable conditions will be created for the peaceful settlement of the Vietnam problem, and it will be possible to consider the reconvening of an international conference along the pattern of the 1954 Geneva conference on Vietnam.

The DRV Government declares that any approach contrary to the aforementioned stand is inappropriate; any approach tending to secure U.N. intervention in the Vietnam situation is also inappropriate. Such approaches are basically at variance with the 1954 Geneva agreements on Vietnam.

## 37   Lin Piao: Long Live the Victory of People's War! (September 1965)

*As President Lyndon Johnson indicated (Reading 35), the power of Communist China was never far from the thoughts of the policy-makers who were increasing American participation in the Vietnamese conflict. The fears of possible Chinese involvement in Vietnam and Southeast Asia seemed to be borne out by a statement of Peking's Minister of Defense, Lin Piao, which was issued to commemorate the twentieth anniversary of the defeat of Japan in 1945. But like all important diplomatic documents this statement requires very close read-*

*ing. At what point does Lin Piao indicate that China, indeed, will enter the Vietnamese conflict? Most important, where in this statement does he say that China will actively assist a "people's war?" Does he say whether such "people's wars" must depend upon internal strength or external assistance?*

---

The Chinese revolution is a continuation of the great October Revolution. The road of the October Revolution is the common road for all people's revolutions. . . . Naturally, the Chinese revolution had its own peculiar characteristics. The October Revolution took place in imperialistic Russia, but the Chinese revolution broke out in a semi-colonial and semi-feudal country. The former was a proletarian socialist revolution, while the latter developed into a socialist revolution after the complete victory of the new-democratic revolution. The October Revolution began with armed uprisings in the cities and then spread to the countryside, while the Chinese revolution won nation-wide victory through the encirclement of the cities from the rural areas and the final capture of the cities. . . .

Comrade Mao Tse-tung's theory of people's war has been proved by the long practice of the Chinese revolution to be in accord with the objective laws of such wars and to be invincible. It has not only been valid for China, it is a great contribution to the revolutionary struggles of the oppressed nations and peoples throughout the world.

The people's war led by the Chinese Communist Party, comprising the War of Resistance and the Revolutionary Civil Wars, lasted for twenty-two years [1927-1949]. It constitutes the most drawn-out and most complex people's war led by the proletariat in modern history, and it has been the richest in experience.

In the last analysis, the Marxist-Leninist theory of proletarian revolution is the theory of the seizure of state power by revolutionary violence, the theory of countering war against the people

SOURCE: War. "Peking, Lin Piao," Long Live The Victory of People's Foreign Languages Press, 1965.

by people's war. As Marx so aptly put it, "Force is the midwife of every old society pregnant with a new one."

It was on the basis of the lessons derived from the people's wars in China that Comrade Mao Tse-tung, using the simplest and the most vivid language, advanced the famous thesis that "political power grows out of the barrel of a gun."

. . . . Why can the apparently weak new-born forces always triumph over the decadent forces which appear so powerful? The reason is that truth is on their side and that the masses are on their side, while the reactionary classes are always divorced from the masses and set themselves against the masses. This has been borne out by the victory of the Chinese revolution, by the history of all revolutions, the whole history of class struggle and the entire history of mankind.

The imperialists are extremely afraid of Comrade Mao Tse-tung's thesis that "imperialism and all reactionaries are paper tigers," and the revisionists [that is, Nikita Khrushchev and those in Russia who sympathize with his views] are extremely hostile to it. They all oppose and attack this thesis and the philistines follow suit by ridiculing it. But all this cannot in the least diminish its importance. The light of truth cannot be dimmed by anybody.

Comrade Mao Tse-tung's theory of people's war solves not only the problem of daring to fight a people's war, but also that of how to wage it. Comrade Mao Tse-tung is a great statesman and military scientist, proficient at directing war in accordance with its laws. . . . It must be emphasized that Comrade Mao Tse-tung's theory of the establishment of rural revolutionary base areas and the encirclement of the cities from the countryside is of outstanding and universal practical importance for the present revolutionary struggles of all the oppressed nations and peoples, and particularly for the revolutionary struggles of the oppressed nations and peoples in Asia, Africa and Latin America against imperialism and its lackeys.

Many countries and peoples in Asia, Africa and Latin America are now being subjected to aggression and enslavement on a serious scale by the imperialists headed by the United States and their lackeys. The basic political and economic conditions in many of these countries have many similarities to those that prevailed in

old China. As in China, the peasant question is extremely important in these regions. The peasants constitute the main force of
the national-democratic revolution against the imperialists and
their lackeys. In committing aggression against these countries,
the imperialists usually begin by seizing the big cities and the main
lines of communication, but they are unable to bring the vast
countryside completely under their control. The countryside, and
the countryside alone, can provide the broad areas in which the
revolutionaries can manoeuvre freely. The countryside, and the
countryside alone, can provide the revolutionary bases from
which the revolutionaries can go forward to final victory. Precisely for this reason, Comrade Mao Tse-tung's theory of establishing revolutionary base areas in the rural districts and encircling
the cities from the countryside is attracting more and more attention among the people in these regions.

Taking the entire globe, if North America and Western Europe
can be called "the cities of the world", then Asia, Africa and
Latin America constitute "the rural areas of the world". Since
World War II, the proletarian revolutionary movement has for
various reasons been temporarily held back in the North American and West European capitalist countries, while the people's
revolutionary movement in Asia, Africa and Latin America has
been growing vigorously. In a sense, the contemporary world
revolution also presents a picture of the encirclement of cities by
the rural areas. In the final analysis, the whole cause of world
revolution hinges on the revolutionary struggles of the Asian,
African and Latin American peoples who make up the overwhelming majority of the world's population. The socialist countries should regard it as their internationalist duty to support the
people's revolutionary struggles in Asia, Africa and Latin America.
. . . .

Today, the conditions are more favourable than ever before
for the waging of people's wars by the revolutionary peoples of
Asia, Africa and Latin America against U.S. imperialism and its
lackeys. . . . U.S. imperialism is stronger, but also more vulnerable,
than any imperialism of the past. It sets itself against the people
of the whole world, including the people of the United States.
Its human, military, material and financial resources are far from
sufficient for the realization of its ambition of dominating the

whole world. U.S. imperialism has further weakened itself by occupying so many places in the world, over-reaching itself, stretching its fingers out wide and dispersing its strength, with its rear so far away and its supply lines so long. As Comrade Mao Tse-tung has said, "Wherever it commits aggression, it puts a new noose around its neck. It is besieged ring upon ring by the people of the whole world."

When committing aggression in a foreign country, U.S. imperialism can only employ part of its forces, which are sent to fight an unjust war far from their native land and therefore have a low morale, and so U.S. imperialism is beset with great difficulties. The people subjected to its aggression are having a trial of strength with U.S. imperialism neither in Washington nor New York, neither in Honolulu nor Florida, but are fighting for independence and freedom on their own soil. Once they are mobilized on a broad scale, they will have inexhaustible strength. Thus superiority will belong not to the United States but to the people subjected to its aggression. . . .

Everything is divisible. And so is this colossus of U.S. imperialism. It can be split up and defeated. The peoples of Asia, Africa, Latin America and other regions can destroy it piece by piece, some striking at its head and others at its feet. That is why the greatest fear of U.S. imperialism is that people's wars will be launched in different parts of the world, and particularly in Asia, Africa and Latin America, and why it regards people's war as a mortal danger.

U.S. imperialism relies solely on its nuclear weapons to intimidate people. But these weapons cannot save U.S. imperialism from its doom. Nuclear weapons cannot be used lightly. U.S. imperialism has been condemned by the people of the whole world for its towering crime of dropping two atom bombs on Japan. If it uses nuclear weapons again, it will become isolated in the extreme. Moreover, the U.S. monopoly of nuclear weapons has long been broken; U.S. imperialism has these weapons, but others have them too. . . .

38   *Dean Rusk: The Threat of China to the*
     *United States (October 12, 1967*
     *and October 16, 1967)*

*Secretary of State Dean Rusk (1909–    ) issued several warnings in 1966 and 1967 about possible Chinese threats to "the free nations of Asia." In the following statements, how does Secretary of State Rusk indicate that American foreign policy has changed since 1947? Why is he concerned about the "militancy" of Chinese Communism? Could he have used Lin Piao's statement (Reading 37) as evidence for his remarks?*

---

PRESS CONFERENCE OF OCTOBER 12, 1967

[Question.] Mr. Secretary, one of the questions—basic questions—that seems to be emerging in this Senate debate is whether our national security is really at stake in Viet-Nam and whether Viet-Nam represents an integral part of our defense perimeter in the Pacific. . . .

[Mr. Rusk.] Within the next decade or two, there will be a billion Chinese on the mainland, armed with nuclear weapons, with no certainty about what their attitude toward the rest of Asia will be.

Now, the free nations of Asia will make up at least a billion people. They don't want China to overrun them on the basis of a doctrine of the world revolution. The militancy of China has isolated China, even within the Communist world, but they have not drawn back from it. They have reaffirmed it, as recently as their reception of their great and good friend, Albania, 2 days ago.

Now, we believe that the free nations of Asia must brace them-

SOURCE. *Department of State Bulletin*, Vol. LVII, October 30, 1967, p. 563; and *Department of State Bulletin*, Vol. LVII, November 6, 1967, p. 596.

selves, get themselves set, with secure, progressive, stable institutions of their own, with cooperation among the free nations of Asia stretching from Korea and Japan right around to the subcontinent, if there is to be peace in Asia over the next 10 or 20 years. We would hope that in China there would emerge a generation of leadership that would think seriously about what is called "peaceful coexistence," that would recognize the pragmatic necessity for human beings to live together in peace rather than on a basis of continuing warfare.

Now, from a strategic point of view, it is not very attractive to think of the world cut in two by Asian communism reaching out through Southeast Asia and Indonesia, which we know has been their objective, and that these hundreds of millions of people in the free nations of Asia should be under the deadly and constant pressure of the authorities in Peking, so that their future is circumscribed by fear.

Now, these are vitally important matters to us, who are both a Pacific and an Atlantic power. After all, World War II hit us from the Pacific, and Asia is where two-thirds of the world's people live. So we have a tremendous stake in the ability of the free nations of Asia to live in peace; and to turn the interests of people in mainland China to the pragmatic requirements of their own people and away from a doctrinaire and ideological adventurism abroad.

## INTERVIEW OF OCTOBER 16, 1967

[Question.] . . . In your last press conference [of October 12] . . . you seemed to point your finger toward a Chinese Communist expansionism. Now, since we know that Hanoi is getting the least part of its military aid from Peking and is getting the larger part from Moscow, can you assess the position, the role of Moscow, in this war?

SECRETARY RUSK: Well, I believe that the Soviet Union is supporting Hanoi, at least with respect to any action which we ourselves are taking against North Viet-Nam. I think this is, perhaps, not so clear about what is happening in South Viet-Nam.

But in my press conference I pointed the finger at what I called Asian communism because the doctrine of communism as announced and declared in Peking has a special quality of militancy, a militancy which has largely isolated Peking within the Communist world, quite apart from the problems it has created with many other countries. So, I would suppose that if Asian communism, that is Hanoi-Peking, were prepared to move this Viet-Nam problem toward a peaceful settlement it could in fact move toward a peaceful settlement very quickly. . . .

[Question.] Mr. Secretary, since your last press conference, some of your critics have accused you of using the threat of "yellow peril" to justify the allied forces' presence in South Viet-Nam. And, related to that also is the fact that many people have seen what they consider a shade different emphasis in your approach to this, that at one time American forces were there to justify the self-determination of South Viet-Nam, and now you're talking more in terms of giving strength to the non-Communist nations in Asia as a defense against Peking. Could you clarify this?

SECRETARY RUSK: Yes. In the first place, I put out a statement [on October 16] in which I rejected categorically any effort to put into my mouth the concept of "the yellow peril," which was a racial concept of 60 or 70 years ago fostered by extreme journalism of those days. This is not in my mind.

I pointed out that other nations, ranging from Korea and Japan on the one side around to the subcontinent of India on the other, are concerned about their own safety over against the things which are being said and done in Peking and by Peking. These free nations of Asia also are of Asian races. So that to me, this has nothing whatever to do with the sense of "yellow peril" that was built upon a racial fear and hostility 60 or 70 years ago in which the hordes of Asia were going to overrun the white race as a racial matter.

Now, as far as the difference in emphasis is concerned, one of our problems is that people tend to listen to what we say on only one point at a time. We have spoken about our treaty commitments to Viet-Nam. We've talked about our interest in organizing a peace in the Pacific, because of our other alliances in the

Pacific as with Korea, Japan, the Republic of China, the Philippines, the SEATO Treaty, and our ANZUS Treaty with Australia and New Zealand.

So we have a great stake in the integrity of the alliances which we have in the Pacific Ocean area.

## 39   John K. Fairbank: Lin Piao's Statement Is a Profession of Faith (1966)

*Secretary of State Rusk's remarks about Chinese Communism were criticized by a number of foreign policy experts. Professor John K. Fairbank (1907–    ) is one of the most distinguished scholars of China and has had diplomatic experience in dealing with the Chinese. When Senator J. William Fulbright began a special investigation into American policies in Southeast Asia, Professor Fairbank appeared to testify before the Senate Foreign Relations Committee on the question of Chinese intentions. In his testimony he interpreted Lin Piao's statement and came to conclusions that greatly differed from those of Secretary of State Rusk (Reading 38). What role does history play in Professor Fairbank's interpretation as compared with Secretary of State Rusk's? What aspects of China does Professor Fairbank emphasize? Are similar emphases found in Secretary of State Rusk's statement?*

---

DR. FAIRBANK: I think the main point is that in the Chinese cultural scene there is a different function performed by words, and we have to really stretch our imaginations to look at this situation. The Chinese use words to express what ought to be, in their view, and if you do not follow the right words, then your conduct is not correct. In other words, the expressions that they use

SOURCE. U.S. Senate, 89th Congress, 2nd Session, Committee on Foreign Relations, *U.S. Foreign Policy with Respect to Mainland China*, Washington, D.C.: Government Printing Office, 1966, pp. 148-153.

are part of their conduct, and if you have a correct doctrine, as they believe they do, about world revolution, Marxism, and so on, then you should express that correct doctrine, and if you doubt that doctrine you are letting it down, you are a traitor. . . .

Well, now, Lin Piao's statement is an expression of a true doctrine, the revolutionary thing, about how revolution will triumph, and it shows the peculiar parochial nature of the Chinese Communist movement in that it is used in a peculiarly inappropriate way from our point of view, it is remarkably unrealistic.

You see, they came to power in their development in China by taking over the cities from the countryside, surrounding the cities, making them impassable from the countryside, and no food could come in, and gradually controlling the population and winning. Now they apply this to the world scene by that argument of an analogy which, I think, is so inaccurate—the cities in this case are the industrialized nations—that they will take them over through the underdeveloped countries. This leaves entirely out of account the communications systems between the two. When they controlled the roads that led to the cities in the countryside they strangled the cities. How are they going to control the sea lanes of world commerce? This whole thing does not make sense.

Now, this kind of statement of Lin Piao's, to my mind, is an abstraction, a testament of faith, a reassertion of faith in the revolutionary belief that he has. And, I think, it is put out exactly for the opposite purpose to what some people seem to think. It is put out, in my mind, to compensate, to say, "Look we are having trouble. We always have setbacks, but still we believe in this revolution," and that is all it says. It is not a blueprint for taking over the world, in my view, at all; that is, of a practical nature. It is not a timetable, it is nothing of that sort. It is merely a profession of faith by a revolutionary who is still a revolutionary. . . .

THE CHAIRMAN [J. William Fulbright, Democrat of Arkansas]: Would you say that using or comparing it to Hitler's "Mein Kampf" is not a very fruitful or realistic comparison?

DR. FAIRBANK: No. . . . It seems to me that Hitler had a war machine geared for aggression. He was in the middle of a scene where there had been wars before, and he could move across borders. The whole thing was a very practical thing. In the case of China they have not been aggressive outside their frontiers. The frontiers that they have are those of an empire and they include minority groups, and they count the Tibetans as within those frontiers, and they have been very aggressive toward the Tibetans. Given, however, their historic Chinese Manchu empire frontiers, they have hardly gone beyond that. . . .

THE CHAIRMAN: . . . . I think you said this morning that because of their very long and successful tradition in history, it is likely in the long run to express itself in nationalistic attitudes more strongly than a recently acquired ideology would have. Is that a fair statement?

DR. FAIRBANK: Yes, I think so. . . . This is the problem in the Chinese tradition, that they have an all-or-none approach, and this is very disconcerting to us because it means, whether it is a Marxist in Peking or somebody else, they are going to be awfully difficult for a long time to come. But the all-or-none approach they believe in is personal rule. This is a tradition. The Emperor rules personally. He does it by his personal example. He is a good man and does the right thing and, therefore, he rules.

And Mao Tse-tung is this type. He is the example, and he has the right idea, you can follow it. Chiang Kai-shek is this type. It is the Confucian emperor type. . . . Chiang Kai-shek has illustrated this, closing down newspapers and various things. Mao Tse-tung does it all the time, of course. We call it totalitarianism, but it is also an old Chinese custom.

Now this means it is going to be awfully hard to get these people to play ball with our system. And when they have this all-or-none approach, why, on the one hand, Chiang says he wants the mainland and nothing else, Mao says he wants Taiwan and nothing less. They both say China is a unit, including Taiwan, and we are left just over a barrel in between them. . . .

The old American idea that both sides have an interest, that we can represent their interest, they can compromise, just did not work, and it is not in this tradition. . . .

Well, now, insofar as Lin Piao is interpreted this way, I think there is something to it. It is a problem. Insofar as you interpret his statements as being that he is about to move, I think it is foolish. . . .

Today we have the danger of developing a war spirit among ourselves. I think this Lin Piao's statement might be an example of this, to fix on something and build it up unrealistically out of proportion. Why, you can get yourself into a mood which says, "My God, we are under attack. Let us hit first."

# PART FOUR

## Some Implications

## 40  Hubert H. Humphrey: Guns and Butter Are Tied Together (April 25, 1966)

*The American involvement in the affairs of Cuba and the Dominican Republic, and particularly the increasingly costly war in Vietnam, resulted in an attack on United States foreign policies that went beyond questioning these policies in specific areas. Critics wondered, as Walter Lippmann had observed nearly two decades before (Reading 9), whether American society could be economically sound and could protect individual freedoms at home while carrying out such policies in Latin America and Southeast Asia. One of the most ardent defenders of these foreign policies between 1964 and 1967 was Vice-President Hubert H. Humphrey (1911–    ). A long-time defender of minority rights and civil liberties in the United States, Mr. Humphrey [both as United States Senator from Minnesota (1949–1965) and as Vice-President] believed that it was necessary to extend America's domestic blessings abroad if the world was to be stabilized. However, he also argued that the world had to be stabilized if the United States hoped to continue the enjoyment of these blessings at home. The Vietnam conflict challenged this assumption since the longer that effort to stabilize Southeast Asia continued, the worse America's urban, racial, and economic situations became. In this speech, Vice-President Humphrey outlined his belief that domestic and foreign policies are closely related, particularly in the economic area. Do the critics of the Administration policies, such as Senator J. William Fulbright (Readings 3 and 31) and Carl Oglesby (Reading 4), indeed, agree with Mr. Humphrey that domestic and foreign policies cannot be separated? What, then, is Senator Fulbright's and Mr. Oglesby's chief difference with Mr. Humphrey?*

---

Many people feel today, they say, we should not be there in Vietnam.

Well, whether we should or not, we are. And we have been

SOURCE. *The New York Times*, April 26, 1966, p. 38.

there a long time. So I am not going to argue about whether we should have been there.

But I do believe that John Stuart Mill gives us some rational and some moral justification for what we do. Listen to his words: "The doctrine of non-intervention to be a great principle of morality must be accepted by all governments. The despots must consent to be bound by it as well as the free states. Unless they do the profession comes but to this, that the wrong side may help the wrong, but the right must not help the right."

I don't know where you can find a clearer statement of why this nation has had to intervene, not of our own volition, but by request by treaty, by obligation and by commitment.

And my fellow Americans, the day that this nation does not honor its commitments, it is on that day that the whole fabric of international law and order is torn apart and breaks down. . . .

We are being watched very carefully by friend and foe alike, to see whether or not in this period of our prosperity, of our affluence, of our power, to see at this time when it appears that certain Communist nations seem to be less irritating than before, we have the same will.

And those who threaten their neighbors need to know that we will stay and see it through; and they need to know that we take our commitments seriously; that we will resist aggression, and they can't get by with it.

Now, to put this in a more immediate level, and I touch, I know, a sensitive nerve. We have a program before the Congress now called Foreign Aid. It is not popular. Most things that are good for us are not popular.

The struggle in Vietnam is not popular; yet it is important, and the expenditure for the first year of the Marshall Plan was about 2 per cent of our gross national product. It was almost 12 per cent, 11 and a half per cent of our Federal budget.

Today, thanks to the fabulous growth of our economy, our foreign aid request is less than one-third of 1 per cent of our G.N.P. and less than 2 per cent of our budget, about 2 cents out of every tax dollar. This is preventive medicine. It is a part of our national security.

I am not at all sure that it will be effective. I am not at all sure that the bombs that we have will be effective.

But they are part of a system. They are part of a total application of power and strength, and the investment in foreign aid should not be looked upon as a giveaway or as a grant; it is a part of our security structure. And I think that it is a lot less costly than to try to treat the symptoms of massive economic crisis and disorder, yes, of war, when I think of what it costs us each day and each year in Southeast Asia. . . .

We have faith in this country. So do you. Among other things we are united in our determination to accomplish something that no nation ever before has even dared to try, to make every single person, every citizen in our society a full and productive member of our society; no one to be forgotten. And so today we make great investments in our country and our people, investments in productivity and opportunity and enterprise and justice and in self-help.

Now, some people don't agree with these investments. I happen to believe that the best investment that you can make is in your own people and the only way that you can help other people is to make sure that this source of wealth and power is right here that the United States of America is a going concern.

It is not a matter of guns or butter, foreign aid or domestic education. They are tied together. You cannot separate them, because the only way you can have guns at the prices that you have to pay is to have an economy that can afford them, and the only way that you can have foreign aid is to have an economy that is productive enough to pay the bills.

41  *Dwight D. Eisenhower: The Dangers of the Military-Industrial-University Complex in America ( January 17, 1961 )*

*When Vice-President Hubert Humphrey discussed United States economic prowess, he emphasized opportunities opening to Americans. When, in his Farewell Address in 1961, retiring President Dwight D. Eisenhower analyzed that economic power, he emphasized the "threats" arising from it. Although Vice-President Humphrey stressed the beneficent use of power, the retiring President warned that "The potential for the disastrous use of misplaced power exists and will persist." President Eisenhower's speech of January 17, 1961 was a highly-influential critique of an American society that had been increasingly shaped by Cold War foreign policies. Notice his use of historical analysis (particularly in his emphasis on the "technological revolution") to support his conclusions. Is President Eisenhower correct in warning that American universities might be too intimately involved with the Cold War? Or, given the historical record since 1947, should these universities take specific positions on domestic and foreign policy issues?*

---

This evening I come to you with a message of leave-taking and farewell, and to share a few final thoughts with you, my countrymen. . . .

We now stand ten years past the midpoint of a century that has witnessed four major wars among great nations. Three of these involved our own country. Despite these holocausts America is today the strongest, the most influential and most productive nation in the world. Understandably proud of this pre-eminence, we yet realize that America's leadership and prestige depend, not merely upon our unmatched material progress, riches and military strength, but on how we use our power in the interests of world peace and human betterment. . . .

The record of many decades stands as proof that our people and their government have, in the main, understood these truths and have responded to them well, in the face of stress and threat. But threats, new in kind or degree, constantly arise. I mention two only.

A vital element in keeping the peace is our military establishment. Our arms must be mighty, ready for instant action, so that no potential aggressor may be tempted to risk his own destruction.

Our military organization today bears little relation to that

SOURCE. *Public Papers of the Presidents . . . Dwight D. Eisenhower, 1960–1961*, Washington, D.C.: Government Printing Office, 1961, pp. 1036–1039.

known by any of my predecessors in peacetime, or indeed by the fighting men of World War II or Korea.

Until the latest of our world conflicts, the United States had no armaments industry. American makers of plowshares could, with time and as required, make swords as well. But now we can no longer risk emergency improvisation of national defense; we have been compelled to create a permanent armaments industry of vast proportions. Added to this, three and a half million men and women are directly engaged in the defense establishment. We annually spend on military security more than the net income of all United States corporations.

This conjunction of an immense military establishment and a large arms industry is new in the American experience. The total influence—economic, political, even spiritual—is felt in every city, every State house, every office of the Federal government. We recognize the imperative need for this development. Yet we must not fail to comprehend its grave implications. Our toil, resources and livelihood are all involved; so is the very structure of our society.

In the councils of government, we must guard against the acquisition of unwarranted influence, whether sought or unsought, by the military-industrial complex. The potential for the disastrous use of misplaced power exists and will persist.

We must never let the weight of this combination endanger our liberties or democratic processes. We should take nothing for granted. Only an alert and knowledgeable citizenry can compel the proper meshing of the huge industrial and military machinery of defense with our peaceful methods and goals, so that security and liberty may prosper together.

Akin to, and largely responsible for the sweeping changes in our industrial-military posture, has been the technological revolution during recent decades.

In this revolution, research has become central; it also becomes more formalized, complex, and costly. A steadily increasing share is conducted for, by, or at the direction of, the Federal government.

Today, the solitary inventor, tinkering in his shop, has been overshadowed by task forces of scientists in laboratories and testing fields. In the same fashion, the free university, historically

the fountainhead of free ideas and scientific discovery, has experienced a revolution in the conduct of research. Partly because
of the huge costs involved, a government contract becomes virtually a substitute for intellectual curiosity. For every old blackboard there are now hundreds of new electronic computers.

The prospect of domination of the nation's scholars by Federal
employment, project allocations, and the power of money is
ever present—and is gravely to be regarded.

Yet, in holding scientific research and discovery in respect, as
we should, we must also be alert to the equal and opposite danger
that public policy could itself become the captive of a scientific-
technological elite.

It is the task of statesmanship to mold, to balance, and to integrate these and other forces, new and old, within the principles
of our democratic system—ever aiming toward the supreme goals
of our free society.

## 42   Fred J. Cook: The Warfare State (1964)

*The journalist and author, Fred J. Cook, provided one of the best
detailed analyses of the American economy to substantiate President
Eisenhower's warning about the military-industrial-university complex. What is the implication of Mr. Cook's analysis: (a) that the
United States must change its attitude toward the Cold War before
the "warfare state" can be controlled, or (b) that the "warfare state"
must be controlled and reduced before foreign policies can be changed?*

We live, little knowing and sometimes less caring, in the world
of the Warfare State. We live with the images of past ideals that

SOURCE. Fred J. Cook: "The Warfare State" in ANNALS OF THE
AMERICAN ACADEMY OF POLITICAL AND SOCIAL SCIENCE,
CCCLI (January 1964), pp. 103–109. Copyright 1964 by The American
Academy of Political and Social Science. Reprinted by permission of The
American Academy of Political and Social Science and Barthold Fles,
Literary Agent.

conflict with the realities of present power. We live, we Americans, in the delusion that we are the world's most peace-loving democracy and that, if it were not for the evil of rampant communism, we and all mankind might be blessed to live out our normal life spans in peace and tranquillity. This image that we have of ourselves conflicts with the images that others have of us; others see, as so often we do not, the reality of a power colossus whose military budget for fiscal 1963 totals a staggering $56 billion. . . .

There were compelling and dovetailing motives behind the creation and the rapid growth of the Warfare State. The escalation of the military art in the crucible of World War II had made it self-evident that warfare had become a science embracing all other sciences. No longer could a nation depend upon the hasty conversion of plowshares into swords; the highly complicated technology of modern war called for constant planning, experimentation, development. . . . In such an age, inevitably, there was born the concept of the need for a "force in being."

This logic, sound enough in itself, was reinforced by other considerations, more subtle and more selfish. It is doubtful if even a Gallup survey could do justice to the shock inflicted on conservative psyches by the Russian victory at Stalingrad. Here the invincible Nazi war machine was brought to a halt and ground to pieces by a system that the American business classes had been telling themselves for years could never work. Stalingrad dealt a lethal blow to such complaisant rationalizations; it demonstrated graphically that in Russia, at least, the system had worked. And, as the Russian armies swept on, rolling up the Germans in rout before them, there was born in the minds of American businessmen, as I know from personal contact, the fearful reflex that the time would come when we would have to "deal with Russia. . . ."

To these considerations was added yet another—our own prosperity. Only World War II had relieved the trauma of the Great Depression; only huge military expenditures had brought full employment and real prosperity. Big-business interests, which had looked with horror on the New Deal's public works projects and pump-priming innovations, had formed a wartime partnership with generals and admirals who had the dispensation of virtually limitless billions of public funds. Business had never known such a bonanza—nor had the military. Neither would have been human had they wanted to kill the goose that laid the golden egg.

All pressures, then, combined to one end—the creation, for the first time in American history, of a powerful militaristic class allied to powerful business interests. . . .

The effect of such a prodigious outlay has been to chain the self-interest of millions of Americans to the perpetuation of the Warfare State. Vast sections of our economy have become almost utterly dependent upon the military budget. California, now the most populous of the fifty states, is enjoying some $6.2 billion in military procurement contracts in fiscal 1963, roughly 24 per cent of the amount being spent for new hardware. Additional billions are being funneled into the state to pay salaries and upkeep on military installations. In the vast Los Angeles area, it has been estimated that fully half of all jobs depend either directly or indirectly on the military budget. In the nation as a whole, the estimate is that between one quarter and one third of all economic activity hinges upon military spending and that, with continued boosts in the military budget, this figure may in time reach a staggering 50 per cent. . . .

Now we have in our nuclear stock pile [weapons] equivalent in destructiveness to some 22 billion tons of TNT. Each of our 1,300 Strategic Air Force bombers, our intercontinental ballistic missiles, our Polaris submarines is equipped with hydrogen bombs 5,000 times more powerful than the primitive Hiroshima device that exterminated 100,000 lives in one blinding flash. To carry the analogy one inevitable step further, there are only 2,000 cities in the entire world with populations of 100,000. We have enough hydrogen bombs in our stock pile to deliver the equivalent of 2.5 million tons of TNT, 125 times the force of Hiroshima, upon each 100,000 population, not just upon each city—and we can deliver it not once, not twice, but 125 times. . . .

A Department of Defense analysis of military spending shows conclusively that, while all of the fifty states benefit economically to some extent, the vast majority get only crumbs from the table of Mars. Just seven states—California, New York, Massachusetts, Connecticut, New Jersey, Ohio, and Texas—devoured 57.2 per cent of all luscious procurement billions in fiscal 1962. Twenty-six, by contrast, obtained only fractions of one per cent apiece. Clearly, the armaments race is keeping the select few in the plush style of military nabobs, but the majority, whose taxes help to support this complex, are not getting their fair share. Nor will they.

The simple fact of life in the nuclear age is that money goes where money has gone. A Cape Canaveral perpetuates itself. . . . As Senator Hubert H. Humphrey has noted, "Those who have get more; the richer you get, the more you get.". . .

Even the five to six billion dollars funneled annually into California in procurement contracts, a prodigious sum for a single state, has not proved the automatic guarantor of full employment and prosperity. Look at the unemployment figures for Los Angeles, heart of plane and missile country. In 1956 the city had only 74,000 jobless; in 1960, 157,000; in early 1963, 189,000. As munitions spending rose, so did unemployment, a development the Los Angeles *Herald-Examiner* summed up in one word—"daffy."

The apparent daffiness has, of course, a logical explanation. It is simple: military spending, though superficially it stimulates, acts actually in the long run as a stultifying influence, a drag on the economy. Deputy Secretary of Defense Roswell L. Gilpatric pointed out in a speech in early April 1963 that California had benefited from a flow of defense dollars "about double the national average in relation to the labor force in residence there"— yet California ranked ninth among the fifty states in the rate of unemployment. Gilpatric noted that midwestern states that had put their emphasis on the energetic development and cultivation of civilian markets had unemployment rates strikingly lower than California, the behemoth of military production. . . .

This clamor and this obfuscation of fundamental issues are aided and abetted by a power lobby bossed by the military masters of the Warfare State. No less than 175 members of the current Congress hold reserve commissions in the armed services, and these services shamelessly proselyte new members in the effort to bind them into the military claque. The air force is a leader in this endeavor, but it is not alone. One new congressman from a far-distant state, arriving in Washington, found the air force practically waiting on his doorstep, urging upon him a commission, assuring him that, if he would only accept, a service plane could always be available to fly him home at the taxpayers' expense. This wooing of the congressman . . . has reached such proportions that Representative John V. Lindsay of New York has called for "a full and complete inquiry" into the propriety of reserve officers being allowed to hold congressional seats. Lindsay said he had been "appalled," he had found the Navy's overtures to him "insulting," and that he had discovered a number of other congressmen felt as he did. One thing quickly became obvious: the number was not large enough. Lindsay's suggestion appears to have been quietly interred. . . .

## 43   *John McDermott: The Crisis Managers (1967)*

*One subtle but highly important aspect of what President Eisenhower called the military-industrial-university complex is traced out by author John McDermott. Mr. McDermott observes the development of a particular mentality in policy-making circles that tends to blur the line often drawn between civilian and military policy-makers. He begins by analyzing an autobiographical account of decision-making in the Kennedy and Johnson Administrations by Roger Hilsman. Mr. Hilsman had been a university professor and respected scholar of Far Eastern affairs before joining the State Department as Director of the Bureau of Intelligence and Research, and then becoming Assistant Secretary of State for Far Eastern Affairs. While in Washington, he was instrumental in accelerating the American involvement in the Vietnamese war between 1961 and 1964. Could "Crisis Managers" move into power even without the so-called "military-industrial-university complex"? What are the differences between the "Crisis Managers" and the American military establishment? What is the relationship of the "Crisis Manager" to the more democratically-controlled foreign policy-making that Senator Wayne Morse argued for during the debates over the Gulf of Tonkin resolution (Reading 34)? What is the difference between the views of policy-makers in the Kennedy and Johnson Administrations, as given in these readings, and those of President Eisenhower and Secretary of*

*State Dulles in the 1953–1955 period regarding the appropriate policies to meet revolutions in the newly-emerging nations?*

---

The decision to escalate the Vietnam War was not made in 1965. It was made in 1964. It was certainly made within six months of President Kennedy's death. It may even have been made within six weeks of his death. . . .

We need no longer doubt it. Roger Hilsman, Assistant Secretary of State for Far Eastern Affairs, 1963-4, a self-confessed member of the Kennedy "inner circle" and the latest of the JFK entourage to commit his public service to the public record [in his book, *To Move a Nation*], tells us more even than we need to know in order to clinch the case.

According to Hilsman's account the Kennedy Administration was fundamentally divided by the crises in Laos and Vietnam. One faction—[Ambassador-at-large Averell] Harriman, Hilsman, the State Department (minus Rusk [Secretary of State Dean Rusk]), the President himself—favored what Hilsman calls the "political" approach. As did their "military" opposite numbers, these men believed that the insurgencies in South Vietnam and Laos were ultimately attributable to North Vietnamese direction, arms, and personnel. But they believed nevertheless that this threat could best be curbed by limiting the application of American power within the borders of Laos and South Vietnam. . . .

The "Military Advocates" within the Kennedy Administration were more numerous by far than their opposites and, as we have since learned to our dismay, more long-lived as well. They included Secretaries Rusk and McNamara [Secretary of Defense Robert S. McNamara], the Joint Chiefs of Staff led by their Chairman Maxwell Taylor, Presidential Assistant Walt W. Rostow, and the then Vice President, Lyndon Johnson. . . .

SOURCE. John McDermott, "The Crisis Managers" in *The New York Review of Books*, September 14, 1967, pp. 4-10. Copyright 1967, The New York Review. Reprinted by permission of *The New York Review of Books* and the author. Mr. McDermott is a lecturer in political science at the New School for Social Research. He is also Field Secretary for the New University Conference, Associate Editor of *Viet-Report*, and author of *Profile of Vietnamese History*.

Hilsman does not attempt to hide his disdain for the "military" faction which brought about the escalation and especially for the heavy-handed and simple-minded types he finds in the higher reaches of the Pentagon. . . . Hilsman, for example, does not speak of "whiz kid liberals," of "frying cities to a crisp," or even of "nailing the coonskin to the wall." He has never fallen in love with a B-17, never dreamt—as Barry Goldwater has phrased it so wonderfully—of dropping ICBM *nukes* into the Kremlin men's room. "Political" language is cooler, more abstract; it prefers euphemism to metaphor. It is closer to the language of an Ivy League faculty club than to that of the officers' mess. . . .

The truth of the matter is that the two factions are not pressing mutually exclusive courses of action; they do not represent alternative national policies or leadership. . . .

Roger Hilsman is an able and articulate member of a relatively new class of men in American life. He is a Crisis Manager, one of the men who have held and continue to hold the handful of positions in the National Security apparatus. It is their job to manage the still youthful crisis—only twenty-three years old—which we call the Cold War. Hilsman himself represents the newer breed of Crisis Managers, as tough-minded as [former Secretary of State Dean] Acheson but not so "military," and as subtle as [John J.] McCloy but not so closely connected with the older and European-oriented Wall Street business community. Like so many of the younger Crisis Managers he is an intellectual and a Kennedyite, is mildly liberal, and maintains a base within the university establishment. . . .

The Crisis Managers face a peculiar problem in dealing with the armed services and the services' allies within the civil apparatus. They have assigned themselves the task of presiding over a vast military bureaucracy—and its supporting institutions—in a period in which changes in technology have forced revolutionary changes in the military art. With the exception of one or two like Hilsman (a graduate of West Point), they generally lack military training and yet somehow must try to maintain direction over the efforts of their always restive military technicians. Under such circumstances they have become the most ideological of men. Without the presumed superiority of an almost infallible conception of the National Interest they could not hope to force grudging acquiescence from their more technically skilled military subordinates.

Their outlook is a peculiar one and is shaped by this need to keep the military in check. What makes them particularly vulnerable to the pressures of the armed services is the fact that they are themselves ideological militarists as well. Unlike their uniformed subordinates the Crisis Managers do not believe in uniforms and medals. . . . But just like their subordinates within the military they perceive international reality almost exclusively in military and strategic ways; their faith is coercion, and while they use political language often enough, in the end they rely on the military devices which they possess in such great profusion.

At one point in *To Move a Nation* Hilsman is confronted with the necessity to explain why Laos is worth a major military adventure. His answer is both revealing and characteristic, especially for a self-styled "political." There is a road, he tells us, or rather the latent possibility of a road, which follows the tortuous course of the Mekong River from southwestern China, through more than a thousand miles of mountain, jungle, and swamp, to southern Laos and Cambodia. It is a line of communication, he argues using a military terminology that neatly marches along the page, and it must be denied the Chinese. No strong or suggestive evidence is offered that China wants to or is able to undertake this tedious excursion. Hilsman does not even see that that is an issue; instead America's overseas imperatives can be read directly from an unmarked military map. . . .

There is no ethical content to their [the Crisis Managers'] hatred of Bolshevism, nor any sense at all of how they themselves may appear to Communist leaders. The Communists—a capitalized epithet usually lacking distinction as to faction, era, or nationality—are said to have no respect for people or their values, practice terror, possess an insatiable appetite for power. But by Hilsman's own description the US, in the decade 1954-64, committed every imaginable perfidy in Laos. Governments were toppled, international agreements trampled upon, elections fixed, political parties created out of nothing, the Army placed on a monthly stipend, the economy distorted and corrupted, and several varieties of

military adventurers encouraged in their aimless depredations
against the long-suffering Lao people. Hilsman is quite firm in
insisting, however, that the villains of the game are the Pathet
Lao because of their "intransigeance and duplicity," their "vicious"
and "ruthless" opposition to free world influence in Laos.

A liberal of sorts, Hilsman naturally finds McCarthyism de-
praved; a moral man, he was appalled by the "unspeakable" prac-
tices found in Diem's prisons. Yet he was among the earliest and
most persistent enthusiasts for the Strategic Hamlet Program,
which forcibly removed several million South Vietnamese from
their homes and livelihood into what used to be called concentration camps. . . . Any person who remains outside the camps is
assumed to be Viet Cong and may be killed on sight or by means
of saturation bombardment in the "free fire" zones, i.e., the
areas outside the camp. . . . "Political" officials like Hilsman are
perfectly serious in defending these programs as an essential
means of saving the population from communist totalitarianism.
Such behavior on the part of civilized men is difficult to explain.
It does indeed seem to be anti-communism of a particularly path-
ological kind. One gets the impression that the Crisis Managers
conjure up a diabolical caricature of the Communists and then,
to demonstrate how hard-nosed and realistic they are, try to go
the caricature one better.

The Crisis Managers are defined by their relation to power.
They want power but power of a peculiar kind. They are not
interested in power as a form of personal adornment, such as
the image of Mussolini recalls, nor do they seek power primarily
as a means to chosen ends. They call themselves pragmatists
(and moderates, always) intending to convey by this overused
term that they are interested primarily in means taken by themselves, that is, in relative isolation from the ends they bring about.
In Hilsman's book, as in so many Crisis Manager tracts, this leads
to a preoccupation with the process of decision-making. Decisions
normally have both antecedents and consequences, but Crisis
Managers are not particularly concerned with these. They are
interested in the process: who made the decision, when and where,
who was consulted and who wasn't, who was cool and who
agitated, who comes out of it looking good, and who will be the
goat in the next round of memoirs.

The Crisis Managers' relation to power is not mechanical, however, and it is not, *prima facie*, frivolous. They want power in its most immediate forms, power today, power to decide, to move and manipulate now, this moment. But their relationship to the power which they seek so assiduously is pictured in a grimly serious way. The telephone calls in the night, the immense influence of the institutions they control, and the knowledge that they deal always with life and death issues—all these produce in the Crisis Managers a portrait of themselves as lonely and heroic men never quite free of the heavy burdens of their high office, burdens of which lesser and more carefree men, like you and me, are blessedly ignorant. . . .

Agonies reach their climax during crises and, like most Kennedy memoirists, Hilsman has a long and loving section on the Cuban Missile Crisis of 1962. That crisis was naturally the high point in the lives of those Crisis Managers who happened to be working that year. Then, at the height of the crisis, for the first and only time perhaps in history, the fate of all mankind—all the significant power over that fate and all the significant decisions—was in the hands of a few men. Historical reality had been reduced to them, to their actions. For those few heady hours all events seemed obedient to the conscious will of a handful of intimates. Their engagement was complete, their every action was bent to the common task, where they went, what they said, whom they saw, how they appeared to others—all of this counted for those few magic hours. It was a truly beautiful moment. . . .

Crisis represents reality at its best for liberal Crisis Managers like Hilsman, and this simple insight gives us the key to their relationship with the maligned military and "military" types. The Crisis Managers are the moderates between two extremes, peace and war. Their stake is in Cold War, of which they are both children and progenitors. Unlike the generals they have no stake in active war. They don't like war partly for the same reasons you and I don't like war, but also because in war the power to make decisions escapes to the generals and that is anathema for liberal Crisis Managers.

It is then, only by contrast to [General] Curtis LeMay or Walt Rostow that our liberal Crisis Managers appear as sane and reasonable men, just as "advisers" in Laos appear a sane alternative to "nukes" in Peking. Without the terrifying backdrop of the Pentagon, and without the distorting influence of a swollen military establishment in our national life, the Crisis Managers would have too few crises to manage and their true role would emerge more clearly, perhaps even to themselves. Their half-disguised militarism, unprincipled anti-communism, and a bizarre, pretentious, and sometimes comic mystique of power are fully as antagonistic to a stable peace as is the ultimate faith in strategic bombing—in fact more so. Perhaps without knowing it, they have made Cold War manipulation and military coercion in foreign countries a kind of noble calling. It is understandable that the process of making money or enlightening undergraduates should become for them tame business compared to life and death confrontation with the Bomb, the task of policing and redeeming the Third World, smiting Marx and Mao with fistfuls of pragmatism and moderation—as they put it—and of getting the whole of mankind moving again. Thus the Crisis Managers are addicted to Cold War. They cannot do without it. They are the moderates who protect us from the twin evils of Dr. Spock and Dr. Strangelove.

That is why Hilsman did not go to the public in January, 1964. He resigned because the "fools" and the "madmen" had won control of the Government. He *knew* escalation was coming. An insider with the facts at his command and an experienced and respected policymaker, had he moved to attack the Administration publicly in 1964, it is conceivable that the war might not have been escalated, especially if some of those who agreed with him had joined him. But Crisis Managers don't go to the public. The public really has no right to meddle in foreign policy. An informed opinion on foreign affairs ". . . like blue cheese . . . [is] an acquired taste" and the public has never acquired it. But more important by far than any contempt the Crisis Manager may feel for the public is his own commitment to "existential" decision-making. Managing crises is the privilege of a Crisis Manager as managing securities is the privilege of a portfolio manager. To go to the public is unthinkable, it is to exercise a deadly threat against the existence and prerogatives of one's own class (not to mention one's own future as a member in good standing). One simply does not do such things. . . .

We have lived so long with Hilsman's system that we have forgotten how to act. Others are actors and we are only spectators. This state of affairs is now a durable feature of American political life.

## 44 George F. Kennan: Mr. "X" Twenty Years Later (1967)

*Twenty years after his famous Mr. "X" article, George Kennan had become appalled over American policies in Southeast Asia which, so Secretaries of State Dulles and Rusk had argued, were simply extensions of Mr. Kennan's original "containment" thesis. In writing his Memoirs during the mid-1960's, Mr. Kennan tried to provide his own interpretation of the 1947 article, sharply distinguishing the original intent of the article from what "containment" had become by 1967. Notice particularly Mr. Kennan's use of post-1950 historical events to justify his denial of the present validity of the Mr. "X" argument. In the readings in this book do Secretaries of State Dulles and Rusk and Presidents Truman, Eisenhower, Kennedy, and Johnson use the same historical events to justify the continued application of "containment?"*

In writing the X-Article, I had in mind a long series of what seemed to me to be concessions that we had made, during the course of the war and just after it, to Russian expansionist tendencies—concessions made in the hope and belief that they would promote collaboration between our government and the Soviet

SOURCE. George F. Kennan, *Memoirs, 1925–1950*, Boston: Little, Brown and Company, 1967, pp. 364–367. Copyright 1967 by George F. Kennan. Reprinted by permission of Atlantic-Little, Brown and Company and George F. Kennan.

government in the postwar period. I had also in mind the fact that many people, seeing that these concessions had been unsuccessful and that we had been unable to agree with the Soviet leaders on the postwar order of Europe and Asia, were falling into despair and jumping to the panicky conclusion that this spelled the inevitability of an eventual war between the Soviet Union and the United States.

It was this last conclusion that I was attempting, in the X-Article, to dispute. . . . The Soviet leaders, formidable as they were, were not supermen. Like all rulers of all great countries, they had their internal contradictions and dilemmas to deal with. Stand up to them, I urged, manfully but not aggressively, and give the hand of time a chance to work.

This is all that the X-Article was meant to convey. I did not suppose, in saying all this, that the situation flowing immediately from the manner in which hostilities ended in 1945 would endure forever. It was my asumption that if and when the Soviet leaders had been brought to a point where they would talk reasonably about some of the problems flowing from the outcome of the war, we would obviously wish to pursue this possibility and to see what could be done about restoring a more normal state of affairs. I shared to the full, in particular, Walter Lippmann's view of the importance of achieving, someday, the retirement of Soviet military power from Eastern Europe, although I did not then attach quite the same political importance to such a retirement as he did. (In this he was more right than I was.)

. . . . And if the policy of containment could be said in later years to have failed, it was not a failure in the sense that it proved impossible to prevent the Russians from making mortally dangerous encroachments "upon the interests of a peaceful world" (for it did prevent that); nor was it a failure in the sense that the mellowing of Soviet power, which Walter Lippmann took me so severely to task for predicting, failed to set in (it did set in). The failure consisted in the fact that our own government, finding it difficult to understand a political threat as such and to deal with it in other than military terms, and grievously misled, in particular, by its own faulty interpretations of the significance of the Korean War, failed to take advantage of the opportunities for useful political discussion when, in later years, such opportunities began to open up, and exerted itself, in its military preoccupations, to seal and to perpetuate the very division of Europe which it should have been concerned to remove. It was not "containment" that failed; it was the intended follow-up that never occurred.

When I used the term "Soviet power" in the X-Article, I had in view, of course, the system of power organized, dominated, and inspired by Joseph Stalin. This was a monolithic power structure, reaching through the network of highly disciplined Communist parties into practically every country in the world. . . .

Tito's break with Moscow, in 1948, was the first overt breach in the monolithic unity of the Moscow-dominated Communist bloc. For long, it remained the only one. It did not affect immediately and importantly the situation elsewhere in the Communist world. But when, in the period between 1957 and 1962, the differences between the Chinese and Russian Communist parties, having lain latent in earlier years, broke to the surface and assumed the form of a major conflict between the two regimes, the situation in the world Communist movement became basically different. Other Communist parties, primarily those outside Eastern Europe but partly the Eastern European ones as well, had now two poles—three, if Belgrade was included—to choose among. This very freedom of choice not only made possible for them a large degree of independence; in many instances it forced that independence upon them. Neither of the two major centers of Communist power was now in a position to try to impose upon them a complete disciplinary control, for fear of pushing them into the arms of the other. They, on the other hand, reluctant for the most part to take the risks of total identification with one or the other, had little choice but to maneuver, to think and act for themselves, to accept, in short, the responsibility of independence. If, at the end of the 1940s, no Communist party (except the Yugoslav one) could be considered anything else than an instrument of Soviet power, by the end of the 1950s none (unless it be the Bulgarian and the Czech) could be considered to be such an instrument at all.

This development changed basically the assumptions underlying the concept of containment, as expressed in the X-Article. Seen from the standpoint upon which that article rested, the Chinese-Soviet conflict was in itself the greatest measure of containment that could be conceived. It not only invalidated the original concept of containment, it disposed in large measure of the very problem to which it was addressed.

Efforts to enlist the original concept of containment with relation to situations that postdate the Chinese-Soviet conflict, particularly when they are described in terms that refer to some vague "communism" in general and do not specify what particular communism is envisaged, are therefore wholly misconceived. There is today no such thing as "communism" in the sense that there was in 1947; there are only a number of national regimes which cloak themselves in the verbal trappings of radical Marxism and follow domestic policies influenced to one degree or another by Marxist concepts.

If, then, I was the author in 1947 of a "doctrine" of containment, it was a doctrine that lost much of its rationale with the death of Stalin and with the development of the Soviet-Chinese conflict. I emphatically deny the paternity of any efforts to invoke that doctrine today in situations to which it has, and can have, no proper relevance.

\*    \*    \*    \*    \*

*We're Sergeant Pepper's Lonely Hearts Club Band*
*We hope you have enjoyed the Show*
*Sergeant Pepper's Lonely Hearts Club Band*
*We're sorry, but it's time to go.*
*Sergeant Pepper's lonely.*
*Sergeant Pepper's lonely.*
*Sergeant Pepper's lonely.*
*Sergeant Pepper's lonely.*
*Sergeant Pepper's Lonely Hearts Club Band*
*We'd like to thank you once again*

*Sergeant Pepper's one and only Lonely Hearts Club Band*
*It's getting very near the end. . . .*

# BIBLIOGRAPHY

FOR *America in the Cold War: Twenty Years of Revolutions and Response, 1947–1967*

These general accounts of the 1947–1967 era provide factual material plus various interpretations of the Cold War: Desmond Donnelly, *Struggle for the World. The Cold War: 1917–1965* (New York, 1965); William Appleman Williams, *The Tragedy of American Diplomacy* (New York, 1962), perhaps the best interpretive volume on the Cold War; John Lukacs, *History of the Cold War* (Garden City, N.Y., 1961, 1965); Denna Frank Fleming, *The Cold War and Its Origins, 1917–1960,* 2 vols. (Garden City, N.Y., 1961); David Horowitz, *The Free World Colossus* (London, 1965), the most critical of American policy; Edgar E. Robinson et al., *Powers of the President in Foreign Affairs* (San Francisco, 1966), a series of studies on the Presidents since 1945; John Spanier, *American Foreign Policy Since World War II,* 2nd revised edition (New York, 1965).

For the 1947–1950 period, the reader might begin with Harry S Truman's *Memoirs,* 2 vols. (Garden City, N.Y., 1955, 1956), and check them carefully against Barton J. Bernstein and Allen J. Matusow, *The Truman Administration: A Documentary History* (New York, 1966), a model documentary collection; and also against the Truman volumes in U.S. Government Printing Office, *Public Papers of the Presidents of the United States.* Cabell Phillips, *The Truman Presidency* (New York, 1966) is the best biography. The critical events of 1947 are given in Joseph M. Jones, *The Fifteen Weeks* (New York, 1955), which has become almost a classic study; Harry B. Price, *The Marshall Plan and Its Meaning* (Ithaca, 1955), ranging far into the 1950's as well; Robert H. Ferrell, *George C. Marshall,* Vol. XV in *The American Secretaries of State and Their Diplomacy; Pattern of Responsibility,* a collection of Dean Acheson's pronouncements, edited by McGeorge Bundy (Boston, 1952); Acheson's *Sketches From*

*Life of Men I Have Known* (New York, 1959); and Gaddis Smith's soon-to-be-published study of Acheson during his years as Secretary of State. For the events of 1949–1950 and, indeed, for the entire 1941– 1950 era, Harold Stein, ed., *American Civil-Military Decisions; A Book of Case Studies* (Birmingham, Ala., 1963) is a most important source, as are Urs Schwarz, *American Strategy: A New Perspective* (New York, 1966), and Raymond G. O'Connor, ed., *American Defense Policy in Perspective* (New York, 1965).

An account of great interest for the 1947-1950 years but also the record of some internal debates during the Korean crisis is George F. Kennan, *Memoirs, 1925–1950* (Boston, 1967). The Truman and Acheson references listed above consider the Korean crisis and the resulting American policy in Asia after 1950. See, also, Glenn D. Paige, *The Korean Decision*, June 24–30, 1950 (New York, 1968), a virtual moment-by-moment account; David Rees, *Korea: The Limited War* (New York, 1964), the best single-volume analysis of the war; Trumbull Higgins, *Korea and the Fall of MacArthur* (New York, 1960); General Douglas MacArthur's *Reminiscences* (New York, 1964); and for background, Soon Sung Cho, Korea in *World Politics, 1940–1950* (Berkeley, 1967). Critical analyses of post-1950 policies are Coral Bell, *Negotiation From Strength* (London, 1962); Emmet John Hughes, *The Ordeal of Power* (New York, 1963); and Norman Graebner, *New Isolationism* (New York, 1956). American foreign policies in Asia and Latin America after 1952 are treated more kindly in Dwight D. Eisenhower, *The White House Years: Mandate for Change, 1953–1956* (Garden City, N.Y., 1963), and *The White House Years: Waging Peace, 1956–1961* (Garden City, N.Y., 1965); Sherman Adams, *Firsthand Report* (New York, 1961); Robert J. Donovan, *Eisenhower: The Inside Story* (New York, 1956); Richard Goold-Adams, *The Time of Power* (London, 1962), a good analysis by a not totally sympathetic British observer; and Louis Gerson's biography of Dulles in the series, *The American Secretaries of State and Their Diplomacy*, the most scholarly and lengthy biography we have of the Secretary of State.

The best studies of the Kennedy Administration's policies in Cuba, South America, and Southeast Asia are found in Arthur M. Schlesinger, Jr., *A Thousand Days* (Boston, 1965); Theodore Sorensen,

*Kennedy* (New York, 1965); Henry Pachter, "JFK as an Equestrian Statue: On Myth and Mythmakers," *Salmagundi*, I (Spring, 1966), 3–26; Elie Abel, *The Missile Crisis* (Philadelphia, 1966); Henry Pachter, *Collis᾽ n Course* (New York, 1963); and, as in the case of Truman and Eisenhower, the appropriate volumes in *Public Papers of the Presidents*. Analyses of the Johnson Administration are beginning to appear in profusion, but the best on the early years is still Philip Geyelin, *Lyndon B. Johnson and the World* (New York, 1966).

For Latin America see Kalman H. Silvert, *The Conflict Society* (New Orleans, 1961); Gordon Connell-Smith, *The Inter-American System* (N.Y. 1966); Ronald M. Schneider, *Communism in Guatemala, 1944–1954* (New York, 1958), and for different views of the early American policy towards Castro, Theodore Draper, *Castroism, Theory and Practice* (New York, 1965), and William A. Williams, *The United States, Cuba, and Castro* (New York, 1962). The Dominican crisis in detailed in Dan Kurzman, *Santo Domingo: Revolt of the Damned* (New York, 1965), and John Bartlow Martin, *Overtaken by Events* (New York, 1966). On China, see Robert Blum, edited by A. Doak Barnett, *The United States and China in World Affairs* (New York, 1966); Tang Tsou, *America's Failure in China, 1941–1950* (Chicago, 1963); A. T. Steele, *The American People and China* (New York, 1966); and on a crucial period there is an excellent analysis in Allen Whiting, *China Crosses the Yalu* (New York, 1960). The secondary material on Vietnam is enormous, but one place to begin is with perhaps the best critical account: George Kahin and John W. Lewis, *The United States in Vietnam* (New York, 1967). A rebuttal by the Administration is conveniently found in *The Vietnam Hearings*, even though it has an introduction by Senator J. William Fulbright (New York, 1966). Indispensable is the work of the late Bernard Fall, including the collection of essays in *Vietnam Witness, 1953–1966* (New York, 1966), and *Reflections on a War* (New York, 1967). David Kraslow and Stuart H. Loory, *The Secret Search for Peace in Vietnam* (New York, 1968) provides controversial background for the documents of 1965 and 1966.

For some internal American repercussions of Cold War ideology and "military-industrial" complexes, see Clifton Brock, *Americans for Democratic Action* (Washington, 1962); Christopher Lasch, "The

Cultural Cold War," in Barton J. Bernstein, ed., *Towards a New Past* (New York, 1968); Tristram Coffin, *Senator Fulbright* (New York, 1966); Paul Jacobs and Saul Landau, *The New Radicals* (New York, 1966); and a classic account, Norman Mailer, *The Armies of the Night: History As Novel; The Novel As History* (New York, 1968).